0297114 TAYLOR E.
BW 10.8?

940·53

HER
Plea
last

L.32/rev.8

WOMEN WHO
WENT TO WAR

WOMEN WHO WENT TO WAR

1938-46

ERIC TAYLOR

ROBERT HALE · LONDON

Robert Hale Limited
Clerkenwell House
Clerkenwell Green
London EC1R 0HT

British Library Cataloguing in Publication Data

Taylor, Eric
  Women who went to war.
  1. World War 2.   Role of women
  I. Title
  940.53'15'042

ISBN 0-7090-3317-6

Photoset in North Wales by
Derek Doyle & Associates, Mold, Clwyd.
Printed in Great Britain by
St Edmundsbury Press Ltd, Bury St Edmunds, Suffolk.
Bound by WBC Bookbinders Limited.

Contents

Illustrations

Between pages 48 and 49

Section A: Eye-witnesses

1 Connie Brook, Royal Artillery (anti-aircraft)
2 Ada Shevill, WAAF (balloon barrage)
3 Ruth Jewell, Royal Artillery (anti-aircraft)
4 Jacky Burgess, ATS
5 Joyce Taylor, WAAF
6 Betty Cullum, ATS
7 Irene Shaw, WAAF
8 Peggy Farrant, WAAF
9 Nellie Carter, WAAF
10 Pearl Drake
11 Jean Black on coal fatigue
12 'Micky' Butler
13 Eileen Boardman, ATS
14 Anne Hall, Royal Signals
15 Kathleen Loomes, WRNS

Section B: 1939–40

16 Sergeant Margaret Young of 137 (Mixed) Heavy AA Regiment
17 ATS recruits are issued with uniforms
18 Recruits arriving at 15 ATS Training Centre and Reception Depot, Aldermaston
19 Fall in three ranks!
20 Falmer Camp near Brighton, August 1939
21 A Royal recruit – Princess Elizabeth joined the ATS

PICTURE CREDITS

ATS Museum: 17–18, 21, 26, 28–9, 31, 39, 41–3, 55, 64.
Central Press: 32, 52, 58, 60. George Scott: 37, 50–1, 59. *GI
News*: 71. Neil Redfern: 73. 20th Century Fox: 72. Eric
Taylor: 68, 70. The remaining photographs are from private
collections of eye-witnesses mentioned in the text.

Acknowledgements

Among the many people who have helped me in gathering material for this book I should like to thank all officers in the Ministry of Defence who have generously given me of their time, particularly Colonel Robinson WRAC, Wing Commander Evans WRAF and staff of the Directorate of Naval Recruiting.

I must also gratefully acknowledge the very considerable help I received from the staff of the Public Record Office, the Curator of the WRAC Museum, Major (Retd.) Dione Parker, the British Newspaper Library staff at Colindale and the British Library Boston Spa staff.

My sincere thanks go to all those newspaper, magazine and television editors who have helped me contact so many women who served in the war-time Forces, in particular: *The Lady* magazine, the National Union of Townswomen's Guilds magazine *The Townswoman*, The *People*, *News of the World*, The *Yorkshire Post*, The *Northern Echo*, The *Yorkshire Evening Press*, *Bradford Telegraph and Argus*, *Derby Daily Telegraph*, *Kentish Gazette*, *Herne Bay Gazette*, Bridlington Press, *Isle of Thanet Gazette* and Central Television.

It must be evident that I owe a large debt to those women who, through direct interviews with me and through their letters and written accounts, generously provided significant details of Service life and events to illustrate the vast panorama of such a topic as the 'Women who went to War'. I have identified such contributors in the text except where – as for example those engaged in secret operations – they have expressed a wish to go under another name. Also in some few cases for compelling reasons and where it would cause unnecessary hurt, I have refrained from supplying exact names; I have mentioned such instances in the text.

To all who communicated with me I express again the sincere thanks I have already given privately: Eileen Andrewartha, Pam Andrews, Joan Armstead, Doreen Atkinson, Claire Baker, Jean Baker, Pamela Barker, Kathleen L. de Bast, Helen Baxter, Brenda Beeston, Marjorie Bennett, Winifred Blackham, Alice Blanchflower, Doris Boon, Barbara Boyce, Lotte Bray, Dorothy Brody, Connie Brook, Frances Brough, Jacky Burgess, Eileen Burroughs, Cora Calvert, Dorothy Calvert, Phyllis Carter, Joan Chamberlain, Margot Clark, Dora Clements, Vera Cole, Gwen Conacher, Paula Cooper, Thelma Cooper, Sonia Corser,

Christine Courtney, Eva Cresswell, Vera Culley, Betty Cullum, Lettice Curtis, Betty Davenport, Peggy Davies, Joan Daws, Nancy Dawson, Margaret Doherty, Hilda Dopson, Pearl Drake-Witts, Nellie Dumbrell, Joan Dunhill, Joanne Duprés, M.S. Edge, May Elliott, Peggy Farrant, Agnes Ferris, Jessica Godwin, Rose Goldberg, Jenny Gooch, D. Lynne Griffiths, Ann Hall, Jenny Hamilton, Anne Harris, D.M. Hedges, Joan Heyles, Dulcie Hill, Marjorie Hirst, Joan Holden, Elsie Homer, I.R. Hoskins, Freda Howard, Joan Hubbold, Betty Hudson, Monica Jackson, Anne Jamieson, Ruth Jewell, Beryl Kealey, Audrie Kearney, Patricia Keates, Moira Keaton, Betty Kelley, Y.J.T. Kingdon (née Black), Eileen Kisby, Evelyn Light, Peggy Linington, Phyllis Linsdell, Kathleen Loomes, B.R. Marks, Olive Mayall, J. Melrose, Mildred Morton, Cora Myers, Ruth Negus, R.M. Nichols, Stella Pearson, June Penny, Sybille Phillips, M. Priestley, Ellen Purdham, Anne Reeves, Catherine Reilly, J. Richardson, Selina Ringrose, Chris Roberts, Myra Roberts, Peggy Roberts, Brenda Robinson, Mary Room, Kay Rouchy, Peggy Rowe, Gill Rowlands, Ada Ryder, Lillie Saxton, Lydia Sharland, Barbara Shorney, Ruth Sims, Irene Smith, Patricia Smith (Keats), Edith Sowebutts, Betty Stubbens, Jean Taylor, Joyce Smedley Taylor, Margaret Taylor, Vivienne Templeton, Barbara Thomas, Kathleen Thomas, Carol Thompson, Edna Turnbull, Molly Urquhart, Elsie Walker, Molly Waterhouse, Brenda Weeks, Nell White, Norma Whitehead, Judith Whiting, Betty Wilde, Helen Zielenko.

My friend the military historian Charles Whiting has led me to much useful material and periodically yanked me away from documents to get down to the serious business of finishing the book, for which I am grateful, and I give sincere thanks to Sheila Surgener for her invaluable help with research and the meticulous checking and correction of drafts, and my warm appreciation goes to Mrs Anne Milner for the conscientious way she typed the finished manuscript.

Without the generous help of all these people the book would not have been so comprehensive. To all I express my gratitude. The responsibility for any shortcomings or errors is, of course, my own.

Glossary

AA	Anti-Aircraft (Ack-Ack)
ATA	Air Transport Auxiliary
ATS	Auxiliary Territorial Service
BEF	British Expeditionary Force
CO	Commanding Officer
ENSA	Entertainers National Service Association
FANY	First Aid Nursing Yeomanry
HMSO	Her Majesty's Stationery Office
MI	Military Intelligence
MO	Medical Officer
NAAFI	Navy, Army and Air Force Institutes
NCO	Non-Commissioned Officer
QAIMS	Queen Alexandra's Imperial Military Nursing Service
RAMC	Royal Army Medical Corps
RN	Royal Navy
OFC	Operator Fire Control
SOE	Special Operations Executive
VAD	Voluntary Aid Detachment
WAAF	Women's Auxiliary Air Force
WRNS	Women's Royal Naval Service
WTS	Women's Transport Service
WVS	Women's Voluntary Service

Foreword

by Air Commodore
Dame Felicity Hill, DBE WRAF (Retd.)

Eric Taylor's evocative book will take many of us back to a unique period in our lives, and will introduce many more readers to an aspect of their grandmothers, mothers and elderly aunts which may surprise them. For it is now nearly fifty years since World War II began.

I think it is true to say that my generation, though reared on parental memories of the First World War and the books and films which depicted it, was far from militant. We knew about Hitler and Mussolini, but unless we were students of politics or personally knowledgeable about what was going on in Germany many of us did not take it seriously until 1938 and Munich. There were no nuclear weapons to fear, and no TV to prod our social conscience. It was a pleasant time to be young if you were reasonably lucky, and by this I do not mean rich or privileged. But in September 1939 the world changed, and all of us with it. Once it came we viewed the war much as had our 1914 predecessors – almost as a crusade and with fervent patriotism, a word which now in our Common Market days is out of fashion.

Women queued at the Recruiting Offices to join the Services, and though this book deals in the main with work of a directly dangerous or secret nature there were many more servicewomen whose work seemed mundane and devoid of glamour, but without whom the Armed Forces could not have continued the fight. Of course those who were serving on operational flying stations saw aircrew virtually in battle, but for so many women in all the Services the war was a distant matter and their sense of purpose and devotion to duty the more admirable for this, enabling them to face hard conditions, unaccustomed discipline and severance from home and family, and to behave with cheerful confidence under bombing.

Women also proved to possess a strong measure of what we used to call 'esprit de corps'. Not in a big way, for though most of them would have declared their particular Service or Unit to be the best, their real allegiance was to the co-inhabitants of their barrack hut and their working section. They stood together, shared together, covered up for one another, forebore in the main from annexing each other's boyfriends, and formed friendships which have lasted to this day.

Unless you have been part of a nation at war it must be difficult to understand how it felt. A world of shortages and government controls, devastated cities, shining generosity and neighbourliness, unity of purpose – a togetherness which enabled people to make light of all their fears and deprivations and problems. And in after years the enduring memory of great physical courage and comradeship.

Eric Taylor tells the detailed stories of some of the 'women who went to war', and pays tribute to the contribution of all servicewomen to the survival of their country. For them the war was not waged for high political purposes, but for a more deep-rooted reason, the protection of the home territory. This is an imperative which does not change, and I pray it will never again be invoked in the context of a war.

Prologue

Twenty-one centuries ago, an angry column of women marched into the Roman Forum and demanded the revocation of a law prohibiting them from wearing golden bangles and bright gowns.

In the uproar that followed, the dour Senator Cato the Elder sat perfectly still and silent. When the hubbub died down, he rose and looked solemnly at his fellows before giving a warning that must have struck lasting fear into male hearts. He said: 'From the moment women become your equals, they will become your masters.'

Centuries later the issue still vexes society.

Whatever the present status of women in the battle for sexual equality might be, they have certainly proved what they can do under the most trying and terrifying conditions in two world wars.

In World War I, nurses in mobile casualty centres worked as shells exploded around them; so did the drivers of the First Aid Nursing Yeomanry, 450 of them, and 9,000 members of the Women's Army Corps. They took great risks, contemptuous of danger.

But such revelations of women's courage were not new to history; women's fortitude has never been doubted. What was new in the role women took in World War I was the way it liberated them from the social restrictions and moral boundaries in which they had, for so long, been kept. War is a terrible thing but through it women had, it seemed, won freedom and some sexual equality.

Indeed, a social commentator of that time, Philip Gibbs, declared: 'If ever there is another large-scale war, which heaven forfend, it seems to me certain that women will not remain as non-combatants. In such a time these women of courage, these girls of the new age who have such vitality and spirit, will join the air squadrons and take part in defence and attack. It is impossible for me to believe otherwise, because their claim to equality with men does not stop when war is declared. Equal in life, they will be equal in death, if they have any pride – which they have.'[1]

From that First World War, women escaped from Purdah. Or so it appeared.

Symbolically, they abandoned their old-fashioned whale-bone corsets, ignored old social restraints, cut their hair in trim, easy-to-manage styles and enjoyed moving freely in shorter skirts. This new, free woman took to wearing fashions that were pleasing to her personally, and she danced, as one man put it, 'in ways that allowed her partner a near sexual embrace'.[2] She smoked in public and even entered the male sanctum of the pub.

Alas! Much of this freedom proved to be superficial.

Soon, women who had previously been praised for their public service in munitions factories and military units came in for a surprise. They were spoken of as vampires depriving men of their jobs and, though working for only two-thirds of a man's salary, found themselves dismissed by employers under pressure from trade unions. And there was no unemployment benefit then.

Understandably, women were left wondering what it had meant for them, that war. Were they back to the old days of 'the women's place is in the home'? Prospects were not inspiring, for in that twenty-one-year interval between the two great wars there were few opportunities, other than marriage or domestic service, for the less well-educated young woman. And naturally not many women relished the idea of putting themselves under the domination of some 'old cat', especially after tasting the comparative freedom of war-time service.

Then came the Second World War, and once more women came into their own. They elbowed their way through the prejudices of their 'masters' to get to the tough jobs, to prove yet again that they could do work which was supposed to be beyond them. So well did they perform that in July 1944 it really did look as though Philip Gibbs' 1930s prophecy of RAF women pilots would be fulfilled, for no less a person than Air Marshal Leigh-Mallory, of Battle of Britain fame, was urging the Chief of the Air Staff to allow volunteers from the WAAF to train as pilots.[3] But all the weight of his experience and rank availed nothing, even at a time when there was a pressing need for pilots. The barrier against women in combat roles stood firm.

This seems the more remarkable since RAF station commanders were lavishing praise on their WAAF personnel. Typical of the esteem in which they were held was the comment made by one Group Captain: 'I have cause to thank God that this country can produce such a race of women as those on my station.'[4]

Yet the Air Ministry would not budge.

In the Navy and Army, similar attitudes prevailed. 'Women do not go to sea in grey-funnelled fighting ships,' said the admirals. And War Office generals shook their heads in horror at the thought of 'gun-toting girls'.

Nevertheless, in their various military roles in World War II, women without doubt proved their mettle, and the attitude of those senior officers who had actually seen women in action is perhaps best typified in a report from General Sir Frederick Pile, Commander of Anti-Aircraft Defences. He wrote: 'The girls lived like men, fought like men, and, alas, some of them died like men. Unarmed, they showed great courage.'[5]

They had indeed. By the end of the war nearly half a million women, drawn from all classes, were in the Forces. Many were exposed to considerable dangers – nurses in combat zones, plotters in Fighter Command operations rooms, members of mixed anti-aircraft batteries, searchlight and barrage balloon units, in air ambulances, in Bomber Command, in secret Naval and Intelligence units and in the Special Operations Executive.

Their commitment was not without cost. Many lost their lives, many were wounded, and many spent long years in captivity as prisoners of war.

Such bland statement and statistics make little impression. But think of eighteen-year-old Gunner Nora Caveney dying of wounds from a bomb splinter as she stuck to her post on a gun-site till she fell and another girl took her place while the rate of firing went on without a break. Think of Wren Despatch Rider Pamela McGeorge, blasted from her motor bike by a bomb, getting up and delivering her despatches on foot in the midst of a heavy raid. Picture WAAF Sergeant Joan Mortimer issuing ammunition from the armoury at RAF Fighter Station Biggin Hill at the height of the Battle of Britain, as a deluge of bombs fell round her highly dangerous store of explosives. Imagine, if you can, what it was like for PO Wren Lunnon, alone, fighting her way through the blazing wreckage of a crashed Hampden bomber to rescue the pilot. And think of Nurse Gladys Hughes, one of many nurses who died of malaria, persistent diarrhoea and malnutrition in a Japanese prisoner-of-war camp. Now statistics begin to mean something in human terms.

Certainly the contribution to the winning of the war made by thousands of women like these excited not only the admiration of the Allied commanders but also that of the enemy. As former Nazi Minister for Armament Production Albert Speer was later to say to the writer: 'We could never get our women into the Services like that.'[6]

Thus, when the war finally ended, people in Britain were left with the conviction that now there would be great changes in the roles women would play in both Service and civilian life.

But were there changes? A few.

Nearly half a century later, though, the barrier before sexual equality still remains to be demolished completely. Soldiers in skirts can now carry guns and use them in defence, but not in attack.[7] The United States Women's Army Corps has gone a stage further: in 1977 Barbara Kent, a captain in the US WAC who visited the WRAC training depot, said that she had been trained to kill with a large number of weapons and was quite forthright in her views on sexual equality in the Services, saying: 'We don't see any reason why we can't do anything men can do.'[8]

On behalf of the Director of Naval Recruiting, a staff officer now confirms that members of the Women's Royal Naval Service may not take any form of combat role, though some may go to sea in auxiliary support ships.[9] And the Director of WRAF recruiting has explained to the writer at great length the problems and the costs involved in training pilots, and presented many plausible and convincing reasons why women are not being trained for operational flying duties.[10] But she did go on to say that the question is under constant review and that the matter comes up in Parliament year after year.

So much for progress towards sexual equality in the Services.

What did women get for themselves in civil life from their efforts in World War II? After the First World War they were given the vote but after the Second World War women received no similar reward in terms of economic emancipation. No doubt their war service lifted their social confidence and made them more independent, but the great majority of women might still wonder today what exactly had been achieved, especially when they read reports such as the one which appeared in *The Times* on 16 November 1987 under the headline: 'Modern men still see home as women's work'.[11] The report that followed stated that working women still earn less than their husbands, have less free time and spend less money.

Apart from the few at the top of their professions, it might seem that women still have a fairly long way to go before they escape from their subordinate position in society. But, on the other hand, the momentum towards greater equality *has* increased dramatically over the last decade. Who in 1945, for example, would have given much for the political prospects of a Siberian railway worker's thirteen-year-old daughter in the little-known town of Rubtovsk? Or, indeed, for the nineteen-year-old daughter of a Grantham grocer studying at Oxford? Yet now Raisa Gorbachev – an important power behind the Kremlin throne – and Prime Minister Margaret Thatcher can walk impressively upon the stage of world politics.

Be that as it may, it all means very little now to that gallant band of women who went to war these forty years ago. For they have something far more worthwhile than social status to treasure, more than just a memory: a revelation. Their war-time service taught them a lot about life. It was an experience that most of them now cherish. Pam Andrews expressed the feelings of hundreds who wrote to me when she said: 'I'm glad I was young then. I still think of all the boys and girls I was involved with and what fun we had, and with what little money. We learnt something of our true selves, about life and how it could be lived, how helpful and supportive comrades could be when people were not all the time competing with each other as they do now. We were all in it together, trusting one another, making the best of what we had. We made firm friends, many of whom we have kept to this day. We did, in fact, learn how to live happily together. What a pity it takes a war to do that! But you've got to go through it to know what it means.'[12]

This book tries to illuminate 'what it means'.

It is not an objective history of the women's Services, for it would be impossible to include all that the many and varied units did. I have therefore chosen more or less typical examples of the experiences of servicewomen.

For every Violette Szabo, for instance, there were scores of other Special Operations Executive women in other parts of the world. In this Second World War women served in all theatres of operations: North Africa, Italy, Greece, Persia, Iraq, Egypt, Libya, South Africa, Jamaica, the United States, India, Burma, Malaya – to name only those that immediately spring to mind.

I have quoted from hundreds of letters, diaries and manuscripts which women have been kind enough to send to me and wherever possible checked the stories by referring to files in the Public Record Office or documents in the respective Service museums. I have interviewed and corresponded with all the women, and some men, who contacted me. It has been an experience I shall never forget. And I only hope that I have done justice not only to those who responded to my appeals for help through the media but also to the half million or more women who gave so much, so willingly.

Perhaps through their stories we may all begin to understand what it was really like in those fateful six years, from 1939 to '45, for the women who went to war.

York, February 1988   Eric Taylor

British women have proved themselves in this war. They have stuck to their posts near burning ammunition dumps, delivered messages afoot after their motor-cycles have been blasted from under them. They have pulled aviators from burning planes. They have died at their gun-posts, and as they fell another girl has stepped directly into the position and 'carried on'. There isn't a single record of any British woman in uniformed service quitting her post, or failing in her duty under fire. When you see a girl in a uniform with a bit of ribbon on her tunic, remember she didn't get it for knitting more socks than anyone else in Ipswich.

Extract from United States War Department booklet issued to every American soldier entering Britain

1 'Give Us a Job. We Can Do That!'

This war, more than any other war in history, is a woman's war.

John G. Winant, US Ambassador to London

3 September 1939

All over Britain they waited, housewives in kitchens, nurses in hospitals, women in uniform, women with their menfolk, and women alone. Just after nine o'clock on that Sunday morning (and it was such a lovely morning too), a programme on how to make appetizing meals from tinned food was interrupted to warn listeners to stand by for an important announcement. Everyone had a good idea of what that announcement might be, for two days earlier, on 1 September, Hitler had invaded Poland, and consequently both Britain and France, having pledged themselves to go to Poland's aid if she were attacked, had sent Hitler an ultimatum to withdraw his troops from Polish soil. Now that ultimatum had expired. Hitler had not withdrawn and Parliament would no longer listen to Prime Minister Chamberlain's vague talk of peace. Angry taunts had been shouted from both sides of the House, and when Arthur Greenwood, the acting leader of the Labour Opposition Party, had risen to speak, another voice had called across from the Conservative back benches, 'Speak for England!' Greenwood did. He urged the Government to act, at once, and declare war.

Thus, at precisely 11.15 a.m. on that warm September Sunday, just as the bells stopped for matins, Neville Chamberlain broadcast to the world that the British Empire was now at war with Germany. His words, heavy with grief and solemnity, fell like stones on the hearts of the people.

Marjorie Bennett, a newly qualified staff nurse who days before had answered the call for volunteers to nurse the troops, listened that Sunday in the nurses' home of the old, impressive-looking Victorian hospital at Netley. Afterwards the nurses sat wet-eyed and silent. Pat Hall,[1] who would soon be driving ambulances in the Western Desert and Italy, was waiting to go on ambulance duty with the ARP at Epsom when she heard the broadcast in her garden at home. It left her dazed. Doreen Atkinson, an eighteen-year-old who had just returned from an

ATS camp at Falmer near Brighton and who was to be one of the first to cross to France with an ambulance unit, remembers too listening with her parents that Sunday: 'My mother was baking rock buns and apple pies. She stood with her floury hands half raised above the mixing bowl, her mouth agape as if to utter a cry of disbelief. Her eyes brimmed over. She had seen it all before, and memories of her dead brothers came crowding in.'

Phyllis Linsdell of Collier's Wood had also just returned from that ATS Camp at Falmer with instructions that if war was declared she was to report at once to the drill hall in Wimbledon, taking her 'small kit' – underclothes, toiletries and so forth. This she had done but had been sent home to await instructions. Now on that Sunday morning she sat with her mother, her father (a veteran of the First World War) and her married sister with two small boys, waiting for what they already knew would be the inevitable declaration. No one was surprised when it came. But they still sat, shocked, each with his or her own thoughts. The sister hugged her sons apprehensively, knowing full well that their father would have to go. Mother was worried about her son already in the Air Force. Father decided that he too would volunteer, and eighteen-year-old Phyllis ('more than excited, exhilarated!') knew that soon she would be off, doing something which would be worthwhile, new and challenging.

Company Sergeant-Major Ruth Jewell, who had joined the ATS in February 1939 and was to be in the first mixed anti-aircraft battery to serve overseas, had already had her posting instructions and was that Sunday morning busy making all ready at her unit to receive the first new intake of those women who went to war.

But there too, in that army camp, an uncanny hush followed the announcement.

Phyllis Linsdell remembers how in London that hush was broken, a few minutes after Chamberlain had finished speaking, by the banshee wailing of the first air-raid siren of the war. 'Here it comes, we all thought, just what everyone predicted: immediate mass bombing.' People were already familiar with practice alerts but now there was a real sense of urgency. Mothers gathered their children and hustled them under stairs or into shelters. There was no panic, but remarkable sights were to be seen as some ran out from their Sunday morning bath or late 'lie-in' half naked, whilst others, like Phyllis's family, stood out in the garden staring upwards.

The deluge of bombs did not fall upon London that morning, but the sirens rammed home the awful message: total war had come to Britain!

Though that first alarm was false, the idea persisted that congregations of any kind were undesirable. All cinemas in Britain were closed down in a week. When nothing happened in the next seven days, most of them re-opened shyly, but a number of the smaller halls stayed dark for good. Film critic C.A. Lejeune told how it was: 'Nobody was admitted without a gas mask. You couldn't go to church without a gas mask. You couldn't go *anywhere* without a gas mask. The thing became an albatross, our burden and our curse. Fishermen went down to the sea with that bouncing abomination slung across one shoulder, their nets over the other. Schoolchildren stumbled over the square cardboard boxes as they scrambled in the lanes for blackberries. Housewives bundled them out of their shopping baskets to make room for apples or a vegetable marrow.'[2]

It was a war that was to break down traditional barriers as the frontier which divided combatant from non-combatant became completely blurred. Now *everyone* was in it, and as those traditional barriers crumbled, so also did ideas on the role of able-bodied women in war-time. Now, surely, it would be absurd to debar women from military service simply because it might endanger life and limb, since they were in equal danger with men at home, from aerial bombardment.

Women were keen to serve. Thousands queued outside recruiting offices to join the three highly organized women's services: the WRNS (Women's Royal Navy Service), the ATS (Auxiliary Territorial Service) and the WAAF (Women's Auxiliary Air Force). Amazingly, on the day following the outbreak of war, 17,000 enrolled voluntarily in the ATS, pledging themselves to serve their country in whatever capacity and whatever place authorities required.

The Auxiliary Territorial Service had been first in the field, being set up technically in 1938 though its pedigree could be traced back to the Women's Auxiliary Army Corps of World War I. Partly incorporated into the ATS was the First Aid Nursing Yeomanry (FANY), sometimes known as the Women's Transport Service (WTS), and at first a branch of the ATS was the embryo of the Women's Auxiliary Air Force. By 1939 the Navy too had its own women's Service (WRNS).

These three chief women's Services, linked directly with the fighting forces, were to expand rapidly (see Appendix D) with the introduction of conscription by the National Service Act of December 1941, when all direct recruiting was cancelled. Initially, though, there was no shortage of volunteers for all Services.

It is not easy in retrospect to analyse accurately the reasons women had for leaving home to enlist in these auxiliary Services. Apart from the fact that patriotism was a much more meaningful and positive force than it is today, there were other factors: opportunities for tackling jobs that formerly had been considered too tough or technical for 'the weaker sex', and liberation from old restrictions and attitudes, from low paid jobs or from being economically dependent on a husband's hand-out. For the young unmarried woman, exasperated by the narrow confines of home, a future beckoned.

'Our home life, like that of thousands of others, was somewhat humdrum. My parents were caring and perhaps over-protective,' said Irene Smith. 'To be suddenly thrust into the hurly-burly of Service life rather overwhelmed me, and yet there was a feeling of adventure.'

Phyllis Linsdell spoke for many when she said: 'It was an unexpected opportunity to do something different, something really good for the country, a chance to get away from all the dull jobs women had always had to do. It was a way that thousands took to escape having to go into domestic service.'

Hilda Dopson was only sixteen when she realized that life in the WAAF would be far better than being in service in a large Derbyshire manor house. She was accepted, completed her initial training and was posted to RAF Linton-on-Ouse where, ironically, she was sent for duty to Lady Chesterfield's house, Beningbrough Hall, York. Yet she too was to find life more exciting and romantic than anything that had gone before.

Many were the girls like Hilda Dopson who lied about their age. Audrie Kearney remembers: 'Aged seventeen and dying to spread my wings, I volunteered for service in the ATS. By moving the date of my birth from late November to February 1942 I was considered old enough to enlist. Being five feet six inches tall (I grew an inch later), no one questioned my age.'

Brenda Beeston had an amusing story to tell about under-age enlistment:

I went with two friends – mother and daughter – one May afternoon, keeping them company as they went for their medical exam at Cosham Headquarters. I was just sixteen and five months then and just over five foot tall. As we approached the headquarters building, there was an ATS second lieutenant standing on the steps, who called out: 'Jolly good! I see you've brought another recruit.' There and then I said to my friends, 'Don't say a word. If I can get in, I'll come with you.' It was my answer to a prayer. I wanted to be in on the fight. My father was RN all his life, my elder sister was NAAFI, and my other sister a Wren. So the die was cast. In I went, and while the other two went in for their medical, the officer said, 'While we are waiting for them, you might as well sign your forms.' She filled them in for me, no mention of birth certificate, so I never said a word and signed on the dotted line. The nurse took me in to the doctor, a man in his late fifties, who looked at me and said, 'How old?' I said quietly that I was eighteen, thinking it was all over. But no! He just grunted, 'Hm, youngest I've seen. Keep in good health?' I nodded, and he proceeded with a very short examination and said, 'You'll do,' smiled and I walked away.

The ironic bit was neither of my friends passed. One was colour blind, and the mother had a small medical problem. When I got home, my mother was distraught and said, 'You can't go.' My father said that I'd made my choice and now I'd have to get on with it.

Women were keen to show they had a sense of duty and faith in volunteering to make a contribution to the war effort. Who were they to sit back when they saw their brothers, fathers, husbands and lovers prepared to fight the evil menace of Nazi Germany? These women, who had gained the vote only a mere two decades before and since then had been seeking equal rights in every way, now demonstrated indisputably that they were prepared to take the responsibilities that came with such rights.

To some, the prospect of service was more daunting than others. Not all enlisted with the exuberance of Audrie Kearney, as Vera Cole recalls:

In order that the rest of my story can be fully appreciated, I should tell you of my family and personal circumstances. At the age of six my father died but during my short knowledge of him he had been a very strict man and we all went in awe of him. Then he died.

I, young as I was then, didn't know he was dead and I went into the room where he was laid out on the bed. I panicked, rushed out and fell head first down the stairs. My mother came to me but, as I appeared to be all in one piece, she left me to get over it. However, as was revealed later, my nerves had been shattered and I was to suffer for this event for many years to come. Tears were always ready to fall if I was spoken to harshly or too kindly, and whilst I was OK at meal-times at home, it was no use anyone inviting me out because I could not summon up enough courage to pick up a knife and fork or a cup of tea. My nerves got the better of me well into my teens.

One can imagine the courage it took for Vera Cole to enlist. 'For my medical examination I had to report to the local Methodist church. I undressed down to my briefs and then put my overcoat on. I was sent into another room where six gentlemen were sitting. One of them said, "Open your coat." I still don't know why but I was passed A1.'

Vera Cole went on to become NCO in charge of unit motor transport and driving instruction.

Some women had nothing to offer but enthusiasm and energy. Others were already partly or fully trained for the work they would undertake in the Services. For example, Monica Jackson, an eighteen-year-old telephone operator, rose rapidly to become signals officer in charge of all ATS telephone operators in the Army.

Far more unusual – almost unique – was Victoria Drummond.[3]

She held a well-paid, secure job in engineering when war broke out but gave it up immediately to be in the thick of the action within days, for she had joined a service which was to record more war-time dead than the whole of Bomber Command. She had joined the Merchant Service, and she had joined knowing full well the risks she would be taking. Indeed, on the day hostilities began, the liner *Athenia*, sailing to the United States with 1,418 men, women and children aboard, had been torpedoed without warning, and 112 lives were lost. The signal was clear enough to read: Germany was going to fight the war at sea without any mercy whatsoever. But Victoria, as a qualified ship's engineer, was not going to let that deter her from doing her bit. And she certainly did not join for the glamour or the perks – in the Merchant Navy there was nothing like that. Even when she was sailing as ship's engineer on the Blue Funnel liners running to Australia before the war, she had enjoyed few home comforts. Now it was going to be an even more Spartan existence, for she had signed as second engineer on a small coasting tramp in which living-quarters were very cramped. The lavatory was tucked away somewhere under a ladder, her cabin was minute, and in the mess room, for anyone as tall as Victoria, getting round the table was difficult in the extreme. She had to move her head most warily.

Down in the engine room demands upon the lone watcher could be heavy; the bridge was seldom silent for a long period, and though Victoria, as engineer, never knew exactly what was going on above, she did know that much would depend upon the promptness with which she obeyed an order signalled to her. She knew also that she was sailing in the most dangerous waters in the world and that she was sharing all the risks with a tough, cheerful, independent breed of men. What she did not know then was the vital part she was going to play shortly – in rescuing an army.

One young woman who did not join the queue to enlist was Violette Bushell,[4] a tough little tomboy turning into an attractive young woman besieged by young men. Not at all worried by the gloom-mongers talking of war, she had gone off to France for her annual holidays with her French mother's relations at Pont Rémy. When France declared war, the family rushed back to Britain. Her two brothers, Roy and John, volunteered for the Army; their father, an ex-Army sergeant of World War I, who had met his wife while he was on duty in France, was too old. Violette was not moved to join anything and went back to her job as sales assistant at a Bon Marché shop. However, events would lead her from the perfume counter there to the concentration camp of Ravensbrück ...

Although the number of volunteers was significant, what was perhaps more remarkable and indicative of the way that women felt then was that they signed on 'for the duration', not knowing how long that might possibly be and without having the foggiest idea of their rates of pay, for these were not fixed until general mobilization took place. Furthermore, women were not just volunteering for service on land: many of them would soon be facing frightening hazards, gaining awards for gallantry and meeting death in the air and at sea.

'Those early days in uniform were at times quite hilarious,' recalled former Regiment Sergeant-Major Hedges. 'People were not used to seeing "lady soldiers", and on local route marches we often had an escort of small boys.'

In September 1939 Private Black of the ATS felt very proud as she marched through Winchester behind the band of the Royal Hampshire Regiment. 'What a fuss we had made of us but what with our new army shoes and lack of marching training we nearly all finished up with bleeding heels but were too proud to fall out.'

Former WAAF Warrant Officer Jean Baker recalls: 'By that September of '39, with civilian jobs behind us, we assembled at Yeadon Airport, Bradford, sleeping on damp beds in cold Nissen huts. Old men guarded us with rifles that looked as if they had come out of the Boer War. Very frightening. We had no uniforms at first. "You in the purple suit – fall out." It was a lot of fun and there was a good feeling with it all.'

It was not 'fun' for every one. Few were prepared for the primitive living-conditions that awaited them and in those first few days, 'Some stifled sobbing could be heard beneath the bedclothes,' recalled former Section Officer 'Archie' Hall.

Selina Ringrose[5] reported for duty with the ATS at Queen's Gardens, Paddington, in bleak and bitterly cold weather. What a shock she had:

> There were piles of square pallets called 'biscuits' stuffed with straw, three of them to cover an iron bed, propped against walls running with water. We had to put on our waterproof gas capes to sleep on them, with disastrous results. I went down with fibrositis, and three ATS privates were discharged later with tuberculosis. One day, the then unknown General Montgomery, who was living in Hammersmith at that time, came to address us from the stage of the local theatre. His ADC walked onto the stage first and said that we were all to refrain from coughing until after the General had finished speaking, and then he would give us exactly ten minutes, timed to the split second, to let us ask questions and raise any matters that worried us. After listening to his talk one outspoken Yorkshire girl was brave enough to tell him about our poor living-conditions. He paused for a second without saying a word, then he screwed up his narrow little face and said in a biting tone that soon we could expect to be enduring even more testing conditions once we got on active service abroad, and we were not to be so soft. He did not hear the Yorkshire reply: 'Must have been *soft in the head* to have joined this bloody lot!'

It was not usual for complaints to be brushed aside in such a peremptory fashion. Section and unit commanders knew well enough that, if complaints were not dealt with at unit level in a satisfactory way, they would soon appear on the front page of the *Daily Mirror* or in a red-hot memo from higher authority.

Typical of what could happen was the complaint made by a Wren[6] stationed at HMS *Collingwood*. She complained that there were no baths, that roll calls and parades were far too frequent during the day, that they were not allowed to speak to male personnel, that lavatories had no bolts, that there was no privacy whatsoever, that laundry facilities were practically non-existent and that the petty restrictions on dress and working conditions were absurdly strict. All this she put in a letter to her father. He knew immediately what to do. He wrote as only an incensed parent could, to the First Lord of the Admiralty, saying he had brought his daughter up as a God-fearing young woman who respected authority and that she was not one to make groundless complaints; she had a well-developed sense of responsibility, and yet here she was now having to put up with outrageous conditions. He felt that it was his duty to bring this matter to the notice not only of the First Lord of the Admiralty but also of the British public, particularly the parents of young girls considering joining the Wrens. He hoped that something would be done to redress the situation immediately.

When that letter dropped on the First Lord's desk, he was grappling with the problems of Atlantic convoys and the U-boat menace. The last thing he wanted then was to be bothered by the complaints of some Wren and her father. But he also knew that the morale of the service was very important and, furthermore, that if he did not do something, it was quite likely to be blown up by the press into a major news feature. Consequently, although it might now seem like using a sledge-hammer to crack a nut, the First Lord immediately despatched two Members of Parliament to HMS *Collingwood* to investigate and to report what really was going on.

Once down there, the MPs 'officially' found little justification for the Wren's complaints. Privately, however, they were horrified at the way these young women were having to live, in conditions little better than those of Jack Tars of Nelson's day, and the visit was instrumental in bringing about changes, so that everyone was satisfied.

The 'petty restrictions' on dress and working conditions the Wren had complained about, however, were often those made specifically for the safety of the women themselves, for horrific accidents could and did happen when what might seem petty regulations were ignored, as the story of Leading Wren Ann Lambert shows.[7]

She was working at a radial drilling machine, wearing the Navy issue blue kerchief as a protective head-covering. The strict dress regulations laid down that it should be fastened at the back of the head with all ends of the kerchief tucked in, and that on no account must any hair be left showing. Unfortunately women found that to tie the bandanna with a bow at the front, leaving a little of the front hair showing, looked more attractive. Leading Wren Lambert was no exception to this practice but, as her colleagues were later to testify, she was a conscientious service-woman and had certainly not left any wisps of hair free.

It seems, from the evidence given at a subsequent board of inquiry, that Ann Lambert had drilled the pilot hole in the material and was about to change the size of the drill. She must have stooped forward to do this, bringing her head close to the rapidly spinning vertical drive shaft. It was then that part of her kerchief or hair got caught up, causing, to quote from the medical report, 'complete avulsion of three quarters of the scalp, the whole thickness of the scalp being removed to the bone'.

Whilst Ann Lambert was being rushed to the local naval hospital, the unit doctor, Surgeon Lieutenant Kennedy, went back to the drilling bench and unwound the bits of the scalp from the spindle. He took these to the hospital, hoping they could be used to minimize disfigurement.

It is only natural perhaps that neither men nor women thought of such consequences from breaking regulations on dress, which they considered to be merely petty, meaningless restrictions. But they learnt in time that there was usually a reason behind them all. On the other hand, to strike a lighter note on the subject of dress, the hierarchy of high command were always alert to the need for modifying dress regulations when work situations 'exposed' the need for a change, as for example with WAAF aircraft fitters, as Carol Thompson from Durham reveals: 'It wasn't easy for us to climb up to aircraft engines on rickety metal ladders whilst wearing an issue skirt, and the aircraftsmen were always rushing to help in steadying the ladder so that you felt you really ought to be climbing up cross-legged. We were nearly all delighted to read one day on station orders that we could wear battledress trousers. The airmen were not overjoyed.'

Dress was important in all three Services and especially at the initial training depots, where a particularly high standard of turn-out and drill was demanded. There were good reasons for the drill too. Smart reactions to commands on a parade ground helped instil automatic compliance with commands in whatever circumstances women might be in. 'Square bashing' developed not only the ability to march well and move large numbers of women from place to place in an orderly fashion but also the pride in belonging to a unit so essential for morale and operational efficiency.

For many women, forty minutes of marching up and down a parade ground could be sheer Hell which left the front and sides of shins burning with pain, yet, strangely enough, some even grew to enjoy it, as Jean Baker recalls: 'We had church parade every Sunday at Morecambe, 1,200 women marching along the promenade in best blue uniform neatly pressed and brass buttons absolutely brilliant. There was great rivalry between the wings, each determined to put on the smartest show with arms swung high and heels biting into the ground as one. An inspiring sight.'

The hard life and high standards demanded of the women in those early months of training had a subtle and benign effect on them, fusing them together as a unit as they developed an attitude of 'We're all in it together, all in the same boat, so we'd better make the best of it.' And with this attitude came an understanding of human nature, for in one Nissen hut or barrack room there might be twenty or thirty girls drawn from a wide variety of social backgrounds and with violently different views on food, health, sex, love, politics and life in general. Being thrown together as they were, in close contact all day and all night for weeks on end, came as a shock at first, and initially there were indeed problems. Evelyn Light remembers them well: 'Sharing a barrack room with some wild young women was no picnic. There was one awful girl from the slums of Plymouth who was always swearing and was particularly abusive if I refused to lend her my hair brush or comb – I was sure she had nits – and when one day I said I would report her to the sergeant, she came for me with a wooden brush handle in her hand, saying, "Your name might be Light, but by God you'll be dark before I've finished with you!" '

Nits were an outstanding problem in the early years of the war. An exceedingly high proportion of women were found at the initial examination to be suffering from infestation with head lice. The official history of the WAAF, for example, says: 'It came as a surprise and something of a shock to all concerned to find that 25 to 50 per cent of all recruits were affected in this way on arrival. Ireland, Glasgow and the large towns supplied the highest number of these cases, as might have been expected, but the incidence was by no means confined to women coming from poor or overcrowded homes. The disinfection of such large numbers in the shortest possible time presented a serious problem and all the then known methods were tried, but were proved to be of doubtful efficacy.'[8]

A former ATS corporal, PTI Cora Myers, remembers: 'Whenever girls were found with nits, they were immediately kept apart from all the others. They ate at a special table, their hair was cut short, and their heads were painted with horrible-looking black paste, the nearest approach to sheep dip I have ever seen.'

The standard treatment was to soak the head in a preparation of coal tar, paraffin and cottonseed oil, followed by shampooing and combing with a square-toothed metal comb. An alternative preparation when supplies were short was a carbolic acid solution. This method gave excellent results but, as the official ATS history records: 'Success appears to have been largely due to the careful combing by medical orderlies aided by the officers and NCOs of the company. As recruits with infested heads had to be isolated until they had been cleansed, the main task of the company staff for the first 48 hours after each intake, which was on a Friday, was to comb heads so that, when training started on the Monday, the company could parade as strong as possible. Special accommodation, containing six basins for shampooing and a room with special lights for combing and examination, was provided in training centres in 1941, as a cleansing centre.'[9]

To be fair, though, we must put the problem in its proper perspective for, though the high incidence of head infestation might shock the reader today, it is worth noting that the problem is still with us enough for current editions of magazines such as *Health at School* to carry full-page advertisements for lotions for the elimination of head lice in two hours, and for four-page leaflets to be available from health authorities for the guidance of parents.

Hygiene in the women's Services in war-time was considered to be of utmost importance. When women were living in such close proximity, the Service medical officers insisted on regular 'Free From Infection' parades as well as routine inspection for every woman returning from leave.

The routine varied from one unit to the next. Dorothy Calvert[10] described what it was like on the ack-ack gun-sites:

Over to the Medical Room we went, to strip to our panties and bras and stand in a row like a lot from a harem waiting for the chief eunuch to inspect us for his master. The Medical Officer would pull the elastic wide in front of our panties, then do the same at the back, remove our busts from our bras and look at each of them. It was just like 'hunt the bloody thimble'. I suppose he knew what he was looking for but we never did, and he never found it. I detested the 'Free From Inspection' parade; it made me feel cheap. When it was the turn for the men, they would tell us in great detail what the MO did to them, how they had to 'drop 'em' and cough, then bend down; that was I suppose to see if their hats were on straight. Then the MO would shift their unmentionables with his stick. But the way they told it was more like a cattle market than anything else. All very undignified indeed.

Undignified it might have been but it was all part of the concern and care for the health of these young girls. If there was any doubt whatsoever in the mind of an inspecting medical officer, the suspect girl would be sent straight to hospital for specialist examination and treatment. Phyllis Linsdell, a cook in the sergeants' mess on the field stores group at Aldershot, had to suffer from this once:

I was on the usual FFI parade, and part of it was to stick your hands straight out in front of you and open your fingers wide. Now I had some flaky skin on my thumb like a rash. The MO saw it and said, 'We'd better do something about that. You'd better go to the skin hospital.' So I went for my bus pass and set off for the hospital. When the doctor there saw it, he said, 'Oh, scabies! Here's a chit. Go down and get the scabies treatment.' This treatment was that they took off all your clothes – all they left me with was my wedding ring and my cap badge. Then they washed your hair in this Danish lotion, and then they took a large brush and brushed me all over with it. They left me for half an hour sitting in a thing like a sentry box with light bulbs in it and then came back and gave me a second coat. I never saw anybody then for three hours, so I opened the door and peeped-out, and an orderly saw me and asked me what I was doing. I told him and he went off for a pink nightdress. Then I had to get into a bed in a small side ward. The next morning I had to get up and polish the floor with the heavy 'bumper' before they would bring my uniform back to me. Well, you've never seen anything like it in all your days; the buttons were brown, and it was shrunken and shrivelled. It had been 'stoved' – fumigated. I went back to barracks and found that I had been reported as absent without leave.

The next time I had an FFI, the same thing happened. I was told to get down to the skin hospital, and there I saw another doctor. 'Oh, that's nothing,' he said. 'It's just a soda rash!' Back I went to my unit and we all had a good laugh. That was the way it was. Nobody was made to feel rejected if anything like this happened. We all got on well together. We had to.

Living together eventually caused antagonisms to disappear, and a feeling of comradeship developed. Girls grew to appreciate the 'strange sisterhood of war', and even the older women, whom one might have expected to miss the privacy of their own bedrooms, found that they gained a companionship with younger people to which they would never have been admitted in the ordinary way, and it brought a new, uplifting bit of brightness and fun into their lives, a new lease of life indeed. Class distinctions faded too – another barrier crumbling – as the girl from the factory often found that the girl from the 'posh' school, who occupied the next bed space, had not an atom of swank or stand-offishness in her; they found their muscles ached in the same way, picked up the soldier's age-old habit of grousing and eased their frayed tempers by cursing the common perpetrator of all their discomfort – whoever it might be at any particular time.

We listened to each other's problems, learnt from each other and helped each other [said Anne Reeves, a former WAAF teleprinter operator at RAF Finningley]. I remember one particularly sad incident of a girl called Thelma in our barrack room whose boyfriend was 'on the turn' as we used to say – he was paying more attention to an ATS girl from a neighbouring camp than to Thelma, whom he'd been taking out for months. I was asleep in bed one night when I felt my shoulder being shaken frantically. It was Thelma standing by my bedside. 'I've taken a hundred aspirin, a hundred aspirin!' she said. I hurried her back to her bed, saw the empty bottles and dashed as I was to the WAAF officers' mess and opened the first door I came to. The assistant adjutant was lying there asleep. I woke her up and told her what had happened. She telephoned the medical officer, and quickly Thelma's stomach was pumped out.

Now, the interesting thing about all that was not so much the speed with which everyone turned out to help but that afterwards no one said a word about it. Everyone kept quiet. Of course, we were all aware that attempted suicide was a crime. We were like that: sticking together, facing the same problems, commiserating together, even confiding in each other in a way that I have never found anywhere else. For example, one girl, a friend of mind, had caught VD. She was worried stiff but we talked about it, and the next day she started treatment and no one was any the wiser.

WAAF personnel suffering from VD were at first treated at the London Lock Hospital but, as it was undesirable for women in uniform to be seen in such a place, arrangements were later made for them to be treated at the RAF hospital at St Albans and then at Evesham.

Venereal disease was a serious problem in those days, and regularly the medical officer would address all women on the dangers of exposing themselves to the risk of catching syphilis, gonorrhoea or chancroid. These lectures were enough to turn the stomachs of the toughest women. One of them, Chris Roberts, later wrote:

I suppose there was a good reason for it, but these lectures always seem to start at about 11.30 in the morning. Maybe by then the MO would have finished sick parade, done his rounds in sick bay, had his 'elevenses' coffee, biscuits and cigarette in the officers' mess and so 11.30 might have seemed a reasonable time for him to stroll over to the education block to talk to his girls about the dangers of venereal disease. Perhaps with his (or her) medical background he had become so familiar with his 'visual aids' that he never realized what their effect might have upon impressionable minds of girls barely out of their teens. We were all so very innocent. He would have jars showing ulcerated tongues with growths like fungus, pictures of women with half their noses eaten away, photographs of patients with a chancre and syphilitic sores sprouting from their lips – and all this just before we went in for our sausage and chips! I can tell you, it all made the current publicity about Aids seem quite tame.

Perhaps the occasional MOs did go over the top and occasionally took a sadistic delight in watching the blanched faces of his audience turn a sickly green, but VD was a frightening problem then, though the numbers of servicewomen suffering from it is said to be fewer than that among women in civil life. The highest reported incidence of VD in the ATS was 5.3 per thousand at the beginning of 1942, and after that it fell steadily to a level of less than one per thousand.

However, the statistics from the Ministry of Health show that the increase nationally of syphilis and gonorrhoea from 1939 to 1940 shocked the Government. In women syphilis infection had jumped upwards by sixty-three per cent and for men by 113 per cent. A year later the Chief Medical Officer of the Health Ministry warned women in no uncertain terms of what could happen: 'Unless properly treated, syphilis and gonorrhoea may lead to blindness, insanity, paralysis and premature death. *If you have run the risk, seek medical help at once!'*

The contraction of VD by an unmarried woman officer was regarded as a disciplinary matter, and she was called upon to relinquish her commission. At first group commanders were required to render an adverse report, but the practice was discontinued and the officer's application to relinquish her commission, with the medical certificate, was forwarded under confidential cover to War Office. In this way there was minimal publicity. The main effort was put into publicizing means of prevention.

Women were advised to ensure that their partner wore a 'rubber sheath' (few would have known what a condom was in those days; everyone knew it as a 'French letter'). These sheaths were issued free and as a matter of course to soldiers, who were also strongly advised to use them – not so much for safeguarding women against pregnancy as for protecting themselves against VD.

What with the graphic posters and the lurid pictures from some medical officers, one can imagine the fear and worry that were generated amongst young women with very little knowledge of their own bodies and who still thought VD could be caught from lavatory seats and towels. Sex education was sadly lacking in schools then, as one ATS officer was to say: 'There were girls in my section who did not know what to do even about their own periods. They were still using rags which they rinsed in cold water and then washed them ready for the next time. They had never even heard of sanitary towels.'[11]

Some women did indeed have odd ideas about sanitary products, as Agony Aunt Evelyn Home, with her correspondence page in *Woman*, found. She was to write: 'When sanitary tampons began to be advertised in the women's magazines, I was eager to try them, though Mother was quite sure their use would be too risky. "What risk can there be?" I asked. "You'd lose your virginity," she said, "Inserting them. Then on your wedding night your fiancé would believe you'd been cheating him." "I'm not going to marry," I said firmly, "so to hell with my fiancé." Mother was appalled.'[12]

Sanitary towels, however, were a different matter altogether. There was, in the ATS, a free issue of them, but many of the girls didn't bother to draw them, for a variety of reasons. Dorothy Calvert, who was in a mixed anti-aircraft battery, explained why: 'One of the jobs we girls hated doing was collecting the STs from the medical inspection room; when we needed them, we had to sign our names – to put it bluntly, to let the MO know we were not in the pudding club. My pal and I went to collect ours one day and put them all in a plain cardboard box so that no one could see what they were as we walked back to the huts, because in those days we were very self-conscious of being female. We hated the men to know what we were doing, as they would strike up singing "The Red Flag" or "Red Sails in the Sunset" or something equally stupid.'

Women in all three Services were more often than not attended by male medical officers, especially during the early years of the war. For example, at most RAF stations the WAAF formed only a fraction of the total strength, so that the male MO looked after their medical needs in the same way as the doctor in civil life. Women medical officers were posted to as many units as possible where the WAAF population justified their substitution for male MOs, but by 1940 there were still only three women medical officers in the medical branch of the RAF.

Great emphasis was placed on the interchangeability of male and female doctors, though a servicewoman always had the right to see a woman doctor for a special examination if she so wished. This was, of course, something she found out only when she had been in the Service for some time, and it apparently came as a shock for some girls to find themselves being asked by a man to strip off. Kathleen Clarke remembers her moment of terror: 'I had never undressed in front of my mother since I was about seven years old, so you can imagine how my heart thumped when this man, the MO, told me to take off everything except panties and bra.'

All things considered, there were very few problems regarding the medical treatment of servicewomen, though in the main female unit commanders preferred to have female medical officers, for it helped ease administrative matters. One instance springs to mind of the female medical officer who was most concerned for the hygiene of women when she found that hardly any of them ever took a shower. It did not take her long to find the reason and the remedy. The sprays on the showers were set in such a way that when the water was turned on it came with such a force that it battered perms out of all recognition. When she had the sprays modified, there was no further disinclination to take a shower. Women in fact seemed to become very much more conscious of personal hygiene in the Services than when they were in civil life, where a weekly bath seemed to be the norm. It was not just that in the Services time and facilities were more readily available; it also had something to do with men. A war-time survey suggested that, although women were often working on equal terms with men, they still wanted to emphasize their femininity. The writer of this survey, Peggy Scott, reported that girls were none the less feminine because of this comradeship with men, but it was a different kind of femininity in that women were caring more for their appearance than they did before the war, not merely to attract the men but *because they thought more of themselves through doing men's work and being treated as mates by the men* [Author's italics]. Women found they had a fund of energy which it was generally thought before the war belonged to men, and they felt justifiably pleased with themselves.[13]

Service life made women fitter than they had ever been before. Never had the majority had such opportunities for playing games. At school boys had always been favoured with more sports facilities than girls; now girls were coming into their own on the tennis courts, on the hockey pitch and in athletics. Competitions were organized at every level, from section to inter-service. Physical training too was geared to the work that women were having to be fit enough to do. Women who worked in the operations rooms underground or in the confines of the paint and dope-painting sheds were positively encouraged to take part in team games outdoors or join in cross-country runs in order to get as much fresh air as possible; cooks were coaxed to take part in rambling or cycling excursions; women who were on their legs a lot had special rehabilitation exercises for strengthening their feet, and those who had to sit for long periods bent over a desk or bench had special instruction in ways to avoid posture-fatigue. In fact, exercises were designed by experts brought into the women's Services to meet the needs of women doing any kind of unaccustomed work. The women, though, were not enthusiastic:

Few of the girls took kindly to PT at first, [recalls former PTI Corporal Cora Myers]. When I had completed my specialist training at Newcastle I was posted back to my old unit at Chester. There I had to get them up at six in the morning for PT, and that was not at all popular. One day I came back to my room and found that all my clothes had been burnt. They found out who had done it, and we never saw her again. Once they got used to getting up earlier though, I think everyone felt better for the compulsory PT. The girls had brown shorts and orange shirts with brown piping, and in those days they looked quite smart, though to look at the photographs today you wouldn't think so. Men used to enjoy watching us limbering up, as you can well imagine.

The purposeful PT helped women in their work, especially when they were being asked to do jobs which previously had been men's. It came as a very pleasant surprise when they found how capable, both physically and technically, they were to cope with this work. Men were not always quite so enthusiastic; some were suspicious about women encroaching upon areas of work hitherto strictly male-dominated. Many believed that, once large numbers of women began to take over technical jobs, there would be no problems: they would be a disruptive influence, and the 'experiment' would be stopped. Others were far more positive, saying that women would be completely unreliable when it came to technical matters, and these few were not always as helpful as they could have been, as WAAF electrician Eileen Andrewartha discovered and was later to write: 'The war did more for women than anyone realized at the time. I was servicing Spitfires, Hurricanes, Mosquitoes and fighter-bombers. Our training was very intensive, having to be crammed into a six-month course due to shortage of technical ground crews. After passing the examination, which consisted of written theory, practical work and oral questions, we were posted to stations where, for the first time, we saw aircraft which actually took to the air. It was here that we had to prove ourselves on the work bench with the men, and be the target for the old jokes, being sent for a left-handed screwdriver, a tin of elbow grease or a replacement bubble for a spirit level.'

But as soon as women found they could stand on their own feet, the demands of Service life came as a confidence-booster: women who had not been allowed to wire a plug at home found themselves accepting tremendous responsibilities for technical work. As Eileen Andrewartha explained: 'Whichever trade you covered, it was your responsibility to check that everything was in perfect working order. There was no room for any short cuts or slipshod work – you signed the log that the aircraft was fit to fly. A pilot's life depended on your work and your signature put the responsibility squarely upon your shoulders.'

Taking over a man's job could raise problems other than the straightforward technical ones – problems which seemed to baffle the Admiralty, the War Office and the Air Ministry. It was, of course, a matter of gender again. Typical was the argument concerning the trade of 'Seaman Torpedoman'.[14] The exchange of memos and minutes between the Director of the Women's Royal Naval Service and the various departments of the Admiralty could have been culled directly from some television comedy programme. Briefly, what happened was this:

At this time the Battle of the Atlantic was being waged, with dreadful losses of naval and merchant shipping, so women ratings were drafted to shore bases to take over the duties of 'Seaman Torpedoman' for which they had been specially trained and would be well qualified. But the Admiralty refused to let them wear the badge for the trade on the grounds that: 'It is hardly a suitable description, "Seaman Torpedoman", for a woman to have on her arm badge.' After another flurry of memos between the Admiralty Director of Personal Services and the Director of the WRNS, it was finally agreed that women could wear the same badge as the men – but then the Naval Director of Victualling put his oar in. 'Ah yes,' she said, 'but if they wear the same badge, they will have to take it on the same terms as the men; they will have to buy it.' At this the Director of WRNS drew herself up to her full height and reached for her pen to send back a sizzling memo pointing out that, if the girls who entered directly into the Wrens could get a badge as a writer or steward free, it was absurd to ask someone who had undergone special training to pay for the badge of the trade for which she had qualified. And then she played her ace: that, as the pay of the Wren Torpedoman was only two-thirds of that of the Naval Torpedoman, the girls should pay only two-thirds of the issue price. At that the Admiralty capitulated and called it a day; game, set and match to the ladies. The badge would be issued free.

There were times, though, when naval commanding officers forcefully resisted attempts to replace women by men, especially in the early months of the war when the women were doing such a fine job on active service and under fire. This was particularly evident when a veritable hornets' nest was stirred up with the publication of an Admiralty Order closing the trade of despatch rider to women. Angry signals flew to the Admiralty from all commands, from Western Approaches to the Orkneys and Shetlands. How magnificently and gallantly the Admirals leapt to the defence of the Wren DRs shows indisputably again that, once women took over a job, they did it well. These despatch riders were using the standard issue Ariel 350-cc motor-cycle, a reasonably heavy machine, in all types of weather, often on cratered roads and under aerial bombardment. The angry Commander-in-Chief, Portsmouth, Admiral Charles Little, signalled Admiralty as follows:

Be pleased to submit for the consideration of their Lordships that the Wren despatch riders on the staff of the Commander-in-Chief here have performed their duties in an outstanding manner. They have covered over 70,000 miles at all times of the day and night and in all kinds of weather. Some cover 400 miles in the course of a day's work with no apparent ill effects. They have taken part in cross country trials over a severe course and won a cup from male competitors. The work of Wren DRs has been of such a high order that it was intended shortly to relieve the remaining male DRs attached to this staff by Wrens thereby releasing the men for sea.

If these Wrens are to be replaced by men they must be young, intelligent ratings of a high standard of physical fitness – in fact the type most required for sea service. To close this category to women would be a retrograde step and I ask that their Lordships reconsider this decision.[15]

He was not alone in expressing such strong feelings. The Commander-in-Chief at Rosyth signalled[16] to say that Wren DRs were carrying out their duties in a most exemplary and courageous manner. Nothing would deter them. Also he reported that they took great interest in the care of their machines and were painstaking and extremely conscientious. The work was not affecting them physically at all, and every one of the girls was perfectly fit and healthy.

Only one accident was reported. A certain Wren Dix had difficulty in starting her bike, and when it did go, it went off on its own, crashing into a fence, the property of the LMS Railway Company. Wren Dix was not on the bike, and the fence was only slightly damaged. She righted the roaring machine and rode on her way.

That nothing would deter these young women was exemplified by the gallantry of Wren Despatch Rider Pamela Betty McGeorge, who, when bombs were falling all around, rode to deliver an urgent message at Devonport. The restrained language of the citation signed by Admiral of the Fleet L.M. Forbes tells all:

Wren P.B. McGeorge 7260

When bringing urgent despatches to the Commander-in-Chief during a heavy night air raid on Devonport on 22nd April 1941 she was badly shaken up by the explosion of a bomb and was thrown from her motor-cycle, which was damaged by flying debris. She abandoned her damaged machine and delivered the despatches on foot and immediately afterwards volunteered to go out again with more. She displayed great gallantry, a high sense of duty and a complete disregard of danger.[17]

She was awarded the British Empire Medal.

It did not take long for women in the three Services to show what they could do. For the ATS the opportunity came first of all in the miserable winter of 1939-40 when contingents were posted to France as part of the British Expeditionary Force. The day on which posting orders came through was a time of great excitement. Girls gathered their little 'extras', their few comforts in addition to the Service issue, and tucked them away in their kit, and they sang a little more fervently than hitherto, 'We're going to hang out the washing on the Siegfried Line. Have you any dirty washing, Mother dear?' not knowing then that it would take nearly another five years before that laundry would be hung out. However, in that winter of 1939-40 the girls left Britain believing that they would not be coming back, except on leave, until the war was over.

It was an inhospitable, bitterly cold continent that awaited them. Everywhere seemed in the grip of an arctic freeze-up. The River Marne, the Aisne and other small French rivers had miniature ice-packs on their banks, but the small ATS units somehow managed to make themselves as comfortable as possible.

Corporal Alice Blanchflower, an ATS driver, was luckier than most:

I took over a feather bed in a farmer's spare room. It had been vacated by his son, who was then serving somewhere on the Maginot Line. I'd never known cold like that before, nor have I since. I was all right in bed, except for my

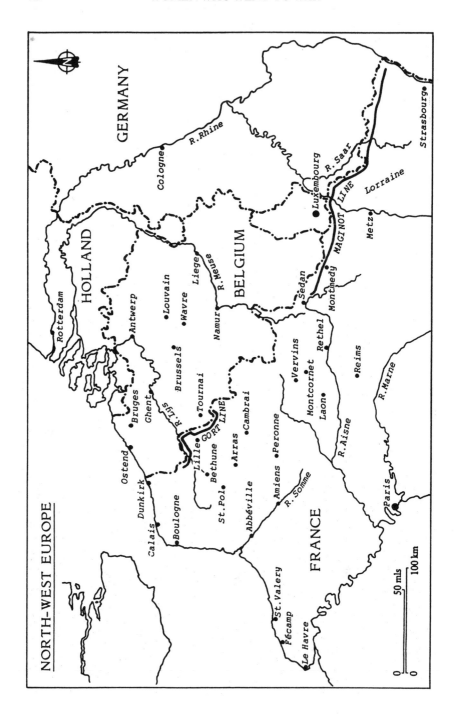

head, and I kept that warm by wearing my khaki knickers on it, pulled down over my ears. Getting up in the morning was awful at first. There was ice on the inside of the windows, and when I rubbed it off to look out on the first morning, I remember seeing the manure heaps in the farmyard steaming in the biting air. The farmer and his wife could not have been kinder. They still had plenty to eat, and every morning they would cut thick slices of streaky bacon from a flitch hanging on hooks from the ceiling and fry them in a pan hanging from a blackened rod above the blazing log fire. Sometimes there'd be a duck egg too, and we washed it all down with big mugs of black coffee. The farmer usually had a glass of cognac with his.

Amongst the nurses arriving in France at that time was Sister Marjorie Bennett, who had been drafted from Netley Hospital for service with the British Expeditionary Forces in January 1940. She remembers those few months in France with remarkable recall:

We had crossed the Channel by night with the 51st Highland Division; singing all the songs of that time, 'Wish Me Luck As You Wave Me Good-bye', and the old ones, 'Pack Up Your Troubles' and 'Tipperary'. We danced Scottish reels to the regimental pipes and breakfasted at dawn in Le Havre. There, in a magnificent gambling casino, we set up our hospital, everyone working non-stop converting the huge mirror-lined rooms into wards.

No sooner did we open than all our beds were filled with soldiers suffering from pneumonia, bronchitis or frostbite. It was so bitterly cold that everything was frozen hard, and I remember seeing a horse standing outside with icicles hanging from its nostrils; its hooves were wrapped in thick sacking to stop it from sliding on the ice-bound roads. We had no heating in the wards except for Valor stoves but we kept the patients warm with plenty of those thick red Army hospital blankets. The soldiers were so glad to see British nurses.

For those next few weeks we were very busy but we did have time to enjoy a few concerts given by ENSA artists. Orderlies would push beds together, bring patients in from other wards and make a kind of stage. We had visits from Joyce Grenfell, Gracie Fields, George Formby, Maurice Chevalier and even film-star heart-throb Charles Boyer.

It was the time of the 'Phoney War' on *Sitzkrieg* for on the outbreak of war France, with her 180 divisions, had taken up defensive positions on the Maginot Line which ran from the Swiss frontier to Longuyon, on the Belgian frontier. This 'impregnable' defensive line, with mutually supporting underground forts, obstacle defences, underground barracks and all the latest scientific devices, was thought to be capable of holding out indefinitely without any assistance from the outside. And the French strategy at that time was rooted in the determination to meet a German attack behind these fortifications and to avoid the kind of bloody encounters they had experienced in the First World War. Unfortunately there was a weakness in the plan: Belgium's determined neutrality prevented complete collaboration in the defensive plans, and therefore this Maginot Line did not stretch its full length to the coast. Instead the French had dug a large and continuous tank ditch as an extension, albeit a feeble one, of the Maginot Line to the coast.

The French manned their line, and the British Expeditionary Force, which had begun to land in France on 4 September, took up positions behind the Belgian frontier. There they waited to meet the German attack. It was to be a long wait. For eight long months, from the declaration of war in September 1939 until the following May, they waited for Hitler to strike.

What did the women of the ATS do during those long months of waiting in France? 'We got our feet under the tables of as many French farmhouses as we could. We helped out with the chores, washed up and helped with the sewing and mending as one of the family,' recalled Barbara Thomas. 'One of the girls used to bring back socks to be darned and shirts for repair from the nearby Army unit.'

Mending clothes was a problem. Though all troops were issued with a 'housewife' ('hussif') comprising needles, thread and darning wool, no one could do the job quite as well as a woman. Air Commodore 'Freddie' West recalled how women used to solve a problem that he had to deal with when he was stationed at Arras during the 'Phoney War'. One morning he asked Number 13 Squadron Commander what arrangements he had made for the washing and mending of socks for his men. There was a moment of hesitation before the question was answered but when pressed the Squadron Commander explained: 'It's a delicate matter. We have our laundry and repairs to clothes done at the local brothel. There are two in the area, and when I was asked to inspect them, we saw "Madame" and the girls all busy washing and mending, and that gave us the idea. We discussed the matter with "Madame" on the spot and made satisfactory arrangements. Our men are not much good at mending socks and pants, and we're extremely satisfied with the work done.'[18]

Women's units and men's too were at that time continually being pestered by visiting delegations from the United Kingdom concerned with welfare, poking their noses in to see how the 'girls' or the 'lads' were doing – Members of Parliament, ecclesiastical authorities, representatives of women's associations and so on. They were all given the usual guff, the careful cover-up, and they went away to write their reports. In the matter of the brothel they were simply told that washing was done privately by a local French laundry.

Brothels were, however, well in the news. In fact, General Montgomery once got his knuckles rapped for his interest in them. He was so alarmed at the incidence of VD that he wrote memos urging soldiers to use rubber sheaths as protection. The High Command held up their hands in horror when they saw the memos. Here was a general actually condoning the use of brothels! He was told in no uncertain terms not to write any more memos on the subject.[19]

As part of the welfare programme, some ATS units were taken on visits. Corporal Blanchflower remembers one visit and how she spent her spare time:

Six of us were taken on a visit to one of the forts on the Maginot Line. Whilst we were there, we heard German loudspeakers informing French soldiers that, whilst they were manning the defences, the English were misbehaving with their wives and daughters at home. When we got back from that visit, some of us got into trouble because we had 'lost' our cap badges and 'found' some special badges issued by the French to their fortress troops.

Sunday was always a bad day for BEF because the French would dress up in their best clothes and parade the streets. Proud fathers home on short leave from the Maginot Line would trail their children round to see their grandmothers. It was then that many of us would feel a little lonely and homesick.

Sometimes on a Sunday, though, we would have a treat from the touring padre, who would take a service and then set up his cinema projector. We would get well wrapped up and enjoy watching a scratched black-and-white film that often had more white flashes across it than black as it jumped on the worn spindles of the old projector. Then, of course, there was always the local *estaminet*, providing some sort of substitute for the pub at home, and there many of the girls would go whereas they would never have dreamt of going on their own to a pub in Britain at that time – unless they wanted to be branded as a hussy on the pick-up!

For the local *estaminet* the cash tills were already tinkling in that bitterly cold winter of 1939-40. Helen Baxter, an ATS driver at BEF headquarters remembers how it was:

Lille was a boom town. Officers and NCOs came driving in on the slightest pretext. And the town itself was already full of senior officers who reminded me so much of those I'd seen in plays on the West End stage, with their red tabs, riding boots, medals and moustaches. Frankly they looked faintly absurd, like men playing at war.

One evening a group of English civilian women with hard hats, and white-haired men, descended on us to enquire about the welfare of ATS women. A bewhiskered old gentleman invited me to dine with him at 'Chez Maurice', and he spent the whole evening pumping me about what girls were doing in their spare time. I'd been to 'Chez Maurice' several times before and got on well with the flat, wheezy proprietor. I liked the place because somehow it had escaped the herd instinct of British Army officers which could turn a good restaurant into a bedlam of braying and 'haw-hawing' goons.

If Lille was a boom town, Paris was even more so. In the spring of 1940 a platoon of ATS bilingual telephone operators was posted to the crowded French capital. With them, fortunately, went a small contingent of drivers. They lived in the comparative luxury of requisitioned houses with everything provided for their comfort and well-being. A YWCA catered for most of their needs: there were French classes, orchestral concerts, indoor and outdoor games evenings and sing-songs, not to mention entertainment of a different kind afforded by gallant Allied military staff officers.

Those happy 'Phoney War' days for the women of the BEF changed suddenly at daybreak on 10 May 1940, when German Panzer divisions rushed the frontiers of the Netherlands and the Luftwaffe attacked cities with an intensity never experienced anywhere in the world before. In five days the Netherlands were beaten, the Dutch royal family in London.

With the Netherlands gone and Belgium about to fall, there came another thrust from the German armour through the Belgian Ardennes. British troops now moved in many directions at once, some up through Belgium, others towards the coast. ATS ambulance driver Doreen Atkinson has never forgotten what happened next – the terror of the Nazi dive-bombers:

It was paralysing. We were in a small convoy making our way to a field ambulance unit but we got held up behind a Royal Artillery battery of twenty-five pounders on the move – or rather, not on the move, for they had stopped to brew up tea! We hadn't had any breakfast, and it was now about mid-day, so we brewed up too. I was sitting on the running board of my ambulance with a mug of sweet milky tea in one hand and a thick chunk of cheese in the other when I saw a sergeant ahead jump to his feet, move into the middle of the road and stare up into the sky. Then I heard what he must have heard and was now looking at. German planes with their unforgettable high-pitched, intermittent note of the engine. They were high in the clear blue sky, nine dots, tightly packed together in arrow-head formation. And they were coming towards us. The sergeant spun round and yelled at the top of his voice: 'Off the road ... take cover ... off ...'

Some of our drivers jumped into the ditch alongside the road. I jumped over it and kept running, away from those vehicles as far as I dared in the time available. About fifty yards into the soft ploughed field I flopped panting onto the ground. But even then curiosity was stronger than the fear. I rolled onto one elbow and, propped in this way, stared upwards. The front plane seemed to waggle its wings, and then it banked over and came screaming straight down towards me. It was a deafening high-pitched screech of wind tearing through structures and of straining engines and goodness knows what else besides. That was enough. I buried my chin and nose as far into the soft earth as I could and lay petrified. It was awful; a succession of sharp explosions, flashes, cries, showers of clods, sods, stones and powdered earth landing all round. And in the midst of all that came the scream of the next dive-bomber, more earth-shuddering bangs, cries and showers of debris, and then the next, and the next, and the next. And then it was over. Silence, except for the far-away drone of the departing Stukas.

Three gunner stretcher-bearers carried their bloody, motionless loads into the first two ambulances, and then we edged our way past the guns, glad to be clear of such a target.

The German dive-bombers were operating strictly according to plans drawn up months earlier, plans which had been practised on manoeuvres and which had actually fallen into Belgian hands when a German staff major's plane, on its way to Cologne, had crashed into Belgium in January 1940. The objective of the dive-bombers was to paralyse the artillery, and it was just very unfortunate that these women ambulance-drivers had been too close to a gun battery on the move.

Sometimes, though, the dive-bombers did mistake their targets, as happened to a group of public-spirited ladies who were not exactly members of the women's Services, but who wore a khaki uniform of sorts, well tailored and figure-hugging. They were of that gallant band of troubadours in BEF controlled from the Drury Lane Theatre, London, known as ENSA, the Entertainments National Service Association. They had been operating from a base at the Hôtel de l'Univers in Arras, touring units and presenting all types of entertainment, until that morning in May when the war for them, and for the Western Allies, began in earnest, whereupon they received an urgent signal to return to Arras, where the base party would provide accommodation and further instructions. Unfortunately the Luftwaffe decided to send the dive-bombers into Arras, and by the time the first of the returning ENSA parties arrived, those who had remained at base were just emerging from the dust and debris. There were effusive greetings of old comrades addressing each other in the usual theatrical way as 'darling' or 'dearest'. One of them, jumping out of her fifteen-hundredweight Bedford truck, ran towards them all shouting, 'But my dears, they must have been throwing things at you last night!' Once again these women were putting on one of the greatest acts of their lives, an act to hearten any of the soldiers there.[20]

Travelling was getting extremely difficult. The great exodus from cities and towns packed the roads westwards with a confused mass of refugees. Old women, mothers with children, men young and old, who a day or two earlier had been cheering the arrival of British Tommies into

Belgium, were now fleeing in panic and fearing German atrocities as much as the bombs. They had every conceivable type of wheeled vehicle: trucks, cars, horse-drawn carts, prams, barrows, handcarts and bicycles, all heaped high with personal belongings and precious bits of furniture. At times, when the road narrowed, it became a seething mass of people pushing and shoving with the strength and endurance that could have come only from sheer terror.

And well they might. It was now a matter of life and death, as many women of the ATS and nursing Services were later to recall vividly. 'Refugees presented such an easy target for dive bombing German planes and they were the first patients in our Casualty Clearing Station near Lille,' said its matron, Miss Jean Mitchell. She remembered quite clearly one morning when a small girl was carried in with her grannie. They had been taken out of a ditch where they had been sheltering with the child's mother. The child and the grannie were both wounded, and the mother was dead.[21]

There were some pathetic sights amongst those driven forward by the same impulse, a blind instinct for self-preservation: an old man in a wheelchair being pushed by his elderly wife, a farm cart piled high with furniture and on top of it an iron bedstead with pillows and blankets round a propped-up old lady.

Now, in those first few weeks of May 1940, women of the British Services were seeing death for the first time in some of its most awful forms. Generally they accepted it all in the same way as the men, maintaining a high standard of morale and discipline.

On roads in the west and north of France, which were now becoming impossibly congested with refugees, the British Army was carrying out one of the most difficult and dangerous operations of the whole war – a long withdrawal with both flanks in danger and with communications so hampered that few units knew the complete picture. Doreen Atkinson, in her ambulance section, was finding driving through the night almost impossible. 'At times,' she recalled, 'intense firing seemed to be going on both flanks, and occasionally huge flames lit the night sky. By dawn there were long hold-ups as the road became totally blocked through one reason or another. For example, I saw some French horse artillery troops ahead cut the traces of the guns and leave them blocking the road as they rode away, two soldiers on each horse.'

Ambulances evacuating the wounded from the forward areas had a particularly hazardous time of it. One section turned a corner and ran straight into an enemy convoy, but the Germans were in such a hurry that all they did was order the ATS drivers to turn round and join their column. For three days they had to go along with the enemy convoy, stopping when it did, and at night the women were too vigilantly guarded to make plans for an escape. There was also the problem of the wounded

Section A: Eye-witnesses

Connie Brook, Royal Artillery
(anti-aircraft)

Ada Shevill, WAAF (balloon
barrage)

Ruth Jewell, Royal Artillery (anti-aircraft). Taken in Brussels just before the
battery broke up

Jacky Burgess, ATS

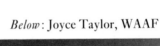

Below: Joyce Taylor, WAAF

Betty Cullum, ATS

Irene Shaw (now Bennett), WAAF

Below: Peggy Farrant, WAAF

Nellie Carter (now Dumbrell), WAAF

Pearl Drake who farmed on during
the flying-bomb raids as cows were
killed

Jean Black (now Kingdon) on coal
fatigue (*on right of picture*)

Eileen Boardman (now Kisby), ATS

'Micky' Butler (now Jackson)

Anne Hall (now Harris), Royal Signals

Kathleen Loomes, WRNS

Section B: 1939–40

Sergeant Margaret Young (now Elsby) of 137 (Mixed) Heavy AA Regiment. She met her future husband on her first day in the ATS and stayed with him in the same unit throughout the rest of her service in Britain and Germany

Try this on for size. ATS recruits are issued with uniforms

Recruits arriving at 15 ATS Training Centre and Reception Depot, Aldermaston

The last peacetime camp for the newly-formed ATS, Falmer Camp near Brighton, August 1939

Fall in three ranks! No uniforms yet but well turned out at Slough Drill Hall

No. 230873, Second Subaltern Elizabeth Alexandra Mary Windsor. Age 18, Eyes: Blue, Hair: Brown, Height: 5 ft. 3 ins. HRH pursued the ATS Vehicle Maintenance course, working in, on and under cars and trucks. She learnt to drive in convoys and how to strip and service an engine. Seen here, King George with Princess Elizabeth during her training in their ambulances, who needed constant attention.

On the fourth morning, for some reason, the Germans changed the order of their move, and the ambulances were put right at the front of the column, behind one leading German truck. Soon after starting, the German truck immediately behind the last ambulance slackened speed, leaving a gap that grew minute by minute. The ATS ambulance-driver saw this through her mirror and realized that here was a heaven-sent opportunity. She gained speed, signalled the driver in front of her and shouted instructions. The message went forward. The leading ambulance driver recalled how she decided to take a chance. There was a short cut, a little lane that cut off the main road just short of a sharp bend and rejoined it later on. She passed word back to the others to follow whatever she did. As they approached a right bend, she waited until the truck ahead had disappeared round it and then shot up a lane to her left. The others followed. But at such a high speed, the ambulance-driver hated to think how the wounded soldiers suffered as they bumped along the lane. Afterwards, however, all agreed it was worth doing.[22]

That small ambulance company got back safely through Dunkirk to Britain, and when it re-formed as 5-0-2 Motor Ambulance Convoy ATS it was posted to the Middle East, where we shall next see them.

Another ambulance-driver heading for Dunkirk told how she got to a point where the road was completely blocked by abandoned vehicles. She drove across fields, down railway tracks and across a burnt bridge. There were wild horses cantering about the streets. Finally she arrived at another bridge with a traffic block preventing her from crossing. There was an order that all BEF personnel must be over the bridge by daybreak, when it was to be blown up. She had to spend all night, helped by soldiers carrying wounded, laying them out in rows of stretchers on the other side. They finished the job just before daybreak. As one might have expected in that confusion, it was decided not to blow up the bridge after all.

When, on 27 May, Doreen Atkinson arrived at Dunkirk in her ambulance, she had a nasty shock:

Never had I seen devastation like that before. I knew it had been bombed but never realized what bombers could do. We had only just entered the town when there was a screaming roar of engines that made us jump and cringe. I looked up and saw about forty grey-green aircraft with black German crosses under their wings flying very low above me. Behind them more still were coming in. I dived under a flight of stone steps leading up to the doorway of a bombed house and crouched down waiting for the bombs. They rained down all around, flinging debris and dust everywhere. The strange thing was that, long after the noise of the aircraft had faded, bombs were still exploding and bursting into fierce, bright white flames. By a miracle I escaped being hit.

I crawled out, shaken to the very core. Later I learnt that along with the 500-pound screaming bombs the Germans were dropping hundreds of small delayed-action and incendiary bombs. They had barely stopped exploding before the next wave of bombers came in.

By that time it was obvious to everyone that something had gone seriously wrong. Everyone began talking about ships, but that seemed pointless because the harbour had been practically destroyed. Then came the news on the 'grapevine': 'The BEF is getting out!'

'Even then,' says Doreen Atkinson, 'it never sank in that it was all over until a major came hustling along banging his leather-bound swagger cane on the mudguards of trucks and ambulances shouting for all transport to be destroyed. Behind him came a section of Royal Engineers, and they made short work of wrecking my poor old ambulance that I had nursed along so carefully for the last few months. Another strange sight was to see Belgian civvies hanging about despite the shelling and bombing, grabbing whatever they thought might be worth saving. All around them soldiers were having an orgy of smashing things up and burning records.'

Doreen Atkinson had at least made it to the coast.

In the base hospital at Le Havre at that time Sister Marjorie Bennett had a grandstand view of the new air war:

There were dog fights between Spitfires and Messerschmitts right about our heads; we saw planes spiralling down in flames, and sometimes the rescue launches would bring in young pilots, British and German, terribly maimed and in great pain. Brave young men.

Early one evening in May there was a massive air raid. The glass chandeliers on our old casino hospital swung crazily in the loft ceiling, the ornate wall mirrors cracked and shattered, whilst we nurses hastily covered the patients in blankets and slid them under their beds. I had many an invitation to get under with them but I went to my own little office where I knelt down and prayed to God.

At dawn orders arrived. 'Evacuate the hospital at once!' Patients were got ready and put into ambulances, and everybody worked together packing whatever could be taken in the short notice. Remarkably quickly it seems now, we were on the road heading for a *château* fifty miles north of Le Havre. By nine o'clock that evening we were all settled in, patients in beds and weary staff sitting down to their first meal since early morning – bully beef and ship's biscuits. And if anyone does not know what ship's biscuits are like, they should try eating a dog biscuit – they're almost the same. As I left the table, my orderly, Private Evans, came to see me and said, 'You look dead beat, Sister. I've found a small box-room and put your camp bed up. You get some sleep and I'll call you at seven in the morning.'

It was not to be. Some time in the early hours of that night, good old Private Evans came dashing into the little room saying, 'Wake up, Sister. Get up quickly. The Germans are coming.'

What a blessing that he had remembered where I was, for nobody else knew, and everyone was so busy rushing about loading again that I could easily have been left behind and not missed. I should have most likely been there when the Germans arrived if it had not been for Private Evans. Alas, I never saw him again.

As we drove away from the *château* that morning, I remember hearing the larks rising high in the clear blue sky, and, as I felt the warmth of the sun upon my face, I thought how good it was to be alive. We were heading back to the casino hospital in Le Havre but we could have saved ourselves a journey. The elegant building we had left but twenty-four hours earlier was now a mass of flames. The docks at Le Havre were battered and burning too. There was no way in which we could have sailed from there. We drove to the railway station and waited. At long last a hospital train arrived, and after loading all the patients into whatever narrow space a stretcher would fit, we clambered aboard ourselves.

. Now the patients were no longer our responsibility: the train medical staff took over. We flopped in the corners but, tired as we were, we could not sleep for the crashing of bombs and the crack of the anti-aircraft guns.

Slowly, it seemed, the train chugged through one small station after another. The platforms were packed with refugees, old people and children begging for help and angry that we could not stop for them. When we did stop at last, it was at the dockside at Cherbourg. The first thing I saw there shocked me. Stern down at a lop-sided angle in the harbour water was a white-painted hospital ship. Those hospital ships with a huge red cross standing out against the white background are unmistakable. At night they are always so brightly lit. Whoever had bombed that ship had done so deliberately.

Fortunately for us there was another one berthed nearby. Whilst loading the patients aboard this, I heard my name called in a well-known voice. It was my younger brother, Steven. We hugged and then parted, each getting on with the job in hand. Once aboard the ship, the nurses with me were given a hot mug of tea, and I guess it was laced with rum for within minutes we were all fast asleep.

By that time, the rest of the British Expeditionary Force had but one objective in view: to retreat to a defence perimeter around the beaches of Dunkirk so that evacuation could begin.

Privately though, Prime Minister Churchill had little hope that more than a handful of BEF troops would escape, and for that reason he had already issued orders for units to select six of the most experienced and highly qualified men 'for immediate return to England', to be used in the re-organization and training of the new Army at home. Unit commanders did not need telling what this meant for them. They were 'for the bag', years in a prisoner-of-war camp, whilst Churchill tried to salvage something from the wreck. Thus, when the Prime Minister rose to address Parliament on 23 May 1940, he gave warning that, 'The House should prepare itself for hard and heavy tidings.'

But for the women of BEF, and for many of the men too, that eventuality never arose, thanks to the intervention of Adolf Hitler. On the day following Churchill's gloomy forecast, Hitler gave an order which stunned his commanders and left the leader of his Panzer Division, General Guderian, speechless with anger. Later, though, he was to say, 'It was an order which had a most disastrous influence on the whole future course of the war.'

That fateful order for which so many women and men were to be thankful said that the German Army must halt; troops were forbidden to cross the Riva Aa. The final words were: 'Dunkirk is to be left to the Luftwaffe.'

So it was that General Guderian, who had smashed his way through northern Europe with contemptuous ease to fling the Allies back to the one port on the French coast still usable – Dunkirk, had to sit frustrated and fuming as he watched 'the nine days miracle of Dunkirk'. In those nine days the seafaring population of Britain rose to the emergency in a great wave of defiant anger, bringing to the rescue operation of the BEF every vessel that could float: naval craft, merchant craft, private craft – everyone who could sail wanted to take part. There were tugs, destroyers, corvettes, dinghies, trawlers, barges, paddle-boats, pleasure-boats, even rowing-boats. Anything seaworthy. The shallow-draft vessels got in close; troops came wading out to them; they loaded up to the gunwales, took them off to a destroyer and went in again. Back and forth they went, those craft of all shapes and sizes, all day and all night, and all the next day, on and on. Just as long as the boats kept afloat, there were crews to sail them. As the *Daily Telegraph* reported later: 'Everybody wanted to take part, not only boatmen but women and lads wearing school caps, who brought their own motor-boats and fetched as many soldiers as they could'.[23]

In this remarkable feat of organization, known as 'Operation Dynamo', women performed acts which gained them awards for gallantry. One of these was the quiet, unassuming young woman from Lambeth whom we have already met – Miss Victoria Drummond.

2 All Together Now

Women are deceptive. Some of the toughest to look
at turn out to be the softest, and some of the sweet
little ones, with girlish laughs and big blue eyes, will
take the toughest treatment in their stride.

Captain Allan Dixon RN
to the author

May 1940

At the time when Britain was on the threshold of one of the greatest
crises of her history, Victoria Drummond lived in a modest
semi-detached house down a long Lambeth street – when she was not at
sea (see p.27). She was a tall young woman with a gentle face, quiet
voice and painfully shy manner. She was not well known to her
neighbours, but a few of them had occasionally noticed her leaving home
with a small suitcase in her hand and turning to wave good-bye to her
sisters, Jean and Frances, who always stood at the garden gate until she
was out of sight. The neighbours assumed that she was living away from
home in a hostel, earning good money in a munitions factory or as a
member of the Women's Land Army.

Nothing could have been further from the reality of Victoria's life.

When she left home in the same way on 28 May 1940 it was in
response to a telegram recalling her immediately to her ship. It had been
requisitioned by the Admiralty for service in 'Operation Dynamo'.
Within hours of Victoria's reporting back for duty in the engine room,
the ship sailed and was that very afternoon edging alongside the East
Pier at Dunkirk. There, the columns of battle-weary troops began to
shuffle on board and pack themselves in any space they could find below
deck. Only fifty of them had got aboard when the German artillery
found the range of the pier and systematically began to rake the lines of
soldiers moving slowly forward.

The bell rang in the engine room for Victoria to give the engines full
power. Amidst a shower of shells the small tramp left the battered pier
and anchored about half a mile off shore. From there, the crew could
look back and see the tens of thousands of men waiting, huddled
amongst the sand dunes for cover against air attack or standing in

orderly queues up to their armpits in water waiting for the armada of small craft to ferry them out to destroyers and larger ships further out. That night Victoria's ship crept back to the pier, loaded up and slipped away just before dawn.

When the captain ordered all troops below, many were reluctant. They had seen too many ships hit, set on fire and sunk within minutes. Getting out from below in a packed ship was an almost impossible task. Eventually, however, the mass of men moved down below, their soaked battledresses steaming. Some of them panicked with a horror of suffocating and a feeling of claustrophobia. In her engine room Victoria Drummond was hemmed in completely. For her there would be no chance whatsoever if the ship were to be hit and founder.

Fifteen minutes after sailing, a German aircraft approached the starboard bow at about 4,000 feet. It circled and dived, ignoring the fire from the Lewis guns on deck. Bombs straddled the ship, rocking and lifting it in the water. Close by, a paddle-steamer caught fire and burned furiously, with flames shooting upwards and glowing orange through the portholes. The sea around her was littered with wreckage: smashed lifeboats, rafts, ropes, planks and bodies. She was listing heavily to one side as men scrambled over the rails and stretcher cases were lowered into lifeboats. Suddenly, as if another bomb had exploded under her stern, the paddle-steamer turned turtle and sank.

By now Victoria had given the captain full power, and the little ship surged through the debris, the mass of smaller craft and the fountains thrown up by the bombs in the bright morning sunshine. Down in the engine room she was aware each time a bomb fell near enough to make the little tramp lurch. Bombs bursting near small ships nearly always broke some of the gear: engines were lifted from their mountings, gauges and fans smashed, compasses deranged and feed pipes broken. It was a terrifying experience for those down below. Soldiers and a few ATS drivers sweated and prayed until, imperceptibly at first, the clamour grew fainter and only the throbbing of the engines could be heard.

Meanwhile, other British women were busy in various ways at Dunkirk. Perhaps the most bizarre story involved a woman who happened to be living in Dunkirk at the time.[1]

Picture the scene. From the north end of Dunkirk harbour there runs a 900-yard stone causeway, and from its seaward end there was a strong pier thrusting into the sea for another 1,400 yards. It was mainly from this pier that the bulk of the Allied Armies was to be lifted. Consequently it was under constant bombardment from field artillery and the Luftwaffe. Yet at the shoreward end of this pier a jolly British woman took up her quarters in a deep cellar from which she was able to make tea for the weary and help the wounded. This she did for the duration of the evacuation operation. Neither bombs nor shells could deter her.

It was the same with the nurses on the hospital ships and carriers: nothing could discourage them – neither machine-gunning nor dive-bombers. On 20 May Sister Dora Clements had sailed from Southampton in a hospital carrier to pick up wounded from Number 16 Hospital, Boulogne. The ship berthed just before midday. There were scores of fires, smoke from burning dockyard buildings had deposited a layer of fine ash and cinders on the water, and an air-raid siren was wailing.

Sister Clements went ashore. The town was packed with refugees asking the way to the ships that would take them to Britain. When she got to the hospital, she found that despatch of the wounded had been delayed because many of them had been wounded yet again in a recent air raid, and she immediately began helping with the dressings. Today she remembers that pathetic scene vividly:

There was one young man with a neatly trimmed fair moustache and a quiff of very fair hair. His hands gripped the black rail just above his head, and sweat glistened on his pallid face. He was only partly in this world, for a mortar shell had removed his leg and shattered his hip. He had had what we call a hindquarter amputation. He had also lost part of his colon. He was suffering acutely; morphine had not helped. As I approached, his eyes looked searchingly into my face, and he made a feeble attempt to move his position. A doctor came to my side and said in a low voice, 'Give him heroin, Sister.' I looked into the doctor's lined, strained face and knew that this was one patient who would not leave France. An hour later I passed his bed again to accompany the first batch of wounded back to the boat. I saw him lying there, arms now by his sides, completely relaxed, lost in a dream world where the lotus-eaters smiled and pain was never known.

When that first batch of wounded soldiers was loaded, the Number 16 Hospital team immediately set up an operating theatre in the ship, for it did not have its own. Three major operations were performed during the trip across the Channel. Sister Clements does not know how to this day they managed: 'The ship was crowded with patients, and at the last minute the captain had allowed on board about a hundred refugees – women and children mainly. Below deck the stench was awful. The wounded were lying with dull, scarlet-rimmed eyes, faces smeared and unshaven. Through the normal reek of disinfectant came a pungent smell of sweat, dirty dressings and damp, mud-caked uniforms. Many just lay there, eyes closed at grips with their pain.'

This hospital ship was well marked with red crosses, yet it was bombed several times and machine-gunned. As the bombs fell alongside, great gouts of water erupted and dropped across the decks, drenching the crouching refugees and 'walking wounded'. Then the dive-bombers swooped and the sea was flecked with small plumes as bullets came cracking down, gouging pieces out of the woodwork.

Such surprising accounts were confirmed by another nursing sister who sailed on 29 May from Dover to Dunkirk. She wrote: 'We were attacked at 0530 by several enemy aircraft, including dive-bombers; the attack was severe, lasting an hour. The decks were machine-gunned at close range. The vibrations of the explosions caused damage to the ship's engines. The ship was alone when the attack began but then two destroyers came up and engaged the aircraft with gunfire.'[2]

One must remember though what Dunkirk was like at that time. As Britain's Poet Laureate, John Masefield, was to record: 'There was so much smoke from the burning oil tanks in Dunkirk which covered beaches and town alike that it was difficult for the enemy to see what was going on. Visibility was so poor that even our own ships were colliding with each other and sinking.' It is not surprising that hospital ships were mistaken for legitimate targets.[3] Masefield again writes:

Hospital ships and carriers suffered a good deal during the lifting, though showing the illuminated Red Cross and flying Red Cross flags.

Two hospital ships sailed to bring off the wounded. The *Worthing* was attacked by twelve bombers and forced to return. The *Paris* reported that she was bombed, badly hit and in danger. Tugs were sent to her, but she was sinking and went down after midnight. The bombing that wrecked her took place in full daylight, somewhere about 7 pm. Men in a ship just astern of her at the time 'Saw the German aeroplanes machine-gunning the boats which contained nurses and medical personnel.' A Master Mariner who went to the rescue says: 'We had a job of work with the hospital ships. *Paris* survivors had been bombed and machine-gunned. Rendered assistance to ninety-five survivors, *including five nurses who were seriously wounded*' [Author's italics.]

Despite all the hazards, however, 1,300 nurses got home safely from France.

In no other war had nurses been called upon to work in such conditions of extreme danger, hardship and endurance. And they would go on to other front-line service, staffing such medical and surgical units as mobile casualty clearing stations for succouring Allied wounded on the battlefields of Western Europe, Italy, Burma, Singapore, Hong Kong and North Africa. At one time in the Western Desert they were so close to the front line that a nurse said, laughing: 'We are the most forward women in Africa!'

Among the nurses back from Dunkirk was Sister Edna Turnbull. On landing at Dover she was given a morale-boosting cup of tea and a packet of cigarettes by women in the green uniform of the Women's

Voluntary Service; she had her name and rank noted by a smart sergeant with a green-blancoed belt and a knife-edge crease in his battledress trousers, and received a first-class railway warrant with instructions to go home and await posting orders. With minimal delay she travelled to London, dressed as she was in her badly creased grey and scarlet uniform, splashed with mud and blood. Eventually she found herself in a packed train heading north. Servicemen sat on kitbags in the corridors of the third-class carriages. In her first-class compartment sat immaculately dressed commuters.

Suddenly Sister Turnbull felt stunned as realization dawned. The urgency of the war situation had not yet penetrated the 'business-as-usual' attitude of Phoney War Britain. These men with their rolled-up umbrellas and their bowlers on the rack sat reading their newspapers as if the victorious German Army was thousands of miles away. Through the train window she could see pairs of men in yellow and blue sweaters strolling around the golf course with their caddies, farmers working with no sign of haste in the fields, and shopkeepers painting bargain signs with whitening onto the windows of their shop fronts. No hint of war to be seen.

She opened her copy of *The Times*. Debenham & Freebody had a quarter-page advertisement for an attractive ensemble: a dress of white romaine and coat of black crêpe. Harrods offered a dozen bottles of sherry, Pale Dry, for 62 shillings, and seamless Axminster carpets, 12 × 9, for a mere 10 guineas. At the bottom of the page her eye was caught by a letter from a Member of Parliament, Ian Fraser, who was getting hot under the collar not about the prospect of an imminent German invasion of Britain but about behaviour in the women's Services. The letter read:

Officers and Other Ranks in the WRNS, ATS and WAAF are rendering most valuable service but should they not be subject to some form of military law? I understand that some of these women are engaged upon important and even secret work and yet they can leave the service without notice. This is surely dangerous and wasteful.

Discipline and behaviour throughout these women's services is, I believe, admirable. Would it not be easier to deal with occasional lapses of duty if there was an official and recognised code of law and practice for commanding officers to follow?

> Yours faithfully,
> Ian Fraser[4]

Edna Turnbull felt she had entered a strange new world where reality no longer existed.

She closed her eyes and rested her head against the warm,

buttoned-back upholstery, and immediately visions of the casualty clearing station she had just left in France came crowding back: the yellow-faced eighteen-year-old soldier whose liver was torn in two, rambling insanely between snatches of the Lord's Prayer, a bewildered look on his face as she held his hand until he died; a middle-aged sergeant lying on a stretcher, his clammy skin covered in sweat, his breathing deep and raucous, hands plucking at the blanket, crying for air and asking for more light. Elsewhere there was row upon row of stretchers with scarcely room to walk between them; these were the cases with reasonable hope of recovery, young men lying in odd, grotesque attitudes, rubber tubing running from arms, from legs, up into noses and stomachs, sucking up the contents. All these men were dirty, unshaven, battledresses gashed and stained, tired beyond belief. At the end of the marquee there were the rows of stretchers bearing those for whom there was no hope, their passing eased with morphia.

Opening her eyes, she stared uncomprehendingly at the neat black jackets, white collars and cuffs, pinstripe trousers, shiny brief-cases, polished shoes. Didn't anybody know what was happening across the Channel? They did not.

Newsreels had not shown pictures of weary troops fleeing in front of the Nazi armour, nor anything of the ships taking a defeated Army off the beaches. People in Britain were still going about their business with little disruption of their daily life and without loss of confidence in the impregnability of their 'sceptred isle', their 'demi-paradise'. Little did they know then what a fool's paradise it was, for they were still living in a country that always thought of wars and of 'the front' as being in some far-off country.

Soon, very soon, that feeling of impregnability would vanish, but in the early summer of 1940 Britain still had little suspicion that everything would change dramatically. In the post-Dunkirk days, a strange mood of euphoria gripped the nation, a condition that can be compared with the feelings soldiers get coming out of a bloody battle when the mere act of surviving, of escaping death or mutilation, produces a curiously moving and even exhilarating effect upon them. It was the same with the nation at large: the whole of Britain seemed to be sharing vicariously with the British Army these primitive emotions, and for a few weeks the wave of gratitude and relief appeared to blur the harsh outlines of the country's predicament – that France had fallen and Britain was alone. In that hot summer of 1940 only Britain, of all the nations that had taken up arms against Hitler, stood unconquered and defiant.

Doreen Atkinson, the ambulance-driver who had escaped from France, remembers how uplifted she felt after listening to Prime Minister Churchill's memorable broadcast to the nation on 4 June 1940:

I was sitting in the NAAFI canteen on the edge of the parade ground in the old Victorian barracks on top of the hill in Lincoln which then was Number 7 Infantry Training Centre. The NAAFI was full of the usual noise, the clatter of cutlery, men whistling, shouting, singing, and in the background was the music of some dance band or other. Suddenly the music stopped, and all other noise subsided. What had been said to achieve this I don't know but there was silence, and then came the voice of Churchill. He told us that we had come through a great defeat, but then he voiced a promise that made us feel really excited. The words of that promise, later to be parodied by music-hall comedians, were:

'We shall go on to the end. We shall fight in France, we shall fight on the seas and oceans, we shall fight with growing confidence and growing strength in the air, we shall defend our island whatever the cost may be, we shall fight on the beaches, we shall fight on the landing grounds, we shall fight in the fields, and in the streets; we shall fight in the hills; we shall never surrender.'

Doreen Atkinson stood up and turned to her friend. 'Come on then, let's fight our way back to the cookhouse. There's a job to be done.'

There was indeed. All over Britain women officers and other ranks of all trades were 'mucking in together' in what later came to be called 'the spirit of Dunkirk'. They were cooking, washing up, cooking and washing up again until they were dropping with fatigue, but the battle-weary troops from Dunkirk had their much-needed meals. In clothing and equipment depots women worked all day and night issuing new clothes and kit; ambulance-drivers spent hour after hour at the wheel; maintenance mechanics greased and serviced the few precious vehicles left to the Army.

At the end of it all, in that hectic summer of 1940, it was clear to everyone that the women's Services had gained a new stature, a new dignity. They had come through the fire, and they were the stronger for it. Well might the visiting Australian Prime Minister say at that time that his outstanding impression of Britain was 'the courage, the action – and the endurance of the women'.

The 'courage and endurance' of women was going to be sorely needed in the weeks that immediately followed Dunkirk, and the range of their duties was to be greatly enlarged to include more commanding and exciting ones, for during that time the British Army was desperately trying to raise a 'Field Force strong enough to fight off the imminent German invasion. Already German assault barges were assembling on the French coast. It seemed only a matter of time, and the big question was: Would there be enough time to find men for the new army and to equip and train them to meet the crack and confident troops who had swept so swiftly to victory in France? Where were the soldiers for this new British field force to come from? They would have to be taken from training camps, offices, base headquarters, lines-of-communication units and non-combatant units of all kinds and drafted for duty with front-line units.

At the same time as this regrouping was happening, there was another pressing need to be met. The anti-aircraft defences had to be considerably strengthened to cope with the intensive air bombardment that would certainly precede any sea invasion. Yet Anti-Aircraft Command was already being denuded of men to reinforce the field units; it was patently clear that there were simply not enough men to go round – demand was outstripping supply. Consequently, to make up for this deficiency in manpower, there was only one course of action open to the Ministry of Labour and National Service: more use would have to be made of womanpower.

From this realization came a new policy: the total manpower resources of the country from then on were to be assessed by counting men and women together. The Secretary of State for War explained this new policy to the House of Commons, prefacing his exposition with the words: 'The Auxiliary Territorial Service has proved so valuable to the Army in the replacement of men that the Government has decided to enlarge the range of duties which it performs.'

Similar expansion policies were pursued by all the women's Services and, as the manpower situation became increasingly acute, women took over more and more duties and trades to release men for active service. In the ATS, for example, from the five categories of trades open at the outbreak of war there quickly grew over a hundred. For the first time in history women were overcoming doubts about their ability to replace men much needed for other duties. Women became armourers, carpenters, coach-trimmers, draughtsmen, electricians, plotters, radiographers, sheet metal workers, vulcanizers and welders, to quote but a few of the new trades taken over.

Once she was in a trade, though it was difficult for a woman to transfer to another, unless discharged for inefficiency. Mildred Morton joined as a driver and instead found herself in a steaming hot kitchen early in the morning and late at night, cooking. She did not like this at all. 'I applied many times for a transfer,' she recalls today, 'but I was always told that there nothing else available at the moment. After a few months I was so fed up I was ready to try anything, so I started by burning the porridge, serving soggy chips and lukewarm, weak tea. There was no need for any more applications to change my trade. I was sent on the next Motor Transport Course that came up.'

This way of getting out of the cookhouse was, it seems, not uncommon. A War Office account tells of rice pudding being served with large quantities of mustard in it and that, 'After a few days of similar occurrences there was little for it but to allow the young women cooks who wanted a transfer to change their employment. Better no food than continual wastage of good food.'[5]

A most welcome opportunity for getting out of a dull ATS trade and into something more exciting came in the summer of 1940, when women were asked to volunteer for training in duties with anti-aircraft batteries. Tests carried out as early as 1938 by a woman engineer, Caroline Haslett, had convinced Anti-Aircraft Commander General Pile that women could easily manage this job. Events were to prove him right. The one barrier that had prevented this so far had been the Royal Warrant which limited women to a non-combatant role. Now, as long as they were not actually employed on the firing of a gun, women could take on all jobs as full members of an anti-aircraft battery. As Prime Minister Churchill was to say when he insisted upon equality of status: 'A gunner is a gunner.' His daughter Mary was one of the first to volunteer for duties with mixed batteries of Anti-Aircraft Command.

The idea of men and women marching, eating, drilling and working together, all under the auspices of the British Army, was not without a certain revolutionary tinge, but for once the Army was astute in the way the first of these mixed batteries were formed for training. ATS volunteers started training with men who had just joined the Army, men fresh from civilian life and who had no military experience whatsoever. Such men did not find the atmosphere of a mixed battery so hysterically unorthodox, for until recently they had been used to working alongside women in factories and offices. This tactic worked: men and women took each other for granted, and the new units settled down very well.

Soon they were to appreciate to some extent the significance of that well-known dictum that, 'War consists of long periods of unutterable boredom, interspersed by moments of intense excitement.' They were also to learn very quickly that one mistake by one person during one of those moments of intense excitement could ruin all the efforts of hundreds of other people. Consequently, during the period they were not in action, the women and men of the AA units trained hard, so that they were one hundred per cent efficient in their own jobs and also capable of taking over the job of someone else who might be wounded or sick. They learnt too that the object of Ack-Ack gunnery was not just to shoot down enemy aircraft but to protect people and military objectives by causing bomber pilots to take such evasive action that their bombs could not be aimed accurately and therefore miss the target. Instructors explained this in simple language and to the women sitting there it all seemed reasonable. The patter would go something like this. Information is taken from WO AA Training Manuals and talks with women.

To drop bombs accurately on a target the bomber must fly on a constant course for a period of between thirty and sixty seconds before the bombs are released – can you hear me at the back there? This is necessary so that the bomb-aimer in the aircraft can adjust his bomb-sight according to the height and speed of the aircraft and wind conditions. He must then align his bomb-sights on the target, just as you follow an aircraft in the telescopes of the predictor or other visual instrument. Thus, during what is called the run-up, the pilot must fly on a constant course to allow the bomb-aimer to make these adjustments.

Now, if we can put up anti-aircraft fire so accurately during this period that the pilot is frightened and is forced to alter his course, the bombs will not be aimed accurately and will almost certainly miss their objective. If so, the gunners have achieved their object – the protection of the target being attacked by the bomber. Ah, you will say, wait for it, wait for it, you will probably say, 'But the bombs will fall somewhere and do damage just the same.' That is true. In large areas such as London, a bomb aimed at Buckingham Palace might easily hit the Houses of Parliament. But remember this: the guns are always sited for the defence of a particular area. It may be a large area such as the London Docks, or it might be a small area such as an important factory. If you prevent any bombers accurately aiming their bombs during that very short period before they are released, you will have succeeded in your object – the protection of the people and the material you are there to protect. Right? Fall out for a smoke.

Now all that sounded reasonable to the young ATS women listening to the officer or sergeant instructor lecturing in the Nissen hut but out on the gun-site things were somewhat different, and putting up accurate fire to harass the pilot enough for him to have to take evasive action was not quite as easy as it had been made out to be.

To burst a shell near an enemy bomber many things had to happen almost at once: 'First of all you have to recognize it as an enemy bomber, secondly to know exactly where it is at that moment, thirdly to calculate where it will be in a few seconds time, fourthly to fuse the shell to make it burst at exactly the right moment alongside the bomber,' explained Connie Brook, formerly of 510 (mixed) Heavy AA Battery, Royal Artillery.

There were instruments which in theory provided all this information, but if any one of the operators made a slight error, this was magnified many times by the instruments passing it from one process to another, and so the work of all the other operators was of absolutely no avail. Consequently training for these operators was rigorous and demanding in many ways, as Ruth Negus found, but there were compensating moments to it all and there was certainly no time to be 'unutterably bored' as one general's description of war had suggested:

When several of us were selected to train as radar operators or operators fire control (OFCs) we went off for six gruelling weeks of training at a large camp near Oswestry. There we learnt about electricity, radar, radio, maintenance of equipment. It was all very secret then. One of the instructors was a terrifying, red-faced colonel who used to jump up and down with rage, slapping his leggings with his cane! We had to get up at 5.30 a.m. and were often still working at 9.30 that evening. Luckily it was summer-time. After that we went to a firing camp at Anglesey and joined the remainder of what was to be our AA battery of the future: gunners, predictor operators, height-finders, spotters, telephonists, cooks, orderlies and, of course, our officers.

I found the noise of the guns at such close range ear-splitting at first and never really did get used to the crack of the 3.7s.

Little did Ruth Negus know that the target her battery was firing at was being towed by the record-breaking, intrepid solo flier Amy Johnson, who must have been keeping her fingers well crossed that nothing drastic went wrong.

Having become used to working together as a battery [Connie Brook remembered], we went home on fourteen days leave and then to a new AA site near Manchester, called 'S' for Sugar. We became known as the Sugar Babies. We had to set up the site from scratch, laying paths, wires and cables, getting used to working out of doors and sleeping in Nissen huts. We were allowed to light the stoves only in the evenings, and we had to collect the coke for them ourselves. Of course, from the time we had joined up, beds had to be 'barracked' – that is, blankets and pillows folded in the prescribed manner, huts cleaned, lino floor 'bumpered' to a high polish, kit laid out for inspection.

At that time we had only one half day pass [out of camp] a week. We were always very busy with teams on watch, and we in the GL12 Radar Sets had to be searching for targets. The radar would transmit the present information to the predictors which added wind speed and future position, the height-finders the information to the guns.

During the night two of us would go to the cookhouse for a bucket of cocoa, and we would bang loudly on the doors before we went in, to scare the rats. During the day we had to maintain all the equipment – cleaning and greasing it and so on. In addition to all this operational work we had to do cookhouse duties, guard duties at the main gate, spud-bashing, scrubbing out the NAAFI, which always smelt of old beer and stale tobacco, and cleaning the ablutions – the most hated chore of all. And, almost as though it was feared we did not have enough to do, we had to spent a lot of time on aircraft recognition.

Aircraft recognition was not easy. Mistakes were made by RAF aircrew even at close quarters, as well as by AA gunners, as one RAF rear gunner, Ken Williams, recalled to the writer: 'We were on our way to Cologne when one of our bombers, a Whitley, got very close behind me. With its twin engines and twin fins, it looked for all the world just like an ME 110, so I let him have a burst from my guns. He made off.' If it was so difficult at close range, one can imagine how difficult it was from a distance of several thousand feet! No wonder mistakes were occasionally made by Ack-Ack crews too. Connie Brook remembers how they plastered the sky round an RAF Wellington one day: 'We were protecting the big Dorman Long iron foundry at Middlesbrough at that time, when the aircraft came over and our guns engaged him. He had forgotten to give the friendly signal to radar but soon rectified the situation when the shells were bursting round him. Cease-fire was called but the shells were in the guns and fuses set, so they had to be fired. Fortunately we did not hit him but we certainly gave him a big fright.'

Work was hard and discipline was strict: 'The chief offences,' recalled Ruth Negus, 'were getting in late or burning one's boots by the stove. Punishments ranged from "confinement to camp" to "cook-house fatigues". Washing up for 400 people wasn't funny.'

Connie Brook knew all about this: 'The water was not always hot, and there were no detergents or washing-up liquid. You were up to your elbows in grease in deep aluminium sinks, and it was tacitly agreed that you got first chance of a bath afterwards – if there was hot water to be had. So scarce was it that my friend and I sometimes got into the bath together, and no one thought there was anything funny or lesbian about it. In fact, there did not seem to be any "unhealthy" relationships that I saw.'

It is perhaps worth noting here the nation's attitude to homosexuality at that time, for it does concern the situation in which servicewomen – as well as servicemen – found themselves. Robert Graves, and Alan Hodge in their book *Social History of Great Britain*, put the matter clearly: 'Homosexuality had been on the increase among the upper classes for a couple of generations, though almost unknown among working people. The upper class boarding-schools system of keeping boy and girl away from contact with each other was responsible. In most cases the adolescent homosexual became sexually normal on leaving school; but a large minority of the more emotional young people could not shake off the fascination of perversity. In university circles, homosexuality no longer seemed a sign of continued adolescence. Shakespeare, Caesar, Socrates, and Michelangelo were quoted in justification of the male practice; Sappho, Christina of Sweden, and the painter, Rosa Bonheur, of the female.'[6]

However, male homosexuality was still an offence punishable by law then, and therefore homosexuals in high places were particularly susceptible to blackmail. They were, consequently, a greater security risk. The extent to which the nation's security was in fact put at risk by the laws and by the general attitude towards homosexuality in men during the Second World War will probably never be known; files will remain closed, and books will be banned. With women, however, the situation was different.

The number of cases of lesbianism reported in the ATS was exceedingly small. Though it was not a criminal offence, there was, nevertheless, a disciplinary aspect to be considered. Fortunately for all concerned, the matter was dealt with in a remarkably sympathetic way, and action to be taken was explained in a memorandum called 'A Special Problem'.

This memo was mainly the work of a woman medical officer who analysed the issues with great wisdom and balance. She looked upon relationships between women as matters of degree, distinguishing between the 'adolescent crush' type, of the young girl having great admiration for another woman's personality and prowess; the normal friendships between women who could share each other's confidences, worries and pleasures, and what the official ATS history described as 'unhealthy friendships and true promiscuity'.

Having looked at the problem carefully and analysed it thoroughly, the memorandum outlined its conclusions on the way to deal with it. But the memorandum was never issued generally. This was deliberate and, as can be appreciated now with the benefit of hindsight, was a wise decision, for issuing it generally might have created a problem by drawing attention to it. As it was, if any ATS commander became aware of dubious relationships which she might consider to be affecting operational efficiency or training and, therefore, asked for advice as to action to be taken, the memorandum was despatched to her.

In the few cases of suspected lesbian relationships reported, the action taken usually resulted in no more than a judicious posting, separating individuals concerned. Only a very few promiscuous lesbians had to be discharged from the Service. Rarely was operational efficiency or training impaired.

'Generally morals and morale were pretty high,' said Monica Jackson. 'We, in a mixed battery, lived cheek by jowl with both men and women. I came across what I realize now was a lesbian friendship, but that was quietly dealt with by a very understanding battery commander.'

Everyone seemed to get on well with each other. That much is clear from all personal accounts and official records. Far from resenting the influx of girls into what had been a male preserve, men spoke highly of them and admired and respected them. It is an undeniable fact that, the more people had to do with the mixed batteries, the more enthusiastic they became. Final reports on run-of-the-mill batteries under training invariably carried comments such as: 'There is good material in this battery among the rank and file both male and female. They have worked hard and made good progress. The turn-out and marching of both men and girls was of a high order. There is an excellent spirit throughout.'

All right, men might have been inclined to say, but what would these women be like when it came to the real thing, when the bombs were dropping and shrapnel was whizzing around? It was well known that gunners firing in action for the first time were inwardly excited whilst appearing outwardly tense but cool.

The sceptics soon had the answer to that question. The women of 481 (mixed) AA Battery, RA, under the command of Major Jim Naylor, proved themselves so proficient in the use of their predictors and radars on location that they were posted with the battery for front-line duties in one of the most active bombing areas in the country at that time – Merseyside. They had an air raid to deal with on the first night in their new site. The battery commander had not welcomed the idea of having 'a bunch of giggling females to deal with', as he phrased it, but his attitude soon changed. 'There was no hardship the men faced that the girls weren't prepared to endure,' he was later to say. 'Their devotion to duty was really remarkable.'[7]

In that battery was Violette Bushell (by then Mrs Szabo), the half-French daughter of a World War I British Army sergeant. When she heard that the German Army had overrun her aunt's farm in Pont Rémy, she was roused into action. She returned home one night and declared, 'I cannot sit back and do nothing.'

Her resolution had been strengthened by a whirlwind love-affair with and marriage to a gallant young officer of the Free French Army whom she had met in London, Captain Etienne Szabo. After the wedding – on his embarkation leave for the Middle East, Violette had joined the ATS and was posted to 481 Anti-Aircraft Battery. There she quickly attracted attention for the speed with which she mastered the new technical skills, for her pretty face and coy modesty, and because of her unusual and attractive French accent. She enjoyed being part of an efficient team, though she badly wanted to fire the gun. To one section officer she once said, 'I only want to have some Germans to fight and I should die happy if I could take some of them with me.' That day, which would earn her the George Cross, was yet to come. For the time being she had to be content to be a member of one of the most efficient Ack-Ack batteries in the country.

When the alarm went in these mixed batteries, there was no question of the men having to wait for the women. They were out there, dressed in whatever was nearest to hand. Once, during a raid, Major Jim Naylor saw Violette busy at her predictor '... dressed in pale blue pyjamas and a pair of red slippers; from her shoulders hung her greatcoat; on the back of her head was perched her tin hat. The action lasted three hours or more. The girls had no cover at all and were liable to be hit by falling bombs and shrapnel.'

Violette's battery was not unique in its courage. The official history of the ATS records: 'On one occasion two auxiliaries aged 19 and 22 were engaged in working with electrical apparatus when bombs fell upon the site. Although knocked to the ground by the blast they remembered, as they got up, to switch off the electric current and thus averted danger to their detachment. The auxiliaries working on the predictor and other instruments were covered in mud from head to foot but they never hesitated in their work and throughout the raid the guns never ceased to fire.'[8]

The first ATS woman to be killed was Private Nora Caveney, aged eighteen, formerly a factory worker. She was following an enemy plane and was on target when she was mortally wounded by a bomb splinter, but she held onto the target until she collapsed. Her place was immediately taken by another woman, who followed the track of the German raider, and the guns continued firing without a moment's delay.

Accidents were not uncommon. Connie Brook recalls how at Sher-ringham Firing Camp a gun barrel burst open like a banana skin when a shell exploded inside it. On another occasion her own battery major was killed in a most unfortunate way which was to have terrible consequences. A fuse wrongly set in one gun exploded just after leaving the barrel instead of in the sky alongside an enemy bomber. Unknown to the gun crew, the major was at that time walking across the fields to them. He was hit by flying shrapnel. No one saw him fall. He bled to death as colleagues in the mess thought he was in the plotting room, and staff there thought he was in the mess; consequently for some time he was not missed and he was dead when they eventually found him. But that was not the end of the story: the gunner who had set the fuse wrongly was so upset that he killed himself.

Accidents were bound to happen even with the most efficient units, and the mixed Ack-Ack batteries certainly had a well-earned reputation for efficiency. They were tremendously proud of this reputation, as former Junior Commander Ruth Jewell recalled: 'It was a matter of pride for the girls of a mixed battery to do well in everything – on duty and off duty. Everyone was so keen that we never had any problems with discipline. And what might seem remarkable in these days was the way everyone took such a pride in behaving themselves. We did have one male officer who misbehaved when he was drunk, and the men were furious with him; they made their feelings known in no uncertain way. It was all part of this feeling of belonging to a unit of which they were proud. One girl who was pregnant when we were stationed at Shoreham, Sussex, had her baby on the site, went into hospital, had it adopted and came back for duty with the battery. Such was the feeling that pride in a unit engendered.'

The high regard these women had for operational efficiency and for their own self-discipline had a most beneficial influence on the way off-duty and social activities were organized. There were many advantages in belonging to a mixed battery. It was easier, for example, to form their own concert parties and band.

Connie Brook, a radar-set operator, joined 510 (mixed) Heavy AA Battery on a bleak site on the coast beyond Britain's most bombed port – Hull: 'I played an accordion on Saturday evenings in the battery dance band at Headquarters and on Sunday evenings at outlying sites. For this I got 10 shillings a week from battery funds – very welcome in those days. Sometimes our evenings were rudely interrupted. Naturally when the alarm went, the adrenalin began to flow and everybody ran.'

Former gunner Audrie Kearney also recalls that odd mixture of apprehension and excitement: 'Waiting to go into action we were usually very excited but too busy to be afraid. I always used to say a little prayer asking that, if we were hit by the enemy, I should be killed outright and not left crippled or maimed.'

Women gunners quickly gained a reputation not only for their courage and efficiency in action but also for the high standards they set themselves in the maintenance of the equipment on their charge. The officer commanding the first mixed battery to bring down a German bomber said: 'As an old soldier, if I were offered the choice of commanding a mixed battery or an all male battery, I say without hesitation I would take the mixed battery. *The girls cannot be beaten in action, and in my opinion they are definitely better than the men on the instruments they are manning. Beyond a little excitement which only shows itself in rather humorous and quaint remarks, they are quite as steady if not steadier than the men.* [Author's italics] They are quite amazingly keen at going into action, and although they are not supposed to learn to use the rifle they are as keen as anything to do so.'[9]

Nothing succeeds like success, we often hear, and in the ATS this was particularly noticeable with the mixed AA batteries. The women were handling the complicated equipment so well that in April 1941 an experimental women's searchlight troop was formed. Their training was deliberately rugged, with long, testing periods of PT and intensive drill on the barrack square culminating in a fifteen-mile route march. On one occasion as they swung onto the barrack square, having accomplished their route march in the scheduled time and without casualties, they were met by the Commander, 2 AA Division, who told them that, having proved their physical endurance, they were to continue straight away with their technical training. They were to pack and be ready to move off immediately. At the crack of dawn the next day the order came, and the women, dressed in male battledress and black tank berets, were given their movement orders. They had to locate a site twenty-two miles away, tow replacement equipment to it and become operational as soon as possible. When they arrived, they were horrified to find that the men of the previous unit had all moved out, leaving old equipment still in the pits. Now it was the women's task to remove this equipment and replace it with the new models they had towed with them. The pits were deep and the towing chains rusty but, nothing daunted, the women set to and got the job done. Whilst all this was going on, hidden observers were making notes.

For the next month the women operated the site, doing everything the men had done: digging, gardening, maintaining equipment, doing guard duties and at the same time carrying out training practices. At the end of this trial period the official report said: 'The standard reached by the women was higher than that of most men operating searchlights.'

In the summer of 1941 ATS were manning searchlight sites by themselves. Audrie Kearney is not likely to forget the night a German bomber pilot caught in the beam, flew directly towards her, firing machine-guns: 'He was so near I could see his helmet and goggles. He shot out the light and pulled out of the dive to safety. I couldn't help thinking what a brave lad he was.'

The women stood by their equipment from sundown to sunrise, when they returned to their huts for a wash and breakfast. They had a few hours snatched sleep and were often at work again by midday. In the winter it was bitterly cold work on the Ack-Ack and searchlight sites, and they were certainly glad of their 'teddy bear' coats and mittens.

One interesting result of work at night and loss of sleep was that women auxiliaries lost their fear or nervousness of the dark, and they preferred to go on sentry duty alone rather than work in pairs and so lose more sleep by being on duty more often. These women adapted to everything quickly, and when German planes started to dive down searchlight beams, adopting the tactics of Britain's own bombers in machine-gunning the site, they asked for an anti-aircraft machine-gun they could fire themselves. But they were refused – women were not allowed to use weapons without alteration to the Royal Warrant.

Women of the Auxiliary Air Force had similar experiences of being under fire. A WAAF sergeant wrote:

One Saturday we were clearing up the billet when the crackle of machine guns and cannon guns was heard. The men grabbed their rifles and dashed out to the Balloon site. The sky was full of AA shell bursts while machine guns were going off everywhere. Several balloons were coming down in flames, ours included. The next balloon to us was being hauled down just as fast as the winch could pull it. It was about 800 feet off the ground when one of the Messerschmitt 109s decided that he would try and get it. He swept over our heads and brought it down all right. But as he turned and banked away to sea again he seemed to be standing still in the air for a few seconds. The range was about 700 feet. The NCO yelled 'Fire!' Everyone pumped as many rounds as he could into it. The plane kept straight on with his dive out to sea, while a thin trail of smoke poured out from behind. When we last saw it, it was going down behind a breakwater out to sea. We did not stand about wondering if we had got it as we had a new balloon to inflate and fly. It was when we had finished this and had the balloon barrage up again that we learnt we had been given the credit for shooting down a Messerschmitt 109.[10]

Balloon barrages formed a crucial part of Britain's air defences, acting as a kind of stockade against enemy aircraft – the idea was to prevent low-flying bombers attacking targets. It was also reassuring for civilians to have a ring of these balloons round their town. But the handling of barrage balloons was both difficult and dangerous; it required skill, team work and considerable strength. One of the greatest potential dangers was lightning, for the balloon, attached as it was to the end of a metal cable, formed an efficient lightning conductor, and when the cable was struck, the electricity passed straight down the cable to earth through the winch gear. Consequently whenever thunderstorms were forecast, balloons were immediately bedded down. There was another reason for this: lightning often set fire to the highly inflammable hydrogen with which the balloons were filled. In the summer of 1940 eighty balloons fell blazing to the ground.

One can easily imagine the risks these women ran when hauling down the balloons in a race against time before the thunderstorm struck. There was a high risk of being burnt by blazing fabric or through their bodies conducting a deadly electric discharge to earth. It was for this risk that one of the standard precautions which women crew members had to get into the habit of observing at all times was to jump on and off the winch – never leaving one foot or hand in contact with the ground whilst another part of the body was in contact with the winch to form a body bridge to earth.

Ada Ryder recalled:

The balloon could behave very dangerously, and the weather was the number-one enemy. In high winds we had to 'storm bed' it; that was, to bring it down to the concrete base and anchor it with concrete blocks, each one weighing fifty-six pounds. The nose had always to be in the wind, otherwise it would break away, dragging thousands of feet of steel cable with it. That cable was lethal. The corporal would stand on site, eight of us each by a concrete block, and at her command we'd all move together about six inches at a time. The wind would be howling, rain and hail lashing us, and it would take about two hours to get the balloon into wind. We'd just finish, all tired out, and the wind would change, so out we'd go again. It wasn't funny, I'll tell you, in tin hat, pyjamas, greatcoat over the top, and big boots on our bare feet! Sometimes we were machine-gunned trying to fly the balloon as a raid came in.

The efforts of these women and their achievements on gun and balloon sites did not go unnoticed and '... brought about a remarkable change of attitude towards service women, particularly with commanders who had witnessed at first hand the superb bearing and coolness of women under fire. They had seen girls, most of them under 21, staying at their posts despite strafing, bombing and scenes of horrific carnage, and they recognized that their refusal to quit was even more praiseworthy when it was remembered that during those first years of the war each girl had it in her own decision whether to call it a day and desert without punishment, or remain among such terrifying conditions'.[11]

Unfortunately for women generally, the enlightened commanders who had seen that women could do most men's jobs were few and far between. With the others, the old prejudice against women was still firmly entrenched – so much so that in the summer of 1940, when there was a desperate need for pilots, the Air Ministry flatly refused to countenance the idea of women flying in the Royal Air Force, no matter how well qualified or experienced they might be. The Cabinet backed this attitude: 'On no account will we allow women to carry lethal weapons', conveniently turning a blind eye to the hundreds of WAAFs employed in armament manufacture and repair and driving tractors towing bomb 'trains' from airfield dumps to dispersal areas. Other diehards simply stuck to the old lines that flying was 'just not women's work' and 'It takes a lot of money to train a pilot. What if they got pregnant?' A more extremely biased attitude was blatantly expressed by C.G. Grey, editor of *Aeroplane*, who wrote at this time:

We quite agree that there are millions of women in the country who could do useful jobs in war. But the trouble is that so many insist on wanting to do jobs which they are quite incapable of doing. The menace is the woman who thinks she ought to be flying a high speed bomber when she really has not the intelligence to scrub the floor of a hospital properly, or who wants to nose around as an Air Raid Warden and yet can't cook her husband's dinner. There are men like that too so there is no need to charge us with anti-feminism. One of the most difficult types of man with whom one has to deal is the one who has a certain amount of ability, too much self-confidence, an overload of conceit, a dislike of taking orders and not enough experience to balance one against the other by his own will. *This combination is perhaps more common amongst women than men.* [Author's italics.][12]

Faced with such irrational prejudice as that, what chance was there for women who wanted to fly on equal terms with men in the RAF, as they had in civil life? Even the most famous of women pre-war pilots who had proved their worth on long-distance record-breaking flights had to make do with the more mundane of the flying jobs.

Thus it was that on 20 May 1940 a thirty-seven-year-old woman wearing the navy blue jacket, trousers and jaunty forage cap of the Air Transport Auxiliary reported for duty at Hatfield Airfield.[13] She did not, however, have the air of a new girl but the serene, confident look of a woman who knew well what she was about. There was, too, something familiar about her face that made people turn to take a second look, as if to confirm a sudden feeling of recognition. It was not surprising, for the face of a smiling, triumphant Amy Johnson had often been pictured on the front pages of newspapers all over the world from 1930 until the outbreak of war. 'Wonderful, wonderful Amy!'

After graduating from Sheffield University she had gained her 'A' and 'B' pilot's licences, which permitted her to fly for 'hire or reward', then qualified as a ground engineer and gained her navigator's licence, which involved mastering subjects such as meteorology, maps and charts, direction-finding, W/T navigation, visual signalling and international legislation. And to back up all the qualifications she had logged 2,285 flying hours and had flown, solo, 11,000 miles, breaking the record to Australia and also to South Africa. Why, then, were her talents and experience, and those of other well-qualified women pilots, not put to better use? When we consider what exactly the skills of Amy Johnson were, her feeling of frustration in what she described once as 'the role of air taxi driver' – a ferry pilot – is not in the least surprising.

Although she had already clocked up many hours of target-towing with a civilian firm, as a mere female she was summarily dismissed when the RAF took over her duties. When she tried to use her 'knowhow' for the service of her country, she met with little encouragement. On one occasion she even begged Lord Vansittart of the Foreign Office to give her some work to which she could dedicate herself. She pleaded with him, in vain, to 'take her on for some dangerous mission in the Secret Service' but again she drew a blank.

By 1940, however, both the authorities and the public had changed their attitudes to the employment of women flyers. Lettice Curtis, the first woman to fly a four-engined bomber, recalled: 'When things started to happen they were desperately short and wanted every pilot they could lay their hands on, men and women.' She vividly remembered the dangers of war-time flying: 'In particular the hazards of having to fly with poor radio communication, in conditions of rain, snow, ice, wind and storm.'[14]

She remembered also one horrifying moment when the pilot in front of her landed in a soggy patch of the grassy airfield: 'On hitting it, his plane went onto its nose and then right over onto its back. I landed alongside but there was nothing one could do until enough people arrived to lift the tail and so release the cockpit hood. When eventually the plane was lifted, the pilot was dead, not from a broken neck, but from drowning.'

Altogether Lettice Curtis flew 222 Halifax bombers between 1940 and 1945, as well as numerous other planes including Wellingtons, Spitfires, Mosquitoes, Tiger Moths, Hurricanes, Stirlings and Lancasters.

Amy Johnson did not achieve such a tally. On the bitterly cold morning of 7 January 1941 she crashed in the Thames estuary. Her body was never recovered. Altogether, fourteen women ferry pilots, out of a total of 138, were to die before the war ended.

Shortly before that fatal last flight, Amy Johnson had written to her parents saying: 'Did you see they're having women as pilots in the French Airforce? They'll never do that here …'*

How prophetic her words were to be! 'They would never do that' despite the fact that women were already showing as much grit, courage and devotion to duty as the men. Typical was the example set on 18 July 1940 by WAAF Corporal Joan Daphne Pearson.

She was standing by the runway of her airfield when an RAF bomber crashed on take-off and burst into flames. She ran towards the aircraft, knowing there were bombs aboard, stood on the burning wreckage and helped the pilot get clear. That was not all. When the pilot was being laid on the ground about thirty yards from the blazing wreck, a 120 pound bomb exploded. Thinking others would follow, she flung herself on top of the injured pilot to protect him with her own body. Her action and the award of the medal of the Military Division of the Order of the British Empire were reported in the *Daily Telegraph*.[15]

In general, the newspapers had little to say about the war – sport and entertainment still occupied much of the columns. There was no real sense of urgency in Britain, despite the fact that she was alone and facing imminent invasion. In the strange lull that followed the Dunkirk miracle, Britain had once again begun to slip into an almost peace-time routine. No wonder pilots such as Amy Johnson were unable to enlist as RAF aircrew: war was not yet affecting people enough to stir them into positive action.

Betty Wilde, who was later to join the ATS, was amazed at the way in which life went on as if there was no war at all. At that time she was a very young civil servant evacuated from London to the safety of Blackpool, where she found that women were having a great time: 'The

---

* The Frenchwomen had to be between the ages of twenty-one and forty and have a minimum of 300 hours solo flying (*Daily Express*, 31 May 1940).

place was full of young Air Force boys, and Polish airmen too. No shortage of entertainment, the ballrooms were packed, ice rink going strong, cinemas, music halls, concerts and all the social activities of peace-time. It really seemed as though there had never been a war declared. I decided that I was not "doing my bit" amongst all that revelry, and so I volunteered for the ATS and joined up with friends from work. It was better that way, for you took your friends with you and did not have to face the loneliness and homesickness met by girls who had joined alone.'

Even in the south of England the situation was little different, apart from the aerial dogfights way up in the sky where a few white trails marked the path of aircraft in mortal combat. It was all very far away.

The war came much nearer with 'shattering' suddenness when, at precisely 9.30 on the evening of 22 August 1940, the first long-range shells landed on the southern counties. Britain then entered a new phase in her military history. For the first time in centuries it looked as though she was going to have to wage war against an invader on her own soil. The German legions, flushed with victory, were just over twenty miles away, and the shelling seemed an indication that a German invasion could be expected in the Dover area.

So serious was the threat of invasion that former ATS Private Kingdon was one day asked a startling question by her commanding officer: 'I note that you qualified as a proficient bren-gunner. Would you like me to remove that entry from your pay book, AB64? Otherwise you might be classed with the men and shot by the invading enemy.' Her reply was typical of the women who had this qualification: 'Leave it in the book. I'd rather be shot than suffer a fate worse than death.'

German long-range guns, hidden in tunnels on the French coast between Calais and Boulogne, hurled their 1,500 pound shells 40,000 feet into the air, so that they fell without warning.

Pam Andrews was with the ATS there in those days: 'We were billeted in a bungalow at Broadleas, Dover, and we used to go to the pictures at the bottom of Castle Hill, but after 22 August we rarely saw a complete performance as we all had to leave during the shelling. We used to plod our way back up to the billet with the "flaming onions" screaming overhead. On reaching the top of the hill, it was a sight to behold. Red and yellow flashes across a moonlit Channel. We forgot the danger altogether, marvelling at it all.'

Leading Wren Ellen Purdham remembers how, 'As the shells began to fall, the ground trembled. Spout after spout of smoke and flame leapt up from the ground, and I suddenly thought of what my uncle Harry had once said. He'd been in the First World War and he had told me what to do: "Just press your nose into the ground, clench your fists and pray. That's the only answer to shellfire." So that's just what I did. It was like all Hell let loose.'

Daily, after that first onslaught of shells, the thunder of the bombardment increased, as more and more guns were put into position on the French coast. Tension mounted. 'Invasion' notices appeared on walls and hoardings, emphasizing the nearness of the enemy and the threat of landings by sea and by air.

'On a clear day you could actually see with binoculars German tanks and trucks drawing up into fields across the water. People were worried but nowhere near a panic,' is how former ATS Corporal Joan Richardson remembers the situation. Indeed, the people of Britain were all remarkably calm. Perhaps too calm for their own good.

Just because the national flag still fluttered above Dover Castle, citizens felt secure; typical 'Business as Usual' signs came up over boarded shop windows. Women pinned notices to the gateposts of shattered houses which read: 'Our fronts may be down but our backs are up.' Women in all walks of life were determined to carry on; they just altered their daily routines somewhat.

'In that summer,' wrote Agnes Ferris, 'it was great fun being in the ATS. We had our usual military chores and duties in the early part of the day but after the eleven o'clock NAAFI break we went out working on farms, getting in a second crop of hay. We drove old cars towing rakes and sat on top of swaying loads of hay, piling it up still higher as men forked it up to us. We worked late into the evening and then – and don't ask me where we got the energy from – we biked down into Dover for a drink at the "Crypt" or for a meal at the "Oyster Bar". You could eat very well there, a plateful of lobster, tomatoes and lettuce for 3s. 6d. At other times we'd go dancing, and there were always plenty of partners.'

Ballroom dancing was in its heyday, never before or since so popular. The *Dover Express* carried a notice which read: 'The enemy is but twenty miles away, but dances will be held every Monday.'[16] On the average Dover held three dances per week, and seldom were they postponed through war causes. One occasion saw the band vie with German gunners as to who could make the most noise; dancers remained swaying to the rhythm of war and a 'hot' band. Public houses also did a roaring trade; evening shelling was their best time. And women were not made to feel unwelcome or as if they were 'on the loose' in going to a pub. Service life certainly helped women overcome the traditional conventional barriers to going for a drink in the same way as men.

Shells did not deter anyone from their routine visit to the pictures either. In that last week of August 1940 when the shelling began in earnest, orderly queues formed nightly outside the Regent Cinema to see Marlene Dietrich in *Flame of New York* and at the Plaza for Joan Blondell and Dick Powell in *Model Wife*, whilst at the Granada those wanting a laugh waited to see Wallace Beery in *Barnacle Bill*.

The Hippodrome, which had been due for demolition before the war, was now a thriving front-line theatre, attracting not only record audiences but big-time stars who otherwise would never have graced its stage. Prime Minister Churchill's actress daughter Sarah appeared there with her husband, comedian Vic Oliver; Evelyn Laye, Albert Whelan and many other stars of stage and radio came to show that they too were real troupers and not afraid of a few shells. After the show people crowded into the artists' bar: 'The place was heaving, thick with smoke and barely enough room for anyone to stand. It was packed to the door, not just with soldiers, sailors and airmen but also with servicewomen. There were Wrens, ATS, WAAF, VAD, nurses from the Casualty Clearing Hospital and Fannys', recalled journalist Frank Illingworth.[17]

It was just the same with the daytime shelling: life went on as usual. Airwoman Brenda Robinson of the WAAF remembers drinking coffee with two of her friends in Woolton's café on the morning the window fell in with the blast of a shell bursting nearby. 'It all happened so quickly there was nothing else to do but carry on drinking our coffee and smoking our cigarettes. If that shelling was intended to soften us up before an invasion or to batter our morale by disrupting our daily routine, it failed completely,' she said.

Morale was high even amongst casualties – and there were many. Frank Illingworth wrote then: 'A constant stream of mutilated men passed through the tireless hands of Sister Nora Maylan. And those of us who helped will never forget either the energy of nurse or doctor or the fortitude shown by the wounded. Two Auxiliary Firemen were detailed to lift a wounded Guardsman. One slipped his arms under his shoulders and the other took his legs but when he lifted only the bedclothes came up. The poor devil had lost both legs but he said, "Under me behind, Fireman, me legs is evacuated." Another soldier, his right leg missing, said he'd "have to play left back next season".'[18]

Typical of this high level of morale and the contempt for the shelling in those days was the attitude of servicewomen to sport. Matches went on regardless of what was thrown at them from across the Channel or from the Luftwaffe bombers: 'Wrens in one match were machine-gunned and on another occasion a mixed hockey match between Wrens and Naval men was interrupted by Messerschmitts. And on yet another occasion bombs dropped on a service pitch caused several casualties. If long-range guns disturbed play the temporary return of peace saw games taken up from where they were left off,' wrote a local sports journalist.[19]

It was not all 'beer and skittles' though. For some women, witnessing war at close quarters for the first time, there were some horrifying experiences.

After one night of savage shelling [recalled former Airwoman Brenda Robinson] I had to walk back through the town picking my way warily over all the debris. In the half light I came across a shocking sight. A gang of men was working in the flickering light of a fire blazing through the roof of a nearby house. They moved great pieces of masonry and charred beams, moving them carefully to avoid the rest of the pile from collapsing onto bodies pinned beneath it all. Some had already been moved to the other side of the road, and ambulance men were lifting them onto stretchers. I came across a young woman lying face downward on her arm, a pool of blood on the pavement under her chest. She moved her free hand slightly as I touched her shoulder. She was dying. I stayed with her until she too was lifted gently onto a stretcher and taken away. I often think of that poor woman now ...

But then Airwoman Brenda Robinson had more urgent matters to occupy her mind for she went back from leave to RAF Manston, where the Battle of Britain was now being waged with frightening ferocity.

3   The Back-Room Girls

Until my experience in London I had been opposed
to the use of women in uniform. But in Great Britain
I had seen them perform so magnificently in various
positions, including service with anti-aircraft batteries, that I had been converted. Towards the end of
the war the more stubborn die-hards had been
convinced and demanded them in increasing
numbers.

Dwight D. Eisenhower,
Crusade in Europe (Heinemann, 1948)

August 1940 – May 1941

The mists of early morning were curling upwards from the lush green
fields which banked in ridges towards a soft grey-blue sky over the
Channel. In the thick-walled coastal radar stations women operators
were sitting silent and subdued before their secret, delicate instruments.
A sense of foreboding hung in the air. They had been warned and knew
what to expect. For weeks following Dunkirk the RAF had waited and
wondered when Hitler would lose his temper and attempt to force a
quick decision with a vast terror raid on London. But that raid had not
come.

Now these highly trained women saw something happening before
their eyes that was more than formidable: the build-up of a massive
enemy formation over the Pas de Calais. Could this be the moment of
Hitler's decisive attack? A daunting thought, enough to send a tremor
through those young WAAFs now searching the skies: an awareness of
risk, a realization that this present spell of duty might end with sudden
death.

That morning they knew for sure they were in the front line: they had
been told they would be the principal targets for the German bombers.
And those bombers were now rapidly approaching the coast.

Inexorably the formation moved closer.

Confidently, a few hours earlier, Hitler had passed to his Air Force
commanders the codeword to attack – '*Adlerangrife*' ('Operation Eagle').[1]
Understandably, he was confident of victory, for already Germany
dominated Europe from North Cape in Norway to the Italian Alps, from

the Atlantic to the River Bug in the east. The Soviet Union was Hitler's neutral friend, Italy his ally, and the United States stood aloof, a hostile neutral but offering no real threat.

To the world it seemed futile for Britain, with most of its weapons and equipment lost in France, to fight on. Nevertheless, despite the odds against continued resistance. Churchill had contemptuously rejected Germany's peace offer of 19 July. Hitler was shocked. The German people had not been led to expect a long war, and he had not reckoned on waging a war across the sea. Nevertheless, he immediately ordered 1,600 invasion barges to harbours of northern France and Belgium ready to embark his crack assault troops. Unlike Napoleon, who, 140 years earlier had faced the same problem, Hitler had an Air Force, the world's largest, with 3,500 war planes whose crews were flushed with victory in the skies from Warsaw to Brittany, from Narvik to Toulon. That Air Force, he was convinced, could shatter the RAF with the same hammer blows that had smashed the Air Forces of Poland and France, to clear the way for his triumphant Panzers. Justifiably confident then, he had sent a strong directive to his Luftwaffe chiefs. It read: 'To establish the necessary conditions for the final conquest of England I order the German Air Force to overpower the English Air Force with all the forces at its command.'[2]

In his reply, Chief Reich Marshal Goering arrogantly boasted that his Air Force would do more than this. It would bring Britain to its knees without any help from the German Army or Navy.

So it was then that on 12 August 1940, in the firm belief of a speedy victory, the whole might of the German Air Force was launched exclusively against the secret nerve-centres of Fighter Command, its airfields and radar stations. There the women were waiting and watching, locating, tracking and passing on the information to controllers of the fighter squadrons.

The governing principle for the defence of Britain was that a sufficient strength of fighter planes be assembled at the required height over a given place where it could intercept an oncoming enemy raid and break it up before it could reach its objective. To keep a sufficient strength of fighters in the air to guard British shores from attack was then beyond the powers of the biggest air force imaginable. Consequently the fighters were kept on the ground in the interest of economy of effort and ordered airborne only when raids appeared to be imminent. In this way fighter pilots could go into an attack with maximum fuel available.[3]

Women played a vital part in this Air Defence Plan by providing information about approaching enemy formations. Especially important were those women working on the new and secret radio-location instruments.

Why women?

It was mainly because the man who developed the system, Sir Robert Watson-Watt, believed that women had qualities which made them ideally suitable for the job. 'The good operator,' he said, 'needs a well developed conscience, a sense of duty, patience and freedom from any tendency to panic. Qualities in which women predominate.'[4]

Not all women, however, could satisfy the rigorous selection procedures for this duty; those who did were chosen for their perfect eyesight, clear voices and integrity of character, as well as for those other factors which went to make a reliable and responsible operator. They had to work long hours and often under conditions of considerable strain. And it was a strain they could not talk about, for they were sworn to secrecy. They were part of a chain of secret radio-location units, each with 300-foot-high masts built along the south and east coasts of Britain.

Naturally the Germans had been puzzled about these masts, which had gone up shortly before the war, and as early as the summer of 1939 a Zeppelin had flown over them, a flying laboratory to spy on these odd contraptions. The Germans suspected they had something to do with the same kind of research they too were carrying out to detect and locate airborne raiders. Consequently these units became primary targets along with the fighter airfields.

By nine o'clock on that morning of 12 August the vital south coast chain of radar stations was already under heavy attack: heavy bombers, dive-bombers and fighters hurled themselves at six stations between Dover and the Isle of Wight. Situated on the very coastline, these stations were extremely vulnerable.

Relentlessly, savagely and incessantly throughout that day the sites were blasted by bombs and machine-gun fire. At times the buildings were almost invisible behind a pall of dust and smoke but inside the women worked on; there was no doubt in anyone's mind of their determination to carry on.

'There was no pretence at any kind of joking that you sometimes see in war films, and there was a good deal of honest funk. At times we were, to put it bluntly, "scared witless", but somehow we saw it all through,' said a former WAAF sergeant.[5]

At the end of that day the RAF wondered how long they could carry on against such an onslaught if the Luftwaffe continued to hurl its full might against the radar stations and airfields.

Back on the German bases the High Command was congratulating itself on the success they were having. Reports from pilots showed that they had already destroyed sixty RAF fighters and literally wiped completely off the map all the targets given to them for that day.

Fortunately, those reports were not quite accurate: the RAF had lost twenty-two aircraft, the Ventnor radar station at Bembridge was out of action, and so was the fighter airfield at Manston.

Nevertheless, full of confidence, the Luftwaffe pilots went into the attack again and again in the days that followed, determined to blast the RAF from the skies and runways, hammering away at fighter airfields. On Thursday 15 August, the day that saw the heaviest fighting of the battle, the Luftwaffe sent 1,800 aircraft in massive assaults against Britain's air defences. From early morning until dusk raid followed raid, yet the women monitoring them seemed indefatigable. It took a German bomber only six minutes to cross the Channel, so there was never a moment to lose.

In the control room of Number 11 Fighter Group, WAAFs plotted the course of the incoming enemy formations. One of these women was Grace Archer, a former Section Officer. She remembers the scene well: 'This enormous room, 72 foot underground, was dominated by its huge centre table covered with a map of southern England, round which we plotters wielded long croupier sticks moving little arrows around showing the direction and numbers of enemy aircraft crossing our coast, as passed on to us through headphones or on teleprinters. The Controller, a Group Captain (surrounded by other high ranking officers of the other services), sat in a glass dome overlooking the table, ordering up fighter squadrons from all stations in the Group according to what he saw on the table. These were exciting and dramatic days.'[6]

They were even more exciting on the fighter airfields themselves.

Joan Mortimer[7] was a twenty-eight-year-old WAAF sergeant at RAF Biggin Hill, an important sector station of Fighter Command. When the bombs started to fall, she was on duty in the armoury, issuing ammunition to the gun positions – not the safest of places to be during an air raid, surrounded by several tons of high explosive. Whilst the airmen not immediately needed for duty raced for the safety of the shelters, Joan Mortimer stayed at her post receiving telephone messages, relaying information, issuing ammunition and keeping defence posts in touch with each other.

That done, before the 'All Clear' sounded, she dashed out of the armoury with a bundle of red flags under her arm, knowing that at any moment the fighter aircraft would be landing unaware that all over the airfield were unexploded bombs. Hurriedly she marked them with danger flags, as one report states, 'shaming the quaking erks [Aircraftsmen] cajoled into helping her'. It was a race against time. Barely had she placed the last warning flag when the fighters began to come in one by one, weaving their way warily between the bomb craters and the red flags.

Joan Mortimer's action did not escape attention. It was announced later that she had been awarded the Military Medal – 'a man's medal for a girl's bravery in the face of the enemy'. In addition, the citation went on to say: 'This airwoman displayed exceptional courage and coolness which had a great morale effect on all those with whom she came into contact.'

As the airmen and women emerged from their shelters after the 'All Clear' had sounded that day, they stared wide-eyed with surprise – not at the blazing buildings, nor at the ruptured gas main on fire, nor at the rubble around them, but at what was approaching them through a fog of dust and over the razor-sharp hot shrapnel which carpeted the cratered roads – the Salvation Army Mobile Canteen. 'Tea and wads' were up. Never had they been so welcome nor tasted so good; a never-failing morale-booster.*

Not many days later, two high-ranking officers of the WAAF drove down from Number 11 Group Headquarters to see how their Biggin Hill women were faring in the raids and to bolster their morale. They spoke fulsomely to the assembled WAAF officers and other ranks about the superb example which they were giving to the Women's Air Force as a whole, and said it was all in keeping with the best traditions of the Royal Air Force itself. Before departing for the comparative safety of their own headquarters, one of them gave the Biggin Hill WAAF a broad smile and cheerfully remarked: 'Well, now you know what it's like, it won't be nearly so bad next time.' At that time, all the Biggin Hill women could think was, how far from the truth the remark had been. Rather than being 'not nearly so bad next time', it would be worse. It was precisely knowing what it was like that would make the next time all the harder. And there were too many 'next times' to endure!

The women at the neighbouring fighter station at Kenley were to find this true at the end of the week, when they came in for a real 'pasting'.

The raiders came in at high and low level with deadly accuracy on a perfect summer day. First came a swarm of steeply diving Ju 87s with their escorting Me109s above them. Outside the dispersal hut some RAF pilots were sprawled in deckchairs, desperately trying to get some much-needed rest. A panic call came from Ops. But before the pilots were airborne, six Hurricanes and several other aircraft were completely destroyed on the ground, ten hangars were wrecked and gutted, and by the time the last of the bombers droned away into the distance, Kenley was a smoking shambles.

The strain on these Battle of Britain pilots – of operational flying and of being attacked when trying to rest – cannot be imagined, but the effect of it on them is well recorded: 'Some pilots became so emotionally

---

* The Salvation Army and the Church Army were often right in the front line, and we shall see women and men officers in the midst of the Blitz and in the action overseas. A 'wad' was a rock bun with a spot of jam in the middle.

numb that they were like automata, morose, withdrawn, wanting neither food or companionship; dragging themselves through each day in almost a stupor. Others, more highly strung, teetered constantly on the brink of frenzy; talking incessantly, smoking heavily, forcing themselves to loud laughter and feigned high spirits. But among the unfriendly silence on the one hand and the horseplay on the other, were the majority, level-headed, thoroughly professional, in control of themselves.'[8]

Women on the station played a big part in keeping up the morale of these pilots, as they were also to do later with the Bomber Command aircrew. Fighter Pilot Ginger Lacey, 'top scorer' in the Battle of Britain with eighteen enemy aircraft destroyed to his credit, was well qualified to speak on this. He gave a good example of how the WAAF at Kenley helped: 'There was an institution, in those days, at Kenley; a small, good-looking, and warm-hearted WAAF corporal cook, Jean Campbell. Though of much the same age as the sergeant pilots she took their daily dangers to heart as though they were her sons. Nothing she could do for their comfort was enough in her view; and when one was missing she would stay up all night, if necessary, to welcome him back with a cup of tea. It is some measure of what this gentle creature suffered, and of the devil that sat on the shoulders of Fighter Pilots at that dark time, to record that during four particularly dark days at Kenley, the three other beds where I slept each had two different occupants.'[9]

Similar stories are told of women on other operational stations. At Biggin Hill, for example, a report says: 'When the NAAFI manageress, perhaps more responsible than anyone for morale, showed signs of strain the Station Commander, Group Captain Grice, ignored her tearful pleading to be allowed to carry on and brusquely sent her packing on four days' leave. She left behind a gay jumper, souvenir of pre-war holidays abroad, embroidered with names of European capitals. He dropped a hint to his WAAF section. On returning from leave the manageress found the words 'Biggin Hill' emblazoned in scarlet across the back. She was delighted with this accolade.[10]

It was about this time in 1940 that WAAF Flight Mechanic Horton had the flight and fright of her life. That she lived to tell the tale passes all bounds of credibility, but film is there to prove her story.

It was the custom in those days for the WAAF flight mechanic to have two special jobs apart from all the normal mechanic's duties. One of these was to polish the perspex windscreen, and the other was to sit on the tail plane of the Spitfire when it taxied to the runway. On this memorable day, WAAF Horton sat on the tail plane, and when the pilot got to the runway for a practice circuit, he turned and accelerated for the take-off. Whether he had forgotten or just did not know that a young WAAF was sitting there, terrified, as the aircraft gathered speed is not known. 'There was only one thing for me to do,' said Miss Horton in a recent television interview as she recalled that day: 'I just lay flat down across the whole tail unit and clung on. The control tower saw what had happened but made a snap decision that the best thing they could do was to say nothing and not inform the pilot in case he became too anxious and made a bad landing through lack of concentration or too much through being exceptionally nervous. The pilot turned and approached the runway for landing, lowered his wheels and touched down perfectly. I did not know we had landed until I saw the earth going past below my eyes!'[11]

By the middle of August 1940 the shortage of aircraft was becoming serious despite the efforts of Beaverbrook and the aircraft industry. There were not enough first-line aircraft to go round. Just as soon as they had been flight-tested and armed, new fighters were flown to the battle front by women. Graham Wallace writes; 'Hard pressed pilots at Biggin Hill had long ceased to be surprised at seeing a girl wearing overalls of the Air Transport Auxiliary step from the cockpit of a new Hurricane or Spitfire to demand a signature for its delivery.'[12]

These women were most experienced pilots, having qualified before the war. They loved flying the Spitfire. In praise of its handling, Lettice Curtis – who later became one of the first women to fly Halifax bombers – wrote:

In the air the Spitfire was forgiving and without vice, and I never heard of anyone who did not enjoy flying it. It had a personality uniquely its own. The Hurricane was dogged masculine and its undercarriage folded inwards in a tidy businesslike manner. The Spit, calling for more sensitive handling, was altogether more feminine, had more glamour and threw its wheels outward in an abandoned extrovert way. From the ground there was a special beauty about it.

The cockpit of any single seater aircraft is a very snug private world, but to sit in the cockpit of a Spit, barely wider than one's shoulders, with the power of the Merlin at one's finger tips, was sheer poetry – something never to be forgotten by those who experienced it.[13]

There was no hope for Lettice Curtis to fly Spitfires operationally though, even at the height of the Battle of Britain, when so many good pilots had been shot down and killed and experienced replacements were scarce. The Air Ministry steadfastly refused to allow women become RAF pilots.

There was no let-up for these fighter pilots, nor for the women on the radar and plotting duties. For almost a month, from early morning until late evening, massed formations of bombers escorted by similar formations of twin- and single-engined fighters battered away at Fighter Command targets in southern England, the main targets being Kenley,

Biggin Hill, West Malling, Northolt, Tangmere, Manston, Croydon, Hornchurch, Rochford, North Weald, Debden, Hawkinge and Lympne – the inner defence ring around London.

One Sunday morning, just as the WAAF at Biggin Hill were putting the finishing touches to their dinner in the cookhouse, the bombs began to fall. From offices and cookhouse, stores and MT yards, WAAFs scuttled down into the airwomen's shelters, chattering excitedly. Section Officer Hanbury recalled how it was: 'The first bombs fell on the east side of the aerodrome, well away from the station buildings. I was in one of the airwomen's trenches and listened as the explosions drew nearer. One bomb fell just outside. I suppose one feels like this in an earthquake, I thought. Other WAAF there thought their limbs must surely be torn away by the blasts and concussion. The noise outside was indescribable but we could still hear the heartening stutter of the Hurricanes' and Spitfires' guns.'[14]

During another raid she took shelter in an airwomen's trench where they were packed like sardines, and a young WAAF whispered the Lord's Prayer, over and over again until the 'All Clear' sounded. When Felicity Hanbury climbed out of the trench, she saw two men gently laying the body of a girl wearing NAAFI uniform in the shade of a hedge. She began to walk towards them as if to help but one of the men noticed her and said, 'Don't bother Miss, the poor thing's dead.' It was the first dead person she had ever seen. But she was soon to see more.

'The Main Shelter, the one where not everyone could get in, had been hit,' said Aircraftsman Albert Hargreaves. 'There was a hell of a crater there. We rushed over and tried to get people out. There were a lot of casualties. There were heads lying around and arms sticking out of the crater. We were digging away there until three in the morning.'[15]

The Biggin Hill Operations Record Book states: 'The raiders dropped sixteen High Explosive bombs estimated at about a thousand pounds each. Six fell among the buildings rendering them quite useless and shattering by blast part of the airmen's married quarters which were being used as accommodation for WAAF personnel.'

One of the WAAF shelters had been hit. 'There was a frightful smell of escaping gas; they'd hit a gas main. When I got to the trench I saw it was sort of half bombed. The WAAFs had all been blown up to one end of it. Luckily, only one was killed but there were a lot of serious casualties,' said Felicity Hanbury.[16]

There were some funny stories though. At Debden, Aircraftswoman Edith Heap remembers a Scottish girl who was having a bath when a heavy raid started: 'She wasn't sure what to do, so she let the water out of the bath, put on her tin hat and just sat there in the tub until the raid was over.' Most of the fighter stations were by now a sorry sight. Biggin Hill had more than its fair share of bombs, and the women there distinguished themselves. Felicity Hanbury, later to become Dame Felicity Peake, was awarded the MBE for setting a magnificent example of courage and devotion to duty during the very heavy bombing attacks, and two other WAAF non-commissioned officers received the Military Medal.

One of them was a veteran of the First World War, Sergeant Helen Turner, who stayed at her switchboard outside the operations room when the raid began. A bomb fell on the tangle of telephone lines just outside her cubicle, severing all except the direct line to 11 Group Headquarters. Unmoved by this, Sergeant Turner stayed on, relaying messages throughout the raid. The remainder of the exchange by this time was on the floor, flat. Suddenly, when the bombing became even more intense, a huge rugby-playing sergeant took a flying tackle at Sergeant Turner and dragged her forcibly to the ground – just in time, for a 500-pound bomb fell through the roof and bounced off the safe! It exploded in the next building, where Corporal Elspeth Henderson was still tenaciously manning her line to Group Headquarters. The blast bowled her over just as her group captain came into the room to see how his staff were faring. The same blast and flying glass knocked the pipe from his mouth. Cursing the temporary loss of his pipe, he grovelled about until he found it. Then, stuffing it full of tobacco, he took a few puffs and helped Corporal Henderson to her feet, praising her remarkable composure. 'There wasn't much else I could do, was there, Sir? After all, I joined the WAAF because I wanted to see a bit of life.'[17]

By 24 August it was open to question whether the southern fighter bases could carry on for much longer. On that day, just after LACW Brenda Robinson got back from her leave in Dover, Manston suffered a monumental pounding. Packs of dive-bombers came screaming down with frightening regularity. The din was insane; it went on relentlessly and increasingly throughout the day but there was nothing the men and women on the ground could do but take it. At times, whole groups of buildings disappeared beneath clouds of flying concrete dust and shrapnel.

'Towards the end of that day you had this horrid feeling that having survived so far you were going to catch it after all, and you began to wonder if you would be under the next stick of bombs to fall, and then it became twice as hard to sustain your own mental discipline,' recalled Brenda.

By early evening there were officers and other ranks at Manston on the verge of physical and mental exhaustion; in the shelters men sat staring ahead, appearing to see nothing. Fear, long suppressed, came to the surface and affected people in different ways.

Some reports paint a disturbing picture. Whilst Spitfires and Hurricanes were dog-fighting with the Luftwaffe, was there something shameful going on in the Battle of Britain ranks? Some astonishing charges have been made that the morale of the ground crews collapsed. They tell that: 'Many airmen had been sitting in the air raid shelters ever since the attack at lunchtime on 12th August' and that 'terrified airmen would not budge' and that a 'Squadron Leader only just prevented another officer from going into the shelter to shoot the first man who refused to come out'. Subsequently the Squadron Leader fiercely denied that all this had happened, saying: 'At this time we used Manston to refuel and the ground crews came out of the shelters as we landed to do their job before going back into the funk holes – because that was the best place to be.'[18]

Today it is fashionable for the 'warts and all' brigade to strip away heroic illusions and tarnish the memory of those warriors who were killed or maimed for life. Of course, neither the 'Few' nor the ground crew were perfect; they made mistakes, they got frightened – it was a terrifying ordeal, and no doubt some had moments of panic, but that is true of even the bravest of people. These men and women saved Britain, battling against huge odds in that hot, dry summer of 1940. They inspired the nation and captured the imagination of the free world.

Women displayed remarkable tenacity in sticking to their posts. 'When the bombing began and the Germans came down and machine-gunned the station, I think the girls were more frightened of showing they were frightened. They were determined not to let anyone down, no matter how terrified they were,' said Section Officer Felicity Hanbury.[19]

Testifying to this *esprit de corps*, WAAF Brenda Robinson said: 'We had that tremendous feeling of comradeship that comes with sharing a fearful experience. It bound us together and gave us strength. Never had I known such a feeling before, and I have never had it since.'

At the end of that day, Manston, exposed at the south-eastern corner of England, was so devastated that it was abandoned.

The operational situation at Biggin Hill and the neighbouring airfields was little better, and it looked as though Fighter Command would now seriously have to consider abandoning all the southern bases. Retreat was ominously imminent.

Just how critical that situation was, few people knew. Whilst over the skies of southern England airmen were fighting a desperate battle for the survival of the country, elsewhere life went on in its familiar pattern. County cricket scores drew headlines little smaller than the day's score of enemy aircraft shot down – indeed, newspaper boys shouted the score sheet as though it were a cricket score. You would hear: 'Nazis ninety down, with two hours to play.' Incredible as it might now seem, the British people would not accept the serious nature of their position. In London they still flocked to the theatres: Robert Donat, in *The Devil's*

Disciple, played to a packed house every night; restaurants had never known such prosperity, despite the rationing. The war had not hit London. Yet.

But on that critical Saturday 24 August, when the fate of Fighter Command seemed to be in the lap of the gods, something happened that was to change the life-style of Londoners dramatically and at the same time to save Fighter Command from annihilation. The capital was bombed.

It was an accident. A mistake. A simple error of judgement on the part of a German navigator and pilot; the sort of thing that could happen to any aircrew.[20] But this mistake was one of historic proportions.

The German pilot had been briefed to attack an oil target east of London but having lost his way he jettisoned his bomb load before returning home. It fell on the church of St Giles, Cripplegate, and demolished the houses around it. Hardly had the dust settled than Churchill demanded a reprisal raid on Berlin. Reluctantly RAF Bomber Command despatched eighty-one bombers by night. Fewer than ten managed to drop bombs on the German capital. Military damage was nil. The effect was catastrophic.

Hitler reacted like a man demented. In front of an audience of women in the Kroll Opera House, he ranted and he raved: 'Since they have dared to bomb our city, we shall wipe out theirs.' Hysterically the women in the hall cheered him on. Wild-eyed and with saliva flecking his lips, Hitler responded to his audience – drawn from all the women's voluntary organizations of Germany – the 'Duty and Beauty' brigades, the 'Do Gooders' (equivalent of the WVS) and the 'Union of German Mothers'. They stood and cheered as Hitler promised them revenge. 'For every five bombs dropped on Berlin, London will get 5,000,' he promised.[21]

Now Hitler had become obsessed with this idea. It throbbed insistently in his mind for days after that meeting with the women.

Meanwhile the Luftwaffe continued its attacks on Fighter Command's airfields and radar stations. There, British women were showing what they were made of; they were as outstanding on the ground as Churchill's fighter pilots – his 'young chicks' – were in the air. During one raid, 'Wearing soldiers' tin hats – their battle bowlers as they called them – shirt-sleeved girls of the Woman's Auxiliary Air Force kept in telephone touch with the outside world over lines repaired after each raid, whilst other WAAFs plotted the approaching raiders. Even when the bombers were immediately overhead the girls remained at their posts showing devotion to duty which called for more than ordinary courage after the carnage of the previous day. As the bombs rained down the whole airfield shook and trembled as though engulfed by an earthquake.'[22]

By 6 September, Fighter Command was tottering on the brink of defeat, and the women as well as the pilots had been stretched to the limit of their resources. It was then that Hitler became Britain's ally! He diverted the Luftwaffe from Fighter Command targets and directed all its might towards London. Thus it was that on the sunny morning of 7 September 1940 Luftwaffe Chief Hermann Goering and the Air Fleet Commander, Field Marshal Kesselring, stood on the French coast and watched a formidable fleet of 600 fighters and 300 bombers massing overhead and destined for London. Now it was up to the Londoners to take it.

For the women of Fighter Command a respite from intensive bombing was mercifully granted. But not from work. That, if anything, increased in its intensity, especially for the WAAFs on radar units and in the plotting rooms.

The attack on the city at the heart of the British Empire opened with a concentration of incendiaries on London's dockland. It was followed by high explosives that night. Miles of warehouses were set ablaze; flames were fed by thousands of tons of sugar, oil, rum and paint that formed into streams sizzling into the Thames. Soon there was no need for the German navigators to set a course. Another Great Fire of London had started, and it could be seen from the coast.

On this night, on the bridges over the river, Wrens of the special Minewatch units were having their first baptism of fire.

These women had a special duty to perform, a job they didn't talk about. As soon as the air-raid siren sounded, they had two minutes to get from their accommodation to their posts in the centre of the bridges. There, hard against the parapet, were small brick-built huts with observation slits so that the Wren on duty could survey the stretch of river as far as the next bridge. On the 'windowsill' of this slit was an arrow-shaped pointer, which could be used to pinpoint the position of anything landing in the section of the river under surveillance. The sighting of any object splashing down into the river had to be noted, and as soon as the 'All Clear' sounded, the Wren on duty had to run as fast as she could to the nearest telephone box, grope in her purse for two pennies and ring the Port of London Authority, who would immediately have that stretch of the river closed to all waterborne traffic until it had been swept for mines or other explosive devices. Everything had to be done at great speed – especially getting on duty before the bombs began to fall.

Margaret Taylor remembers how it was: 'When it was our turn for duty, we had to sleep fully clothed in shirt, collar and tie and bellbottoms, and most of us, being true optimists, would cream our faces and put our hair in curlers (not of course the large plastic rollers now used, but the smaller metal variety that clipped the rolled-up hair into place and imparted a rather corrugated effect to the finished product when removed). Naturally there was no question of making oneself at all presentable to the outside world by removing cream or curlers when awakened by the siren. On went shoes, jacket, tin hat, gas mask over the shoulder, and off we would set at a gallop, dashing down the street with guns blasting away and shrapnel pattering down through the branches of trees lining the road.'

On 7 September 1940 the bombing by day was so intense and the conflagrations so great that it was impossible to extinguish fires before nightfall, and the flames again served as a beacon for the 235 German bombers that raided London again at night.

Then, at precisely nine o'clock, Wren Moira Keaton at Mill Hill received a most peculiar signal, one that she did not understand at all. Just one secret codeword: 'CROMWELL'. Her commanding officer knew what it meant though. So did all the other unit commanders to whom the message was flashed that night. It meant 'Invasion imminent'.

The women's Services stood by in a special state of readiness all night, tense and watchful, manning signals offices, key positions and telephone exchanges. On moorland, where parachutists might drop, troops stood by with precious little ammunition and with 'mortars' made from drainpipes. Others patrolled beaches along the southern and eastern coastline. But when dawn came, the calm sea off those beaches was empty, still devoid of any kind of invasion force.

On Monday 9 September WAAFs in the radar station were again on special alert, this time from British Intelligence's 'most secret source', where women worked around the clock. Goering had ordered another massed daylight raid on London, and fortunately these women had already read that message and warned the radar units.

About noon the 'blips' appeared on their screens – a thousand aircraft, bombers with a strong fighter escort, heading directly for London.

This time women of the mixed anti-aircraft batteries were ready and waiting too, eager to get at the prey. And get at it they did. Savagely. Their intense and accurate fire broke up the bomber formations, destroyed their cohesion and allowed the Spitfires to come screaming down into the scattered raiders. Those fortunate enough not to be amongst the eighty shot down by fighters were harried ignominiously home by vicious black puffs of exploding 3.7 shells.

Nevertheless, back the bombers came again that night, flying on radio beams, starting new fires in the city.

Wren Motor Transport Driver Nancy Spain was on leave in London that night, riding in a taxi from Holborn to Lambeth when the dive-bombers swooped. It was an experience she was never to forget: 'A mixture between a scream and a snarl and a roar was coming at us, apparently at five hundred miles an hour. Suddenly it changed to the bitten off "whoof" of the Metro Goldwyn Mayer lion, and I knew we were being dive-bombed. I also realised that I was flat on my face beside the taxi driver, who said to me. "After the viaduct". I could not think what he meant. I thought insanely that it sounded like a new H.G. Wells' novel, and then I heard the yell of a screaming bomb. The crash was nothing after the scream. Rubble fell on me. For about a year Hell broke loose all round me. It was like a stage storm. The thunder and lightning never left off for a single instant. Blinding light and blinding dark followed one another in bewildering succession.'[23]

In seven nights, 9 to 14 September, the women of the mixed heavy anti-aircraft batteries had no sleep at all. 'On Sunday morning,' said former ATS Sergeant Maggie Priestley, 'we were all ready to enjoy the luxury of a lie-in to make up for lost sleep when the alarm went.'

There was no sign on the radar screens but there had been a signal from 'that most secret source' – as Churchill called it: Goering was sending his bombers in for a final daylight fling. Now the defenders were ready.

At Number 11 Group Headquarters that Sunday morning the WAAF plotters had been reluctant to leave the bright sunshine for the artificial lighting and cool air of the operations room fifty feet below ground but they were all there, listening, watching, waiting. The room was murmurous with people. Suddenly voices hushed and they were aware of a presence: Prime Minister Winston Churchill was there, and with him his wife. He had a walking-stick in one hand and a half-smoked cigar in the other.

'All is quiet,' said the Group Commander, Air Vice-Marshal Keith Park. But Churchill's eye had already caught the movement of a WAAF 'croupier' as she began to push discs around the French coast. German bombers were massing. Very soon it was evident that Park's remarks had been tempting providence. A serious battle impended.

A lean man of medium height, Park held himself erect, his narrow, triangular face utterly without expression, his small jaw gaunt. He steepled his hands as he gazed at the table. His eyebrows rose. All eyes were on the markers now. When Park finally spoke, it was in his usual quiet, firm voice. He gave orders to squadrons in remoter parts of Britain to fly down to the southern front. At once.

Very soon, and before the droning throb of the German bombers' engines could be heard over the coast, several hundred fighters were sweeping up to meet them. The pilots knew just where to position themselves – as one was later to say to the writer: 'Those women radar operators and the plotters did a fine job for us. They gave us that fine edge over the German raiders, providing those extra minutes to get into the best position to attack.' It took thirty minutes to climb to 30,000 feet, where many of the dogfights took place.)

That day saw 'one of the most decisive battles of the war', wrote Churchill, '… and like that other decisive battle, Waterloo, it was on a Sunday'.[24]

This battle, upon which so much depended, lasted little more than an hour. But what an hour! The busy WAAF plotters pushed their discs this way and that according to swiftly changing situations. Soon not one RAF squadron was left in reserve. Then, just at a critical period when the fighters were having to break off engagement to refuel, something happened which brought a look of relief into the anxious faces of the women round that table. The discs they were moving now seemed to be turning eastwards. They were going home! The German bomber formations were disintegrating. It seemed as though the tired and overstrained German pilots had decided that the legend of their invincibility was now well and truly shattered. They had had enough; bombs were jettisoned, and many of them were heading for home with throttles wide open.

After the war, that Sunday, 15 September, was recognized as the climatic point in the Battle of Britain, and it is on that date that traditionally the British nation gives thanks for its delivery from invasion.

What would have happened if that invasion had succeeded? The programme of SS Colonel Dr Six would have become operative, and all able-bodied men between the ages of seventeen and forty would have been deported. Britain would have lived in servitude.

The women to whom Britain owed thanks for that relief were not only the WRNS, the ATS and the WAAF: but there was a most important secret sisterhood who helped provide Air Chief Marshal Sir Hugh Dowding, Chief of Fighter Command, with detailed prior knowledge of the Luftwaffe's plans and advanced warning of impending attacks. They were the women who worked with that 'most secret source' mentioned earlier, a source that was not to be revealed for another thirty years – ULTRA.

When, in one of those battles, Diana Payne[25] was bombed out of her home in London, she went to live in Cornwall, where, for a short time, she worked for the Ministry of Labour and pursued her passion for sailing at week-ends. Then it seemed natural for her to volunteer for service in the WRNS as boat crew. However, during her interview at the recruiting office an odd question was put to her: 'Can you keep a secret?'

She replied honestly that she did not know, as she had never had a secret to keep. Despite this non-committal reply, the interviewer then said that she would be considered for 'Special Duties X' – as second choice to 'boat crew'.

Call-up papers came: Category 'Special Duties X'. She reported to

Hampstead, had the usual head examination for lice infestation and then followed a fortnight's recruit training. On the completion of this she was posted to 'Station X' along with twenty other young Wrens. They soon found themselves at a beautiful Tudor house, Crawley Grange, near Bletchley Park – the headquarters of the Government Code and Cypher School. It was there that all those romantic thoughts of the sea and sailors vanished as Diana Payne learnt that she was destined to live with 500 women for the rest of the war, miles from the smell of the sea. Along with the other new recruits she signed the Official Secrets Act, and then the heavily guarded secret itself was revealed, the best-kept secret of the war: Britain was reading German coded messages and had been since Day One of the war! Now Diana Payne was to join that ULTRA team engaged on cryptanalysis of signals enciphered on the captured German Enigma computer-like code machine. A machine which was to be one of the most cogent secret weapons in the Allied commanders arsenal enabling them to follow virtually every Nazi move before it began.

Training began. It was not easy to master the intricate complications of running huge machines, an early type of computer, known as 'Bombes', which had noisy revolving drums that unravelled enemy Enigma code thought by the Germans to be unbreakable. But eventually the technique was mastered, and Diana Payne then began her war-time stint as a back-room girl working round the clock. 'Watches' were from 8 a.m. to 4 p.m., 4 p.m. to midnight, midnight to 8 a.m. As time went on, she operated 'Bombes' that became more and more sophisticated in order to decode messages from all headquarters: Navy, Army, Air Force and German High Command itself, in a remarkably short time, so that Allied Commanders could often make new dispositions of their forces in time to affect the outcome of battles. For example, before the Battle of El Alamein, Hitler sent a message to Rommel, but Montgomery received it first because Rommel's decoding was delayed due to sand in his Enigma machine!

These women therefore had tremendous responsibility placed upon their shoulders: any delay or slight mistake could lead to countless lives being lost at sea, on land or in the air. For this responsibility these Wrens were paid £1.10s. a week (a woman telephonist in the Auxiliary Fire Service then earned £2 a week). They had no status, no rank to speak of and absolutely no possibility of talking about their job whilst on leave. To relatives and friends who enquired what they were doing, they said they were 'writers' – the naval term for a kind of clerk.

'Sometimes it was very difficult having so little to say about one's life,' wrote Diana Payne, 'so my wartime activities were considered unimportant and something of a failure.'

One can easily imagine the tensions and feeling of isolation suffered by those women in not being able to talk about their work. And when that work was finished at the end of their 'watch', what could they do? Social life was naturally limited by their location in the countryside, miles from anywhere, and by the nature of their job. They could go for country walks or cycle rides but they were not allowed in local pubs. Life was far from easy.

Former Wren June Penny remembered how tiring it was: 'We were standing up most of the time as it was a big machine, a lumbering, rattling kind of computer which required a lot of attention. The noise was awful; the stress from ten to twelve noisy machines in each bay was nearly more than we could stand.'

As new theatres of war opened up, the workload increased. New units sprang up in similar mansions deep in the country, with hundreds of women drawn from all three of the women's Services, intercepting messages, breaking cyphers, distributing information through special channels also run by women. 'Watches' worked non-stop for eight hours at a time, with maximum concentration. But not without cost. Girls collapsed unconscious, suffering from overstrain; some were invalided out of the service; others had nightmares. 'There were cases of girls going berserk on duty,' wrote Diana Payne. 'I began to feel that this strange life of secrecy and semi-imprisonment would never end.' But the work did go on, unremittingly, and eventually there were over 2,000 women working on ULTRA. Despite the strain of such work, there were compensations: the comradeship and feeling of exhilaration when things went well.

June Penny remembered: 'It was exciting when we managed to break a code, although we never knew what the actual message was, of course. We learned afterwards that the system was one of the factors that helped win the war as it enabled the War Cabinet to learn of troop movements and naval intentions, also bombing raids, well in advance. In some cases they were not able to use all the information or the Germans would have known that their codes were being broken, and the information was given to only very few commanders in the know.'

Little is known of the worthwhile contribution made by these women to the success of Allied campaigns and ultimate victory, for to date the ULTRA files are not available in the Public Record Office. The secret was also kept by the women, a dedicated breed who proved wrong all those commanders from Shakespeare's *Julius Caesar** onwards who sneeringly declared that women could never keep a secret. Churchill was different. He acknowledged their achievement when he thanked his 'chickens for laying so well without clucking'.

On another occasion Churchill called the women at Station X,

---

* *Julius Caesar*, Act II, scene iv, line 9.

Bletchley, 'the geese who laid the golden eggs but never clacked'. Those golden eggs – the decrypts of German messages – were delivered directly to the Prime Minister by one Mrs Barclay, a member of the First Aid Nursing Yeomanry, a corps conceived in 1907 as one for well-to-do nurses on horseback riding round battlefields succouring the wounded. By 1914, with a more practicable role, the FANYs crossed to France with their own motorized ambulances and so became the first women to drive for the British Army. They set up hospitals, nursed cases of gunshot wounds and typhus and even rescued wounded under fire, when an ammunition dump exploded.[26] By the time the Second World War began, they were known as 'The Women's Transport Service' – a name that covered an extraordinary range of duties. Amongst them were those of the 'back-room girls' – wireless-operators, coders, and agents of 'Special Operations Executive', formed in July 1940 with the specific purpose of fostering active resistance to the Nazi conquerors of Europe. The nerve-racking work of the courageous agents who dropped into occupied countries has received considerable public attention, but little has been written about the 2,000 FANYs who served with SOE in forty-four countries – in Europe, the Middle East and the Far East, performing tasks which were as exciting as they were bizarre.

Because this corps had no particular brief, it attracted many unusual women of high calibre who had a penchant and ability for work of special delicacy and responsibility, often in high places. Mrs Barclay's delivery of ULTRA secret decodes to the Prime Minister was but one example of this. Many FANYs occupied rather exclusive, confidential positions as 'personal assistants' and indeed as lovers. The beautiful fashion model Kay Summersby, who had a passionate love affair with the five-star general she chauffeured (Dwight D. Eisenhower), told how she joined the FANYs: 'The Motor Transport Corps was the volunteer corps that the debutantes and post debutantes flocked to when war was declared. I knew many of them. We had gone to the same dances, watched polo at Hurlingham, together, spent long week-ends in Scotland together but there was a difference between them and me. Most of them were wealthy. I was not!'[27]

She was earning her living modelling for Worth of Paris, and it was quite usual for her to go to one of the great balls in London wearing a new Worth design, lent to her for the evening (as good advertising), and from time to time she would see a girl who was in the Transport Corps fox-trotting by in a gown she had modelled at Worth. The two girls would tell each other how absolutely marvellous they looked and then exchange pleasantries about what they were presently doing. Consequently it was not long before Kay Summersby had exchanged her Worth creations for a smart new uniform. It was June 1940.

There were times, it is true, when troops and civilians would jeer at the 'society girls playing war' but they did have a real part to play, especially in the back-room role and with rather special operations.

It is not surprising that FANYs came to be so closely connected with the Special Operations Executive, for its purpose and operations had to be so secret that the men who were brought in to organize and run operations tended to be known to one another and to come from the closed social circle of the better public schools. Consequently, through this reliance on the higher social class for the headquarters staff (the agents at the sharp end were a different matter), there came a form of recruitment for the women which followed a similar pattern. They 'spoke the same language' and were not overawed walking through the 'corridors of power'; they were known by somebody who knew somebody who worked for somebody at the vicarage of St Paul's Church at 31A Wilton Place, which happened to be the recruiting office for the FANY special units.

Women who were recruited into this work had to measure up to standards set by Dr Hugh Dalton, charged by Churchill to set up the organization, in July 1940. 'We need,' he said, 'absolute secrecy, a certain fanatical enthusiasm, willingness to work with people of different nationalities, complete political reliability.'[28]

Christine Courtney remembers how she was drawn into this mysterious, makeshift, murky world which then went under the unrevealing title of the 'Inter-Services Research Bureau': 'My ex-headmistress of a well-known girls' public school suggested that I should go to a certain address in Knightsbridge. So, off I went with butterflies in my stomach, frankly not too sure what to expect other than that I was volunteering for service with the FANY/WTS' (First Aid Nursing Yeomanry/Women's Transport Service).

She was accepted and found that as a volunteer she would have certain privileges – but there were snags: 'We might on occasion be treated as an officer – but without the same pay. If not actually in the debutante class, we were expected to act as such.'

Clearly after a few months of war the supply of debutantes began to dry up, and the recruiting officers were asked to look out for women with a potentiality for secret service. Nancy Dawson was one caught in their net.

I found myself on a train bound for Euston and told to look out there for a tall man wearing a Cambridge Blue rosette. He took us to Ames House in Mortimer Street, W1, just around the corner from the BBC. From there we were sent to Cornwall House in Waterloo Bridge Road, just across the river from Somerset House. I was joined by six other girls from Scotland, and there we met about twelve other girls who had been educated at very exclusive English schools and who seemed surprised because we Scots had never heard of them. The Officer Commanding told us that we should really have been at a place called Bletchley Park. (We gathered that this was a place like a university, with Cambridge dons sitting about, thinking up things for spies to do.) However, we stayed where we were, and three women came to teach us all about morse code, code and cyphers, typing on teleprinters and the ins and outs of wireless sets. We practised morse with reams and reams from *The Wind in the Willows*. This was sent to us by a delightful lady who had trained dozens of secret agents.

Morse code was part of the basic training of most 'back-room girls'. Usually it was an intensive training course. As Christine Courtney recalled: 'When we were at Banbury, we met a FANY officer called Lawrence who was, apparently, Lady Hailsham's daughter. Viscountess Hailsham was there herself and we were suitably awe-inspired! Lawrence took us upstairs to a room with a long oak table, and in the space of ten days (mornings only) she taught us the morse code down to the last "T". No messing about, quiet efficiency and a calm ruthlessness. We either mastered it or we got out. We mastered it, using all the short cuts, EISH (dots), TMO (dashes), AN, BV, DU (opposites), and the rest of the alphabet, also numbers. The hit tune was then 'Kalamazoo' and we used to spell it out in morse.'

After the morse training was finished, recruits were sent to Fawley Court, Henley-on-Thames, for three months training as radio-operators.

There, in an enormous country mansion designed by Sir Christopher Wren, it looked as though they were in for a life of luxury: there were beautiful gardens through which peacocks paraded, paths down to the river boathouse, and 'stupendous views of the Chilterns', recalled Christine Courtney. But life was not to be so easy. Sergeants of the Royal Corps of Signals saw to that, as she soon discovered: 'We had to learn how to send and receive messages in morse at a speed of twenty-five words a minute ready for our posting to an operational unit where we would be transmitting live coded messages to agents dropped behind the enemy lines.'

One of the 'coders' was Mary Room, who joined the FANY when she was twenty. She found this work totally absorbing, as did many of her colleagues: 'We worked three shifts – always very busy. I particularly enjoyed the night shift when we had a meal break, always egg and chips – they tasted delicious in the middle of the night! The trouble was, though, that we could not help feeling involved with the agents, although we knew them only by their code-names. It was harrowing sometimes when news of an arrest came through.'

Another product of Fawley Court, Audrey Swithinbank,[29] a parson's daughter, spoke of her own distressing experience when she was receiving a message from an agent. Suddenly the dots and dashes turned into a continuous buzz and was then abruptly broken off. She waited in vain for the transmission to begin again. It never did. She learnt later that the agent had been caught at his transmitter by the Gestapo. They had shot him, and he had fallen forward onto the morse key. Hence the continuous buzz.

These women working on wireless/telegraphy found their lives were to be dominated by the 'Sked' – the schedule which dictated the six-hour sessions they had to serve at the bench with its transmitter/receiver and morse keys. Before their eyes was a board on which were listed the call-signs they had to listen for at certain times. Against each code-name and call-sign was the coded message which had to be sent when contact was made. Sometimes weeks would go by before an agent made contact. Sometimes it would never be made. 'You can imagine the excitement when, after an interminable silence, an agent at last came through,' said Audrey Swithinbank.

There were times when a message came through with a garbled coding. Then it was that the decoders rallied to the challenge. It was an added fascination of the job, found Mary Room. No one would think of going off duty until the riddle was elucidated. It did not seem to matter how long they had been on duty or how tired they were. Messages came from all over the world – Patricia Smith (Keats) recalled long periods on duty handling traffic from Japan. Long hours were the rule rather than the exception, but no one questioned this.

What is perhaps most surprising of all about these wireless/telegraphy 'girls' was their age. Some were old. Very old.

> Little Miss Moffat was eighty-two [recalled Nancy Dawson], and when I took over from her once at two o'clock in the morning, feeling more like going to sleep myself than sitting at the morse key, there was Miss Moffat typing gaily on. I used to feel like dying about 4 a.m. but the older people thrived at this time; they seemed to be as bright as buttons and thus well suited to the work they were on. It was exacting and very hard; my hand used to feel like dropping off after hours of writing morse code in groups of five figures or five letters. I often used to wonder if any of the young Wrens who worked as coding or decipher clerks at CMY (the place to which we sent our signals for decoding) realized that some of the people who despatched these highly secret messages were old enough to be their grandparents.

How was it that these old ladies were on this secret service? They had volunteered in response to a Post Office appeal for former counter clerks, used to sending telegrams by morse, to come forward. And cheerfully they did. Many were in their seventies and some past eighty but all eager to 'do their bit for Britain' even if it did mean leaving a comfortable home to live on outlandish farms. 'One even lived in an old bus,' said Nancy Dawson. 'I used to think they were a grand lot. Now that I am a lady of a certain age, I know they were!'

All over Britain by the end of 1940 there were secret radio stations under different umbrellas – Foreign Office SOE, Military Intelligence and organizations which went under misleading names like 'Captain Ridley's Hunting Party', sending and receiving messages to and from the most remote places in Europe and beyond – messages that sometimes precipitated momentous, exciting battles.

Sometimes the messages brought a tremendous feeling of exhilaration into what might have been a dull stint of duty. Wren Kathleen Loomes remembers one such occasion.

After completing her training in wireless/telegraphy at Greenwich Royal Naval College, she was posted to a small radio station on the windswept east coast near the 'bracing' seaside resort of Scarborough. Shortly after her arrival there, volunteers were called for to serve on special duty at Peterhead: 'I knew it was somewhere north of Aberdeen but I thought it could not be more isolated than the old cottage in which we worked in Scarborough. That was miles from anywhere, down a long lane. Well, I was wrong. The unit at Peterhead was more isolated and the situation far more dramatic. Our job, we were told, was to listen for the German battleship *Bismarck*, which was the newest and most dangerous in the German Navy. And it was said to be hiding somewhere across the sea from us in one of the Norwegian fjords.'

On 22 May 1941 Kathleen Loomes was on the night watch. It was bitterly cold in the van, for winter hung on grimly at Peterhead. Inside the van the windows were steamed up, and outside the drifting banks of fog swirled across the high silvery moon, casting strange shadows over the sea.

Time dragged. Kathleen wondered idly what Hitler's deadliest battleship might now be doing. Perhaps even now it was edging stealthily out of some dark, misty fjord into the cold swell of the North Sea. And then what could they expect?

4 'For Those in Peril ...'

Fears and fancies thick upon me came.

William Wordsworth,
'Resolution and Independence'

1941-2

The ship's company on the *Bismarck* knew what to expect. It had all been explained to them in detail and with so much pride by their commander, the dapper Admiral Lütjens. And he certainly knew what he was talking about. Had he not already made a name for himself ranging the Atlantic in command of the battle-cruisers *Scharnhorst* and *Gneisenau*? Had he not already sunk a quarter of a million tons of British shipping? Now they were about to sink at least 2 million tons, and that would be that. Britain could never survive such losses.

In May 1941, before leaving the home port of Gydnia, Admiral Lütjens had assembled the ship's crew and also the special contingent of newly commissioned cadets who were on the ship for one express purpose: to observe the triumphs of the *Bismarck* and relate the success stories to crews of their own ships when they returned to them. Their role was an honour which they would never forget. Or so they were told.

Gentlemen [the Admiral had said], you are now serving in the most powerful and modern battleship afloat. There is not one ship in any of the world's Navies that can face us in single combat. No ship can escape our fire power. In your four months of training here in the Baltic you have proved yourselves worthy of being on this ship today.

Now we shall put that training into practice. We shall decimate the British Atlantic convoys. No merchant ship will dare put to sea. Can you imagine, for example, what effect on the British people will be the news that we have sunk their magnificent troop-carrying liner the *Queen Mary* with ten thousand troops on board?

The British people, whose morale is already shattered by the Luftwaffe's bombing raids, will find themselves slowly starving to death.[1]

As Lütjens warmed to his task, his high-pitched voice, resonant with pride and excitement, carried clearly all over the ship and the quayside. There, coiling a loose end of rope, the last civilian worker to go home

100

heard almost every word. 'The Atlantic!' So that was it. He placed the rope precisely by a bollard and trailed off homewards. But once out of the dockyard he quickened his pace. There was no time to be lost. The news must be sent to Britain. Soon on the London bench of a Wren telegraphist, the keys started chattering.

Britain was well aware of the new menace she was about to face. Coastal Command aircraft had been watching the building of the Nazis' two big super-battleships, the *Bismarck* and the *Tirpitz*. Britain also knew how much of her fate hung on the outcome of the Atlantic battles, and the Royal Navy was very far from complacent. On paper her ships' tonnage far outstripped the Germans', but the unpalatable truth was that most of the British ships were vessels left over from the First World War, few of them as fast or as well armed as the German ships. Hitler had rebuilt his Navy despite the restrictions on the building of battleships placed on Germany by the Versailles treaty. He had built 'cruisers', which were in fact so crammed with guns and heavy armour that they well deserved their name 'pocket battleship'. Now there were these two new tremendous battleships of more than 35,000 tons to contend with. No wonder the British admirals viewed the sailing of the *Bismarck* with apprehension.

The only hope of success now lay in good intelligence for surprise and the best tactical disposition of their forces. In this crucial enterprise the British back-room girls were again to play a key role.

Early in May a London Wren dealing with foreign telegrams received a strange signal which she recognized as being from an agent.[2] It had come via Sweden, Switzerland and Portugal. She sent it by special messenger to the Admiralty. The dock worker at Gydnia had got his information through that the *Bismarck* was heading for the Atlantic. Then came another signal, picked up by a watchful Wren telegraphist at Bletchley Park from her 'Sked' contact in Flekkefjord, Norway, saying that the *Bismarck* was now hiding, camouflaged, in a narrow fjord in the forbidden area north of Kristiansand and was about to sail under the cover of low cloud and heavy rain.

RAF reconnaissance aircraft were despatched, but exhausted pilots came back with the same message every time: 'No luck. Visibility nil. Cloud down to 200 feet.'[3]

Now, taking advantage of her tremendous speed, *Bismarck* was heading for the Atlantic convoys like a fox for the chickens.

A Wren officer in the Admiralty War Room moved the black motif representing the German warship away from the fjord. She turned questioningly towards the admiral, wondering which way to turn the prow. A shrug of the shoulders was his response as he picked up the telephone to ring the Chief of Staff, British Home Fleet, at Scapa Flow.

The response there was more positive. Loudspeakers shrilled, boots clattered on decks, telephones squawked: 'Steam in ten minutes.'

Thirty minutes later, at midnight, the Wren in the Admiralty War Room walked again to the chart and moved two warships from Scapa Flow, the *Hood*, a veteran, a twenty-one year old battleship, and the new, untried battleship *Prince of Wales*.

'They're off!' murmured the admiral. They were heading for Iceland at phenomenal speed, there to await and pounce on the Germans if they tried to break out into the Atlantic. Aboard the *Hood* were 1,341 officers and men; on the *Prince of Wales* were almost a thousand.

And with them were the women.

An eye-witness aboard the *Prince of Wales* wrote:

I wonder whether women realize what a dominant part they are playing in the war at sea – as elsewhere. You think of a warship as a fighting machine manned by men; so it is. But there are women in every ship too. Not flesh and blood women, but the ghosts of women. The men on the ocean wastes have their wives and sweethearts with them in thought more vividly than their wives and sweethearts know.

I honestly believe many men love their wives more when they are at sea than when they are at home with them. For to lonely men at sea their good and desirable qualities are greatly magnified.[4]

These men who spent long lonely nights and days keeping Britain's lifelines open thought much of their women, for there were many hours of emptiness for every minute of excitement as they endlessly ploughed the oceans. These men must indeed have been the world's most prolific letter-writers, producing in the average battleship as many as 800 letters a day. The real-life women of those replicas on the *Hood* were shortly to receive their last and saddest letters of all.

But where was the *Bismarck* now? That was the question puzzling the Naval Chief of Staff. The German battleship had not been seen since slipping out of the Norwegian fjord under the mist of low cloud and drizzling rain.

In the damp and cold wireless/telegraphy van at Peterhead Wren Kathleen Loomes was sitting with five other Wrens wishing the morning would come and with it the welcome mug of strong Navy tea. She wondered if they would ever hear anything of the German battleship which seemed to be causing the brass-hats so much panic. Suddenly her reverie was interrupted; she listened more intently. There it came again, exactly as before, the call-sign XYU. 'I was convinced it came from the *Bismarck* as she sneaked out of those Norwegian waters. Three times I heard it. I reported it to the chargehand,' recalled Kathleen Loomes.

Soon other messages were being fed into the Admiralty exchange.

The cruiser *Suffolk* had sighted the *Bismarck* and *Prinz Eugen* heading directly for the Denmark Strait, north of Iceland and just below the Arctic circle. She alerted the *Hood* and the *Prince of Wales*. Early next morning, in the sombre, murky light, the battle began.

The *Hood* turned and went for the *Bismarck* practically head on, and for what then seemed a long time the two biggest battleships in the world thundered towards each other at a combined speed of over sixty miles an hour.

> Suddenly an orange-gold flame belched from the *Hood*'s great forward guns and almost by return came three puffs of smoke from the guns of the *Bismarck*. The *Hood*'s guns continued to fire as it surged forward leaving fountains of water erupting in its wake.[5]
>
> Then, wrote eye-witness John Nixon, the *Hood* was hit. The shells seemed to fall just before one of the after 15-inch gun turrets, and fire broke out, with thick black smoke. *Hood* continued to race forward, her guns still firing.

What happened next is the kind of nightmare John Nixon did not want to see twice in a lifetime. There came a terrific explosion, and the *Hood* was enveloped in a flash of flame and smoke. Sections of funnels, mast and other parts hurtled hundreds of feet into the sky, some falling on the *Prince of Wales*. Two or three minutes after *Hood* was hit, all that remained, apart from bits of wreckage was a flicker of smoke and flame on the water's surface.

A destroyer was diverted to rescue survivors – and all she found of the 1,421 officers and men[*] were a midshipman and two seamen.[5]

The *Prince of Wales* was hit too, with fourteen killed and ten wounded, but she had got two hits on the *Bismarck*, damaging her fuel tanks. The German ship turned south leaving a wake of oil behind with the *Prince of Wales* on her heels.

Then the worst happened: the pursuers lost touch. They knew the *Bismarck* would race for refuge and repairs in the French ports, sheltered by German coastal defences. She would have to be caught quickly.

At daylight the *Bismarck* was sighted by a Catalina aircraft making for Brest at 22 knots. Now all the Royal Naval forces in the area dropped their convoy work and joined in the hunt. Planes from the carrier *Ark Royal* attacked and crippled the *Bismarck*, then the battleships *King George V* and *Rodney* fired, silencing the *Bismarck*. Finally the cruiser *Dorsetshire* finished the job with her torpedoes. So ended the 1,750-mile hunt of the *Bismarck* – the longest high-speed naval chase in history.

[*] Strength of 1,421 given in *Flagship* Hood by Alan Coles and Ted Briggs (Robert Hale, 1985)

As the 'unsinkable' warship plunged, stern foremost, hundreds of black dots appeared all over the hull. They were the crew making a last effort to escape. A hundred men were saved but, while the rescue was going on, there came another alarm: U-boats in the area. All ships dispersed quickly from the scene – as quickly as they could. The Battle of the Atlantic did not stop for the sake of a few hundred men in the water. It raged on.

Victoria Drummond was in the midst of it.

From the beginning of the war, Allied shipping was 'convoyed' – grouped together for safety and escorted by warships. Sometimes a convoy would comprise as many as sixty ships, and always the slowest set the pace. The escorts would take the convoys out to a given point and then send them on their way whilst the warships accompanied an incoming convoy. Once away from their escorts, the merchant ships had to rely on their own devices for survival – their speed and their anti-aircraft guns.

It was at such a point in the transatlantic journey that Victoria Drummond's ship, the *Bonita*, came under heavy attack. Victoria had signed on as Second Engineer of the *Bonita* shortly after Dunkirk. The crew had been surprised to see a woman on board, and some, being superstitious, looked askance at the prospect of sailing with a woman in the engine room of all places. Everyone was well aware of the warning that convoy commanders gave at the conference before convoys sailed: 'Keep closed up on one another's tails. Any ship that straggles must remember she is in dangerous waters and may be sunk. The main factor in safety is speed.'[6]

Speed would depend on the engineer. Would this woman really be up to the job? Would she be able to coax all the power needed from the old *Bonita* to keep up with the rest of the convoy?

They were soon to find out. At the appointed rendezvous at sea, the *Bonita* took her place amongst the tankers, cargo liners, Liberty ships and Empire Liners. Then, with the convoy complete and with naval escort shepherding them, they steamed towards the west. All this time, Victoria kept the number of revolutions of her engines exactly on target to preserve the allotted cable lengths from the ship ahead.

All went well for the next forty-eight hours as the convoy sailed westwards. On the bridge of the *Bonita* the captain kept a wary eye open for the commodore's signals by lamp or flag.

They were 400 miles from land early one morning when a Nazi bomber swooped down for the kill. Guns of the naval escort split the air but the attacking aircraft did not alter course. A stick of bombs fell across the bows of the *Bonita*. The blast flung Victoria Drummond heavily against the levers in the engine room, stunning her momentarily. Picking herself up, she saw steam spurting from the main engine-room stop valve. The violent lurching of the ship, bracketed by the bombs, had fractured pipes and broken electrical connections and tubes. She saw no reason why the rest of the engine-room crew should suffer death through drowning or scalding steam, so she gave an order – just three words: 'Get out quick!'

Such was the discipline she had already instilled in her engine-room crew that they went rapidly, even though they knew they were leaving her alone to face almost certain death.

For her part she knew that, from her position, already sixty feet below water, she would have only 4½ minutes to get out if the worst happened. But she knew also that her duty was to remain on the control platform until she got the signal from the bridge: 'Finished with engines.'

Now the captain was calling for maximum speed. Never before had the *Bonita* given more than 9 knots. Victoria opened her up. The furnaces roared as never before. One of the ship's officers later recalled[7] how he had seen Victoria through the skylight: she was standing on the control platform holding the spoke of the throttle column, her face screwed up as scalding steam gushed close by her head, one eye was closed with a black streak of fuel oil. With the sensitivity of an experienced and skilled engineer, she juggled with the pressures, keeping one pipe from bursting by releasing pressure on another. All the time she was talking to the engines, urging another pound of steam through the straining pipes.

Gradually the speed crept up: 10 ... 11 ... 12 ... 12½ knots, and now the captain could take action to combat the attacking aircraft. He kept to a steady course until the bomber was committed to its run and then swung the helm hard over to move the ship out of the bomb's path. Each time, survival was a matter of seconds and inches. It was only the increased speed which gave the captain a chance to turn the bulk of the *Bonita* out of the bomber's aim. 'With anyone less skilled in engineering down there, we should never have had a chance,' the captain was to say later, when the ship docked at Norfolk, Virginia, badly damaged but still under its own steam.

On hearing the story from crew members when the ship docked in America, the Mayor of Norfolk wrote to the mayor of Lambeth saying how inspired American women were to hear of 'such a woman's courage and skill'. His letter ended with the words, 'It seemed to us that the very spirit of England spoke through her.'

Her momentous achievement was recorded in an engagingly folksy way by the people of Virginia, who made Lambeth a present of a British-American restaurant and called it 'The Victoria A. Drummond'. It was fitting, however, that the gallantry of the god-daughter of Queen Victoria should be recognized in a more conventional way: she was awarded the OBE.

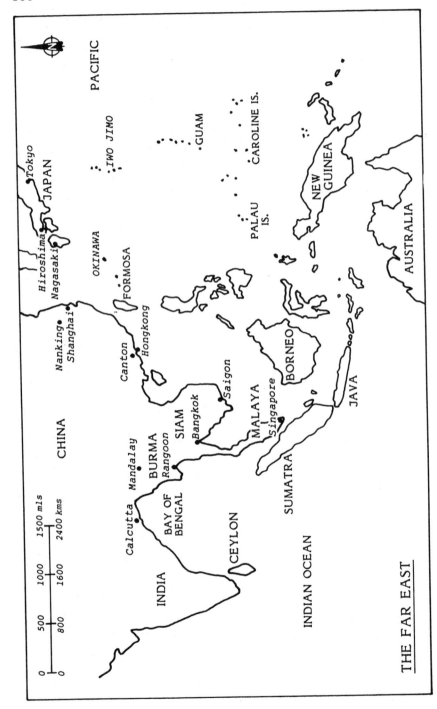

THE FAR EAST

But when Victoria got back to Lambeth, she was not to have the usual home-coming welcome. Her home was no longer there. It had been bombed, and it was only by a hair's breadth that her two sisters were still alive. Jean and Frances Drummond had been on duty in the air raid wardens' post when it received a direct hit. The building collapsed onto the basement control room, where the sisters were, blocking all exits with fallen masonry. In the basement, water and gas pipes burst, and the water-level rose so rapidly that the Drummonds would have drowned had not a rescue team been on hand to burrow into the debris and make a tunnel through which the sisters escaped.

Victoria went back to the sea, to the engines she loved. There were many years of war-time sailing ahead of her, years in which she faced the perils of the U-boat-infested Atlantic.

At the other side of the world, women were about to face perils of a far different kind, perils and atrocities that would stun the whole world and bring the blackest Christmas ever to the nurses and wives of the cosy peace-time garrison of Hong Kong.

Before first light on 30 November 1941 twenty-four warships, the backbone of the Japanese Navy, slipped unseen from their base in Tunkan Bay. Seven days later, without any declaration of war, this powerful strike-force attacked the United States Fleet riding proudly at anchor at the Hawaiian island base of Pearl Harbor. By ten o'clock that same morning it was in ruins. A massive armada of 353 Japanese aircraft had come in low against the blinding morning sun, and the might of the US fleet had been reduced to a heap of twisted, blackened metal. The Americans lost eighteen warships, 349 aircraft, most of them destroyed on the ground, and 3,700 sailors, soldiers and marines. At one stroke, the USA had lost its capacity to dominate the Pacific hemisphere; mastery had passed into Japanese hands in the space of a mere 2½ hours.[8] Immediately, Britain expressed her solidarity with America and declared war on Japan.

Within hours of the attack on Pearl Harbor some of the most unnerving events of the whole war happened to women in Hong Kong. The Japanese attacked the garrison, in which there were several British hospitals staffed by British and Commonwealth nurses. For eighteen days the ill-equipped British troops, never expecting to be asked to fight, surprisingly beat off one ferocious attack after another, as Japanese officers, swinging their swords and yelling 'Banzai!', pushed their troops into the fray without regard for losses. Eventually, on 18 December, the defenders were forced back from the outer defences to the main island of Hong Kong around the St Stephen's Boys' College, converted into a hospital. There, make-shift beds in the corridors were crammed with stretchers bearing the dead and dying. All over the streets outside lay bodies with faces distorted and the blood hard and brown in pools beside them.

Clearly the defenders could not hold out for much longer. Already it seemed that Japanese soldiers had overrun all opposition. They could be seen, elated with their success and with bayonets fixed, half-running in and out of shops and offices, searching everywhere for watches, jewellery, tobacco and booze. Many had obviously found hard liquor already and were indulging all their baser instincts – killing, maiming and raping without restraint.

Watched by grim-faced Canadian soldiers on the roof of St Stephen's, the Japanese began to converge on the hospital, running drunkenly down the hill. They stumbled over bodies that lay sprawled grotesquely in the street, stopping here and there to gulp down more spirits and to vomit against the walls. At last they came to a disorderly halt outside the double-doored entrance to St Stephen's, above which hung the Red Cross flag. There in the doorway, barring their way, stood the civilian superintendent of the hospital, a veteran of the First World War, sixty-five-year-old Dr Black. A rifle jabbed him in the chest, there was a shot, and the lean figure of Dr Black jerked violently backwards, but before it hit the ground another soldier jumped forward and lunged with his bayonet for good measure and further gratification of his blood-lust. Another medical officer had now rushed into the hallway and was about to shout when he too was shot and bayoneted.

Now there was no stopping the slaughter. No Japanese officers were there to check them as the soldiers ran through the wards, dragging bed covers off the wounded and bayoneting them as they lay helpless and horror-stricken in their beds. When a nurse tried to protect a patient by flinging herself across his prostrate body, the two were bayoneted together.[9]

Then, as if the idea had suddenly struck them, a small group of Japanese left the patients and turned towards the nurses. They caught hold of their arms and dragged them, pushed them and prodded them with their bayonets towards a small room in which they were locked. From then on, throughout that Christmas Day, whenever one of those men wanted a woman, he went to the room and pulled out a nurse in her blood-spattered white uniform and raped her.

All this was witnessed by Lance-Corporal Harding of the Middlesex Regiment, who, badly injured in both legs, had been bundled by nurses into a large wicker laundry basket. Through the gap between the sides of the basket and the lid he was forced to watch the sickening violation, unable to do anything to stop it.[10] All that day women were taken out and repeatedly raped.

Other Japanese took their pleasures in an orgy of violent killing. Three young volunteer nurses were killed, and all the Chinese women of the St

John's Ambulance Brigade as well.

Shortly before dawn on Boxing Day some sort of control was established, and the garrison officially surrendered to the most senior Japanese officer who could be found. The formal scene was watched incredulously by Matron Kathleen Thomas who was recovering from her own wounds in another hospital, Queen Mary's, which had not suffered in the same way as St Stephen's. 'I shall never forget,' she said, 'my first sight of our Japanese conquerors; grubby little men, with bicycles, in dirty khaki uniform and white tennis shoes, wearing tin hats. Surely, I thought, a British garrison cannot have surrendered to men like these?' They had, and there was worse to follow.

A few weeks later, on 30 January 1942, a wan-looking, horse-toothed General Percival, commanding the Singapore garrison, looked out onto the pall of smoke that hung over the bomb-shattered dockland of his 'City of the Lion' and at the crackling flames of burning warehouses. He cleared his throat before addressing his troops over the local radio. 'The battle of Malaya has come to an end,' he said, 'and the battle of Singapore has started. In our island fortress we stand beleaguered. We must stand firm until help arrives as it surely will.'[11]

Fourteen days later it was all over, but in those two weeks the nurses there had once again been in the thick of the bombardment. A nurse at Gordon Barracks, Singapore, wrote to her Matron-in-Chief describing what happened:

In spite of large Red Crosses on all buildings and the barrack square, the Japs dive-bombed and machine-gunned us frequently. It was terrible to see the shell-shocked patients and hear their screams as the bullets spattered around us. We moved all patients from the top floors, and all the bedridden ones on the ground floor were put under their beds'.

During one of the worst raids in which one VAD was killed, the officers' mess demolished, the Night Sisters' house badly damaged and an ambulance with its driver blown up, Matron jumped up from under a bed and rushed outside with the bombs still dropping. She shouted that she was going to see if any of the Night Sisters had been hurt. The Sisters' House was blazing fiercely and the planes still diving down and machine gunning. But that made no difference to the Matron. Across the small concrete square she hurried and disappeared in the smoke and dust. Some time later she reappeared, a little out of breath but told the anxious nurses quite calmly that no one was hurt in spite of their quarters being half on top of them. 'They are all on their way up to join us for a cup of tea,' she said.[12]

After that incident the situation became more desperate still, for by that time the Japanese guns were now firing directly at them from the

Johore coast. By this sudden change in the military situation, the hospital was now between the attacking Japanese and the British front-line troops.

On the next day, the nurses were ordered to move as fast as they could to the Alexandra Hospital as Japanese troops had now landed on Changi beach. But as soon as they arrived there, further orders came. This time they were told to get down to the docks without delay. It was no easy task. Shells were landing all around and one time they had to take shelter in a sewer where slimy sewage swirled around their knees. Once through the dock gates the next problem was to find a ship for by now warehouses, offices, abandoned cars and trucks were all ablaze. At last they came across the *Empire Star*, scrambled aboard and at four in the afternoon sailed out of the harbour.[13]

But they were far from safe even then.

Once again the bombers came in. 'For four hours we had one raid after another. Over fifty planes attacked in the last raid and we suffered seven direct hits. Each time it pitched to one side and then righted itself. It was terrifying.'

In that overcrowded ship the nurses had a space well below decks where the frozen meat used to be stored. Washing was impossible, and the only food was dry Army biscuits and the occasional tin of corned beef. At night the nurses climbed up to the deck on a vertical ladder beneath which three soldiers stood on duty to be of assistance should anyone slip.

Many days later they reached Batavia and then Bombay. They were the lucky ones. Nurses who left on the next ship, SS *Kuala*, were all lost when the ship was bombed until it sank.

'Amongst all those killed was our own Matron and Principal Matron,' wrote the nurse. 'No one will ever forget those last days in Singapore.'[14]

The scenes come back to many as nightmares to this day. Memories torment them.

Sister Doris Hawkins,[15] who had been serving in Palestine and was at last on her way home, had an experience which stayed with her as a recurring nightmare. She remembered the date well: 12 September 1942. She was aboard a rather slow liner with a few other nurses, several units of the Navy, Army and Air Force and about 1,800 Italian prisoners of war. Doris Hawkins was responsible for bringing home a fourteen-month-old baby, Sally, and on that memorable night she settled the baby to sleep in her cot and went to the ship's dining-room for dinner. Just as she was about to sit down, there was a shattering explosion. Crockery, glasses, soup tureens and everything movable clattered and crashed to the floor. The whole ship shivered and then stood still. The first torpedo had struck.

Sister Hawkins was one of the first to move. She fled to Sally's cabin, wrapped her in woollies and a blanket, grabbed her 'shipwreck' bag and turned for the door. The second torpedo then struck, flinging her across the cabin. Baby Sally was still in her arms. Now Sister Hawkins began to struggle down the narrow, corridor packed with people pushing and shouting. It was then that the lights went out.

The ship tilted and people fell awkwardly. As they regained some sort of balance, they surged upwards. At last, gasping for breath and with the baby still in her arms, Sister Hawkins reached the lifeboat station at which they had been drilled to wait.

But around her small group pandemonium raged. The second torpedo had burst among the Italian prisoners of war, and those who had survived the explosion had rushed up onto the deck, stormed the lifeboats or jumped into the sea.

After what was probably about fifteen minutes but seemed an age, Sister Hawkins realized that to wait any longer was pointless. There was going to be no lifeboat for them. She hugged the baby girl tightly to her breast, wondering what to do next. 'The baby never cried once either then or through the whole terrible experience, despite all the noise and confusion around; she stayed quite still in my arms, making only gentle talking and cooing sounds,' Doris Hawkins was later to write.

Just when the situation seemed hopeless, Sister Hawkins felt an insistent tugging at her sleeve. It was Squadron Leader Wells, an officer she had got to know on the voyage. He guided her to another part of the ship where, below the sloping deck, there was a lifeboat. A young Fleet Air Arm lieutenant took Sally. He tucked her inside the back of his greatcoat, tied a blanket round his waist below her feet and carried her papoose-fashion down a swinging rope ladder into the crowded lifeboat.

Doris Hawkins scrambled down after him, followed by her friend Mary. Leaving go of the rope ladder, they fell into a heaving mass of panic-stricken humanity whose only wish was to get away from the sinking ship before they were sucked down with it. Already the boat was carrying far too many people; it was leaking badly and filling with water as it banged and crashed against the side of the ship. The Fleet Air Arm lieutenant passed baby Sally to Doris, who then tried to squeeze her way into a safer part of the boat.

Suddenly she sensed the searing shock of ice-cold water striking her stomach. A black mist engulfed her. Sally slipped quietly away. 'I did not hear her cry even then, and I am sure that God took her immediately to himself without suffering. I never saw her again,' said Doris later.

As she came to the surface amid a flurry of thrashing arms and legs, she opened her mouth, gasping for air, but immediately she was grabbed round the neck by a terrified Italian who pulled her under the water again. She kept as calm as she could, let herself sink and then kicked herself free and swam to the surface. This time she was near a thick wooden beam, which she grasped. Another Italian took hold of her clothes to pull himself to the beam. There they both hung for some time before Doris saw her chance. Nearby now was a raft. She let go of the beam and, using all her remaining strength, swam to the raft. Already four Italians were hanging on to the side ropes, and they helped her onto the top of the raft, where she lay panting.

Now they were a hundred yards from the ship. She saw its prow rise majestically out of the water before it slipped, hissing and roaring, beneath the waves. No sooner had it disappeared from sight than there was a tremendously loud explosion which pushed Doris Hawkins viciously backwards, forcing her head right back and her spine to arch beyond its natural limit. At first she thought her back was broken, so excruciating was the pain. Everyone on the raft was now vomiting; their bodies had been tossed about by the sea, by explosions, by floating about on debris, and most of them had swallowed mouthfuls of thick engine oil and salt water.

Through that long first night they all took turns to sit on the raft whilst others slipped over the side into the cold water to hang on to the side ropes. Everyone longed for dawn. It broke, cold, grey and threatening. A savage wind cut through their thin clothing; it hurled cold grey spray at their huddled, crouching backs; it blasted them with such force that they could hardly breathe.

So strong was the wind that it overturned the raft several times. Then they all had to strike out, swimming as fast as they could, to reach it before it drifted away before the wind. And each time they were flung into the water it became all the more difficult to get back onto the raft; fingers were numb and limbs stiff.

The harsh grey dawn gave way to the early morning sun, which restored their circulation, but by midday the same sun was blistering bare skin on arms, faces, necks and feet. Around the raft now were floating corpses and wreckage.

Doris Hawkins lay in the heat with one arm trailing in the water. She counted the survivors on the raft. There were nine. Just at that moment a stabbing pain shot straight up her arm to throb in her armpit. She pulled her arm from the water and saw it swelling up even as she looked. And worse still, she saw what had caused the pain. Wrapped round her forearm was an obscene-looking, long, violet-coloured tentacle. In terror she flung her arm about. The tentacle fell onto another man's arm, stinging him. A sailor hit the tentacle with a stick until it fell onto the raft floor and was flicked overboard. Some time later yet another man picked up the stick by the end which had whacked the jellyfish tentacle and was just as badly stung by the poison on it.

For all who were stung, the pain was intense.

It was Sunday. The first day on the raft was nearly over, and as the

The WRNS was formed in 1917, but when the Second World War broke out there were no WRNS Headquarters staff, no trained unit officers, but there were about 1,000 'immobile' Wrens. Seen above, two Wren minewatchers with an officer of the QARNNS. *Left to right*: Wren 3/officer Morley, Sister Holland and 3/officer Skeggs

Opposite: Riding a motor-cycle by night was hazardous. Note the shield on the headlight directing the beam downwards and providing little illumination of the road ahead

ATS despatch riders competed successfully with men in motor-cycle competitions

Wren despatch riders rode through the heavy bombing raids delivering messages. Pamela McGeorge defied bombs to earn the BEM

FANY/ATS despatch riders learning how to ride the bike to ground

Churchill's daughter, subaltern Mary Churchill, was soon in action on the Hyde Park site of a mixed anti-aircraft battery, RA

A mixed anti-aircraft battery operating in a London blitz, 1940

ATS gunners with kine–theodolite at an AA battery site

'It aint 'alf 'ot, Mum!' ATS in the Middle East

A cartoon satirizing wartime fashions: 'AUSTERITY IN HANDFORTH. ATS Military Modes have recently been severely restricted. We consider it our duty to record for posterity the following popular models before they pass from our gaze forever.'

...UTICAL"
...EL

...tasty, very sweet.
...ar with the younger set.

THE
"EASTER
BONNET"
MODEL

Much favoured by the shy and those who wish to appear so.

THE
"OOMPH"
MODEL

Definitely 'a la Dietrich'. A boon to Yank bashers.

...IC"
...EL

...ted by the 'refaned' type.
...basher's dream. Well-
...ed girl's joy.

THE
"HALO
MODEL

Worn by the cuddlesome type. Uplifted peak obviates 'eye-poking'.

THE
"UTILITY"
MODEL

Followed by studious type. Will replace all others, owing to military encouragement.

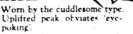

Opposite: WAAF flight mechanics on a Fighter Command station

Woman pilot of the ATA Ferry pool

Not too easy in a high wind. WAAFs operating a balloon barrage unit

Crew of site 48 defending factories in the Widnes area 1942

Nurses on the way to Singapore, 1940

Nurses were aboard this hospital ship bringing troops from the beaches of Dunkirk. They stuck it out on the beaches working under perpetual bombings and under intense shell-fire and staffed the long procession of ambulance trains heading for Dunkirk

evening sun dipped to the horizon, Doris Hawkins pictured her family in her home-town church. She prayed with them. A few minutes later, at dusk, a U-boat surfaced. It headed straight for the raft, seeming as if it was going to ram them, but just at the last moment it veered away slightly. A German sailor threw a lifeline, and they were all nine taken aboard the U-boat.

Doris Hawkins, with legs swollen and stiff, was helped down the conning-tower into the officers' wardroom. Her nightmare, she thought, was over. It was, in fact, only just beginning.

In the U-boat's wardroom, Doris Hawkins was amazed at the treatment they were given. The Germans could not have been kinder: they gave up their bunks to the women, brought them Eau de Cologne and cold cream, gave them lemons from their lockers and supplied dry shirts and underclothes from their own limited kit.

Not once did she hear the words 'Heil Hitler!'

At great risk to its own safety, the U-boat cruised on the surface picking up more and more survivors, collecting lifeboats, tying them together, towing them to a rendezvous where other U-boats were keeping watch, and giving steaming hot drinks to those in the boats.

It seemed incredible. The Germans simply could not do enough, running great risks on behalf of those torpedoed. The U-boat commander broke radio silence to call for help. Vichy France responded by promising that a cruiser would come at high speed. Everything appeared to be going wonderfully well. It was too good to be true.

It was indeed. Things were not to go as planned. A British bomber saw to that! It had spotted the U-boats and immediately dived to attack, dropping a stick of six bombs alongside the submarine which had picked up Doris Hawkins. Naturally the U-boat commander had only one course of action, an emergency dive without the survivors aboard. They were all put back into the sea to swim to the lifeboats. This was when the nightmare really began for Doris Hawkins. She swam, weak as she was, for fifty minutes to reach a boat. She was lucky; many failed to reach a boat and perished just when rescue seemed at hand. Doris was pulled into the boat so scantily clad that a sailor immediately pulled off his vest and gave it to her; an airman stripped off his shirt and handed that over. It was some comfort to Doris to find her friend Mary in the boat with her, and sixty-six men. Only a very few were to survive.

Next morning the boat had drifted away from all the others, and the situation looked grim indeed. The U-boat commander had told them they were 600 miles from land of any kind, and they had only fifteen gallons of water between them. At first they began to row by shifts, but that soon had to be stopped, for they had not the food or water to sustain the effort. By ten o'clock each morning the equatorial sun was beating down on their raw, sun-chafed skin, making physical exertion impossible. Their water ration was two ounces a day – less than an eggcupfull – taken only when the sun had dipped. How they longed for evening to come! In the morning they were allowed four Horlicks tablets and three pieces of chocolate – but not a drop of water.

Days passed with dreadful monotony, one running into the other, and the nights were long and bitterly cold as the wind cut through the thin summer clothing they had been wearing when torpedoed. Huddling together for warmth, they would at first pass the time talking of home and food and what they would do when they were home again. Soon they could not talk; their tongues were brown and dry, their mouths misshapen, their pores closed up completely. So they dozed and dreamed, often of cool drinks, of fruit, of cups of tea and ice-cream. And gradually their condition got worse.

After fourteen days they began to die. Most of them died quietly in the night and would be found at daybreak cold, blue and stiff. 'They just seemed to fade into death,' said Doris Hawkins, describing the passing of her friend Mary. 'On 25th September she realised she could not live much longer. She smiled and thanked me for taking care of her, and then quite calmly she repeated her home address. Then she seemed to fall asleep, facing death as she had faced life, unflinchingly, looking forward and not back.'

By this time all those who were left were suffering from salt-water sores, septic fingers and toes, and suppurating eyes. There was a doctor in the boat, Dr Purslow, but as neither he nor Sister Hawkins had any medical kit with them, all they could do to give relief from pain was to cut open the swollen fingers and boils with pen-knife cleansed in sea-water. They warned their fellow-sufferers to try to avoid infecting each other but with little success. Indeed, the doctor himself developed deep infections in his arms and legs. Doris Hawkins lanced open the worst areas with a razor blade but little pus came out. Red lines streaked his arm and leg, more septic sores erupted and it was clear to the doctor that he now had blood-poisoning. The next morning he struggled painfully to his feet and said that as he could not be of any further help, and as he was likely to infect all the others in the boat, it was better that he should take his leave. Doris remembered: 'He took a long look around the boat and then stepped backwards into the sea.'

Towards the end of the third week salvation came. It rained, a torrential downpour. They caught and saved water in the sail and in every vessel available. They drank as much as they wanted, and their dehydrated bodies took on new strength. Hope revived as the breeze freshened. Then, on 8 October, land was sighted. Four days later their lifeboat drifted onto a sandy beach in Liberia, West Africa. For the sixteen survivors out of the original sixty-eight in the boat, the ordeal was over. But not for long.

The inevitable nervous reaction followed, and nightmares came with awful regularity. She dreaded the nights, for as soon as she closed her eyes, she could see the faces of all those who had once been her companions in the lifeboat. 'When sleep came', she was later to write, 'all the scenes of horror were re-lived with increased intensity. These night terrors were to haunt me.'

Soon she was aboard a liner bound for Britain. Ironically, it was the sister ship of the one they had been in when torpedoed, and they had now to face 3,000 miles sailing unescorted through the same submarine-infested waters of the Atlantic. 'It was a nightmare voyage,' she said, 'every bang made me leap from my bunk.' And she had good reason to be nervous, for the Atlantic battle was far from finished – in fact, in 1942 it was reaching its peak. The Allies were then losing more ships than in any previous year.

This was the time when a new movement started recruiting overseas for the British women's Services. Sybille Phillips was a British subject living in Washington DC when she heard through the British Embassy there of the British Volunteer Movement in New York which was attracting applicants from as far apart as Canada, California and the east coast. Naturally, her friends and relations were not keen to see her risking her life going over to Britain and tried hard to dissuade her. She recalls:

They somehow obtained a training film for air-raid wardens in which all the horrors of the London Blitz were shown. Instead of making me change my mind, it made me all the keener. I volunteered right away.

We had to pass a medical exam conducted by a British doctor, and then off we went to the assembly point at the Spelman Hall, New York.

The Battle of the Atlantic was at its height, and we did not know what to expect. Two pamphlets were given to us, *War Work in Britain*, which held the application form and explained the Government's wish to recruit all available British personnel, and one with the intriguing title *Since You are Going to England*. That did not mince any words and put the facts to us quite objectively, saying what we would be giving up in the material sense and that we would be choosing a harder way of life. It explained rationing and shortages so that we were under no illusions about the choice we were making. It ended with a paragraph which asked us to meet with sympathy and patience the fatigue and possibly the abrupt manner of people we were to live with in this new life.

Finally, on 24 October 1942, we were told to pack and be ready to leave within the hour. In small groups we were taken to the docks, and we boarded the SS *City of Hong Kong*. Our cabins were cramped but warm and comfortable, and we were advised to wear our life-jackets at all times. We went to bed and were fast asleep when we awakened to realize we had quietly had quietly and under cover of darkness and mist slipped out to sea! And if I merely say we were excited, I should be giving a false impression. It was far more thrilling. One thing was very clear. We never once regretted our decision.

On our ship were twenty-five female volunteers and about a hundred naval personnel who had been shipwrecked and were going home to be re-commissioned. Those men being there made us all the more aware of the risks in crossing the Atlantic then. However, we sang, played cards and passed the time as well as we could.

Events started to get exciting after the fourth day out. We had before then become a little blasé about seeing the convoy scatter and hearing the sounds of depth-charges, but on this fourth day we were all sent down below and everything was battened down. Then the depth-charges started exploding. This time, though, they seemed all around us, and they went on for hours. It was no use asking questions. We just carried on trying to act calmly. By this time we all went to bed fully dressed as well as in our life-jackets. The next morning all was quiet but we awoke to a totally different scene. Now we were all alone! No convoy.

Several ships had been lost and we had zigzagged back on our course towards New York.

Another event remained in Sybille Phillips' memory of that hazardous journey. It happened that on board was a petty officer who had been badly burnt when his ship had been torpedoed. The man was now in such severe pain that he needed treatment beyond the facilities aboard the SS *Hong Kong*. Despite all the risks involved in stopping mid-Atlantic, the ship's captain did just that and called for volunteers to row the man across the rough sea to a corvette which had been signalled. Sybille Phillips takes up the story:

Our ship was now completely on its own, and the Atlantic seemed such a wide open space that October in 1942. It was cold and grey and the waves were huge. Not a ship in sight. The corvette had a long way to come. We just waited anxiously at the rails. At last it arrived, and I cannot describe our fears and other emotions as we watched our lifeboat with the wounded petty officer aboard being gently lowered into that hostile, rough sea. As the sailors rowed across to the corvette, the little boat – for so it seemed then – was often hidden from sight by the waves that towered above it. At last, the mission of mercy was completed, our own sailors were back on the ship, and it was full speed ahead again.

Fifteen days later we sailed into Liverpool. It was 9 November 1942, and by that time the city had been pulverized by German bombers. I can still see that awful scene of devastation. It left us all speechless.

The naval boys were taken off by tender before us, and we stood by the rail singing 'Bless 'em all'. Those lads had taught us a few things for our future use. Our eyes were dry, the unshed tears held back. Some hours later, we too were taken off and put on a train for London. In due course we reported to the Officer Commanding No 7 ATS Training Centre at Guildford.

There was much we had to get used to: British money again, the accents and doing PT in shorts, blouse, plimsolls and goose pimples. All of us from the States were hothouse plants from centrally heated buildings, ill-prepared for such Spartan treatment.

When basic training came to an end, we had a party, and I had to get dressed in the Stars and Stripes flag and sing, 'I'm a Yankee Doodle Dandy', despite the fact that I kept protesting I was as British as the rest of them. I was truly thankful for being back in Britain among my own folk and in the ATS.

Basic training was also a thing of the past for Monica Jackson and her colleagues of the new 'rocket batteries' stationed on Wolverhampton racecourse. Only once had she seen those rockets fired, and that was just a trial out to sea. Now Service life had developed into a comfortable routine, as she recalled recently:

Life was certainly novel for the girls of 137 Battery on that racecourse: girls slept in the tote, the men in the stables; the officers' mess was at the top of the grandstand, and the sergeants' mess beneath. Sick-bay was in the jockey's weighing-in room, and the NAAFI club in the jockeys' changing-room. We did PT in the paddock, paraded in the yard and spent our duty hours on the radar sets away in the middle of the course.

We slept in one of the Nissen huts on watch, and our washing water came from a large galvanized tank but we kept a bucketful near the stove in winter so that we did not have to break the ice to wash. The lavatory was a bucket under a wooden seat in a little wooden shed, and it was emptied every morning by two girls in strict rota. We walked a long way, dug a large hole, filled it again, sluiced the bucket out in the canal, used gallons of Jeyes fluid, and I never heard anyone complain. In winter we slept with our uniform clothes between the blankets to keep them aired, and most of us went to bed with a woolly over our pyjamas and wearing bed-socks. Our leather jerkins acted as an extra cover, and at times we topped the lot with a groundsheet when the roof sprang a leak.

We rigged a splendid alarm system for the icy mornings. A call came through from battery office to the sergeant in her cubicle. She then pulled a cord which switched on all the lights in the main part of the hut and turned on the radio, which woke everyone up without anyone having to get out of bed shouting 'Wakey Wakey'.

In London, Wren mine-watchers such as Margaret Taylor were frequently under fire. Dressed in warm duffle coats over their uniforms and perched in bomb-proof observation posts, they kept watch for mines dropped by enemy aircraft. Before enrolling for this job the women had been warned that it was 'highly dangerous' but that they would have the satisfaction of knowing that each of them would be replacing a sailor for sea-going duties. Essential qualifications for women volunteering for the task were that they should be strong physically, strong-minded and able to make quick decisions and keep cool-headed in any emergency.

One night when Wren Madeleine Speed[16] was on duty, a fifty-seven-year-old man threw himself into the river. Sharp-eyed Wren Speed spotted him going under, dived in and brought him back to Westminster Pier, where she applied artificial respiration, but unsuccessfully. The coroner sent a commendation to the flag officer.

At one time, the huge Port of London was almost closed because the sea-going channels were blocked by magnetic mines which exploded not just when a ship hit them but whenever a ship came within a certain distance of their magnetic field. These new mines were attached to a large parachute and floated slowly down, so that they would not explode on impact with the water. Once in the river or sea, they would drift just below the surface and consequently were not visible to the naked eye. It was therefore very important for a sharp look-out to be kept for anything like them dropping during air raids. When the air-raid warning sounded, these women would dash out to their posts at all times of the night or day.

In addition to the usual regulation kit they carried a piece on a chain round their necks. Margaret Taylor explained: 'It was a special, shrill police whistle which we had to blow in case we were molested on the way to or from the post in the black-out. In times such as we now have, it is interesting to reflect that, despite all the dangers and anxieties of war-time living, I never heard of anyone having to blow that whistle.'

Margaret Taylor was lucky. Others were not so fortunate, for uniforms seemed to attract a certain type of man. The problem grew big enough towards the end of 1942 for personnel of all Service departments, the Home Office and New Scotland Yard to meet regularly for discussions on ways and means of dealing with an increasingly alarming situation which could have a most serious effect on morale and Service efficiency. The outcome was that a decision was made that all rape cases should be dealt with by civil courts – even when the assailant was a serviceman under military law – for the offence was a civil one and should therefore be dealt with by the civil police.[17]

This new procedure brought more stress for the woman attacked, for it meant that the police had to be asked at once whether they wanted the woman to be examined and talked to by the police surgeon; if they did, the distressed servicewoman had to be detained comfortably, pending his arrival, and with as little damage as possible to any evidence provided by her clothing or her person. If the police said that action could be taken by the military authorities, the unit medical officer would then be called to carry out the examination. The determining factor was to be speed, the necessity for ensuring that immediate action was taken before evidence was destroyed.

Rape never was an easy problem to handle but the situation in war-time was made worse by the fact that a disturbing number of servicewomen were, in fact, soliciting men. Sometimes they would be in uniform, sometimes in civvies. Most of these servicewomen who were caught acting as prostitutes were absentees who had gone to London 'to go on the game'.

As one of them, a former WAAF, confided to the writer some forty years later:

Once you had done a bunk, you got into a desperate situation. You had to do something for a living but without ration cards or identity card you couldn't get a job, and your money very soon ran out. But there were easy pickings then with so many foreign troops in London, bored and with money to spare. I suddenly found that what I'd been doing for love I could do for money, and I never really thought of myself as a prostitute. I was simply on the run, waging my own little war against 'them', the officers, the sergeants, the Military Police and the government who had taken me into the Army against my will. I was fighting my own little battle for survival. And I won. I was lucky, though. Some of the girls got into the wrong hands and soon found themselves mixed up in all sorts of crimes.

She was right. Some servicewomen did come to a very sad end.

To deal with this problem of servicewomen getting into further trouble whilst on the run, a Special Absentee Reception Centre was set up in London in April 1942, and it was quickly followed by one in Manchester. It was no easy job though. The staff soon found they had to be tough and wide awake to deal with such a bunch of determined women being forcibly detained against their wishes. 'They were ingenious, unscrupulous, inventive and bloody dangerous,' said former ATS Sergeant Gill Rowlands. The Official ATS history is just as forthright: 'Several incidents occurred in which serious consequences might have resulted but for prompt action on the part of the guards. One auxiliary attempted to set fire to a barrack room, whilst others combined to assault the piquets and escape; they cut up the bedding, spoiled their clothes, broke gramophone records and ruined all the books and games provided. On one occasion the covers were removed from the electric light switches so that the piquet or any other member of the permanent staff, feeling for the electric light switch in the dark, would receive a shock.'[18]

So difficult was it to look after these women that the London District Absentee Centre eventually admitted defeat and handed over the task to the Provost Wing, but it did seem that the only way to deal with these hardened malcontents was to discharge them.

Clearly the best action to be taken against the disenchantment that could lead to breaches of discipline was to promote interest through purposeful activity – prevention rather than cure. Consequently more and more emphasis was placed on keeping women busy and happy.

There were some ingenious ways devised [wrote former Wren Margaret Taylor]. We had lectures on seamanship and navigation just in case we might transfer to boat crew; we had trips down the Thames in a launch owned by a playwright and member of Parliament, A.P. Herbert, who had two Naval ratings, Timmy and Tommy, as his crew. The not-so-ingenious ways of keeping us busy were to make us polish all the brass taps and scrub concrete floors.

When ingenuity failed completely, we would be sent on route marches. I remember that on such marches we would often pass the 'Star and Garter' home for the disabled of both world wars. They would be ranged on the verandah facing the road, some in beds, some in wheelchairs, others on crutches. In whichever direction we were marching, we never failed to give them an 'Eyes Right' or 'Eyes Left', with the petty officer in charge of the squad at the salute, and those gallant gentlemen would return the courtesy, those who could stand struggling to their feet to do so. It was surprising and unusual to observe the sudden change in the atmosphere which could then occur at that altitude, with an inexplicable mist apparently rising from the ground, blurring one's vision for the next quarter of a mile or so.

When all else failed there was always foot drill in readiness for some parade like the 'Wings For Victory' ones. It was in such a parade that our contingent was placed halfway between two brass bands – an awful position to be in if one hoped to keep in step, so a certain amount of shuffling and changing step took place at intervals during the march. However, as we proceeded up Birdcage Walk, both bands ceased playing almost simultaneously, except for the drum beating time for the marchers, and as we swung round the corner into Horse Guards Parade, past the throngs lining the pavement, a little Cockney boy, clutching his mother's hand, piped up piercingly, 'Ow look, Mum! lydy sylors!'

The 'lydy sylors' often had the laugh on some of the top brass of the Royal Navy. It was a little known but important part these Wrens played in the Battle of the Atlantic. They were stationed on HMS *Eaglet*, where the Commander-in-Chief, Western Approaches, had his headquarters. Former Third Officer C.J. Howe explained what happened.

We were used in large numbers in the Tactical School in Derby House where anti-submarine tactics were initiated and evaluated. Often the U-boats sank the convoy in the exercises, and the venerable senior officers under training were considerably 'miffed' to find that the U-boat commander was a young Wren. On one well-known occasion, Admiral Noble's successor – Admiral Sir Max Horton who was a notable submariner in World War One – was considering whether the Tactical School was of any use but was persuaded to attend the school during an exercise and asked to take the part of a U-boat commander. After he had been sunk six times by a Wren escort commander, he agreed that the Tactical School performed a vital function.[19]

Undoubtedly those Wrens on the shore-based Tactical School were smart. But what about the Wrens afloat? They were certainly keen to sail and often well qualified. In the early years of the war, recruiting officers were surprised and cynically amused at the number of girls naïvely offering their services to the WRNS on the grounds that they were experienced in boat work, sailing and navigation, little realizing that they would be as frustrated in their desire to sail as were the experienced women pilots in their wish to fly RAF aircraft.

It was still very much a man's world. Even girls who had trained as Sea Rangers on HMS *Implacable* at Portsmouth (with Mrs Laughton Matthews who became Director of the WRNS) found themselves facing the same annoying response to their requests to sail: 'Members of the WRNS do not go to sea.'

But they refused to accept this decision. They would go to sea. And some did.

On 10 March 1941 a Parliamentary Question was put to the First Sea Lord 'Can the Wrens go to sea?' Captain Pilkington, the Civil Lord of the Admiralty neatly side stepped the question by saying:

The answer is that the principle of Wrens serving afloat is not objected to by the Admiralty. I have no doubt that if you gave the Wrens half a chance they would be perfectly prepared to sail a battleship. In fact when the Wrens go overseas now they do take part in service on the ship, and help the men in a good many ways day by day. But the real difficulty about this proposal is accommodation on board. In all designing today the utmost and absolute economy of space has to be effected, and, quite obviously, if men and women are serving alongside, you cannot have the same economy of space as if there are men only. That is the real objection to my Hon Friend's suggestion, but at the same time I can assure him that if when and where it is found practicable to employ Wrens afloat that will certainly be done.

Such a statement would never have been made if the Wrens had not already proved their worth afloat. They had for months been training as boat crews in harbours on the south coast, and they had learnt quickly.

These Wrens were not going to be put off as easily as Captain Pilkington might have thought. They persisted in pushing for sea-going opportunities and soon were serving on troopships on the Atlantic run, doing coding, cyphering and signals work. Twelve Wrens sailed with Prime Minister Winston Churchill for Casablanca in January 1943 when he conferred with American and Russian leaders.

At last it began to look as if the Wrens had breached the red tape and prejudice, but in the end 'lavatories' won the day. It would be too difficult to have women around. It was the same basic argument in all three Services. As soon as the possibility of having women on the unit was suggested to commanders, minds turned to the problem of latrines and ablutions. As one medical commander, Brigadier Clynton Reed, explained in 1942. 'I must admit when, after the battle of El Alamein I was asked by the DDMS [Deputy Director of Medical Services] to have a detachment of six girls and their ambulances with my Indian Field Ambulance in the desert, my immediate thoughts were of the difficulties this would create. Not only were there the problems that would arise from having girls in a vast area of desert occupied by men, but there was also the need for separate hygiene and messing arrangements.'[20]

In face of attitudes such as this, reinforced by the die-hard prejudice of the Royal Navy against women serving at sea, the Wrens made little progress in their fight for sea-going opportunities.

They did, however, win their fight with the First Sea Lord for another 'right' about which they felt strongly. It was about their uniform, in particular their stockings.

In fact, this was a matter which occupied the minds of women in all three Services at that time. The ATS, for example, hated their 'bilious' woollen stockings, which they said vied with their khaki bloomers for the title of 'passion-killers'. In summer many of the girls, determined to add a little more to their looks, cast off their woollen stockings and followed the cosmetic transformation routine of Ruby Morton: 'We used to paint our legs with gravy browning and then draw a line up the back with a black eye-brow pencil for the seam. But the guards at the gate would sometimes send us back as 'improperly dressed' if they wanted to be awkward.'[21]

The Wrens would not indulge in any such practice. They demanded the right to wear black silk stockings.

How they won their battle with the Admiralty was later recorded for posterity in *The Wren* magazine as follows:

One pleasing story about Lord Alexander of Hillsborough has been left out of his formal obituaries.

While he was First Lord of the Admiralty during the war, the Wrens won a battle for silk stockings to become part of their uniform.

Some protested to him about this and asked how he could justify such extravagance in wartime. 'Well,' he said, 'the Wrens like the feel of them and so do my sailors.'[22]

But whilst the top brass of the Admiralty and the WRNS were engaged in this minor battle, a detachment of Wrens which had just left Britain in a convoy bound for Singapore were fighting for their lives in a real battle. Twenty-two of them perished when SS *Aguila* was sunk in a U-boat attack. As a result, plans for sending Wrens to sea were set back yet again, much to their dismay.

5   Blue Skies and Buzzing Flies, Where the Khamsin Blows

Soft sand under my feet, a whiteness of sun obscuring
Distance piled upon distance, as far as human enduring.

Ruth Evans, 'A Roman in Libya' in *Chaos of the Night, Women's Poetry and Verse of the Second World War*, edited by Catherine Reilly

1942-3

Whilst so many Wrens were chafing and fretting about their lack of sea-going opportunities, women in the other Services were embarking in ever-increasing numbers, sailing the seven seas and seeing something of the sharp end of the war.

One of these was Sister Norma Whitehead of the QAIMNS. On 5 January 1942 she was aboard the hospital ship *Somersetshire*, sailing towards a shell-shattered port in Libya, and even at that time of year the rays of the midday sun beat through her tropical kit shirt so fiercely that every movement of her body brought a quick rush of sweat.

Shielding her eyes from the glassy glare which came off the sea, she looked towards the whitened ruins on the quay and to the small town beyond, which stood out so starkly against a background of dull red sand, giving a theatricality to the scene. Sweat trickled into her eyes. So this is Tobruk, she thought.

It was a name well known in Britain at that time. For seven months the British and Commonwealth troops there had withstood a siege, with German troops commanding such a clear view over the whole town and defensive area that it was only at night that men in the advanced trenches could give themselves even the simple pleasure of standing up; in the day they had to lie down all the time, for any movement brought a 'stonking' of shellfire and mortars. Now the garrison had been relieved, but the battle was still raging around the area as Rommel, with tanks and infantry, tried to penetrate the British and New Zealand lines in an attempt to isolate Tobruk once again.

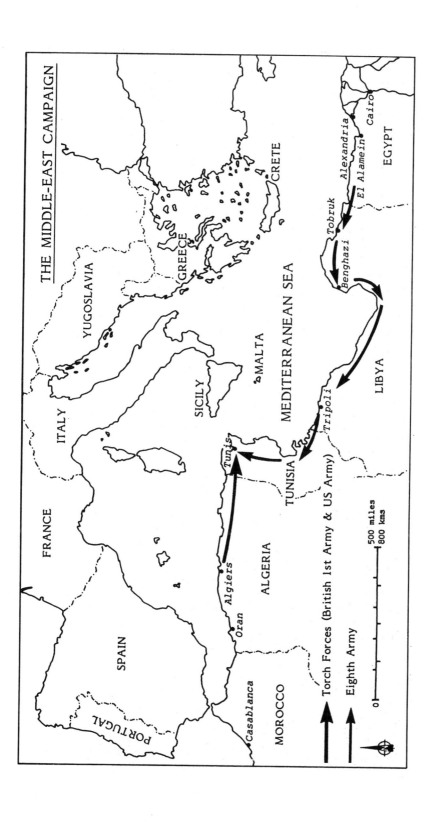

THE MIDDLE-EAST CAMPAIGN

FRANCE

SPAIN

PORTUGAL

MOROCCO

Casablanca

ALGERIA

Oran

Algiers

ITALY

YUGOSLAVIA

GREECE

CRETE

SICILY

MALTA

MEDITERRANEAN SEA

Tunis

TUNISIA

Tripoli

LIBYA

Benghazi

Tobruk

El Alamein

Alexandria

Cairo

EGYPT

Torch Forces (British 1st Army & US Army)

Eighth Army

500 miles
800 kms

0

Sister Whitehead's hospital ship anchored just clear of the port, and immediately lifeboats were lowered to take nurses ashore to help with the evacuation of badly wounded and severely ill soldiers. It was a most difficult task which went on throughout the day, each stretcher having to be lowered from the jetty four or five feet into the waiting lifeboats whilst shells burst sporadically on the foreshore, on the sand dunes and in the water. Darkness fell before all the wounded were embarked, and nurses had to spend the night in the town.

And what a night that was [said Norma Whitehead]. We had eleven and a half hours of heavy shelling. I suppose that the Germans knew that whatever major relief and reinforcement activity there was to be done would be carried out under cover of darkness and so they systematically hammered the whole area.

It was always worse to be shelled at night, your imagination filled in the details of what you couldn't see and it was nerve-racking to hear the screams of those who were hit and to fumble around soggy, shattered limbs, applying dressings to bleeding gashes you couldn't properly see. At daybreak next morning we felt shattered as we sat, with our hands wrapped round steaming enamel mugs of tea. The small group of nurses I was with didn't talk much; we sat tensed watching a section of Royal Engineers some little way to our front, moving slowly forward, earphones to their heads, shoulders hunched as they listened intently, while their instruments swept over the sand detecting German mines. We all knew what to expect, we had seen it happen before, we didn't want to look but we couldn't keep our eyes off them. Suddenly there was a muffled cheer, it was all over. They were through! This time. A cleared pathway lay taped behind them. They got into a jeep, drove back to where we were sitting and jumped off, drawing hard on their 'V' issue fags – that would be killing them in greater numbers thirty or forty years later than the Germans were then.*

We followed them to their cookhouse and refilled our mugs with hot tea into which the cook had stirred liberal quantities of sticky condensed milk. Still puffing hard on their fags and still with a whitish hue to their tanned faces, the young lads told us they usually had a de-mining job at first light because then the blinding rays of the rising sun prevented the enemy from seeing properly. By this time our casualties were all loaded and so we embarked and headed out to sea, relieved to be in a safer place.[1]

That was the first of many trips to Tobruk Sister Whitehead made with her colleagues. It was not so much the shelling, or the bombing, or the fear of excitement of those voyages that remained so firmly fixed in her mind as a simple incident that happened one morning as she was going back to the ship after visiting the base hospital in the town. She

---

* Fifty cigarettes a month were issued free to soldiers overseas, and it has been said that *habits of smoking fostered* in those young men then were responsible for more deaths later through lung cancer than the whole British Army suffered as battle casualties.

was walking on her own when suddenly a young lad wearing the black beret of the Royal Tanks Corps ran out from between two houses and touched her on the shoulder. He said in a bewildered voice: 'You are a woman then. You are real!'

Suddenly overcome with embarrassment, the soldier then stepped back and saluted, saying, 'Pardon me, ma'am, but I thought I must have had one over the eight last night. I haven't seen a woman in ten months.'

Sister Whitehead smiled and exchanged a few words with the soldier, and then went away quite happily. She was seeing what other women were also seeing, the remarkable effect the presence of women had in the forward areas on soldiers' morale. She was later to say:

> Those months aboard the hospital ship were probably the most memorable of the war and indeed of my whole life. Not just for the excitement but for the way that everyone worked so well together, unfalteringly, cheerfully. Being together 'in the desert' forged bonds between us; we were all a long way from home and a kind of affinity grew – a feeling that in our shared plight we had something precious in common with each other, something those at home would never understand. Men and women alike took to their discomforts philosophically, shrugging them off with their own versions of the native Arabic shoulder lift, and a murmuring of 'Mahleesh' – 'it makes no matter' or 'not to worry'. It was a sad day for me when I had to leave my old 'Tobruk Warrior', as the hospital ship was affectionately called, and became a landlubber in a tented hospital.[2]

Life for nurses in a tented desert hospital was more than difficult. There was so much with which they had to contend. To begin with, they were coping not only with casualties inflicted by the German enemy but also with those from another vicious enemy, as Sister Marjorie Bennett, who had two years in the desert, recalled:

> The sun was our enemy too. With temperatures of 100° or more for months on end, life became really exhausting. The wards were always full; there were battle casualties of every description, and we were also treating troops for various tropical diseases – sandfly fever, malaria, yellow fever, dysentery and mumps – and also many skin conditions, such as eczema, impetigo, scabies and desert sores. Desert sores were large sunburnt areas mainly on thighs and arms that had become septic and ulcerated.
>
> Heat exhaustion was another scourge we had to cope with. With little means of reducing body temperature rapidly, due to lack of water and shade, many patients died.[2]

In addition to the stifling heat, nurses had to learn to live with the all-pervading sand. It could not be kept out. When they stripped for a wash in the cool of the evening, they would find sand caked in small ridges in their crotch and armpits; it matted their hair so that putting a comb through it became well nigh impossible even when the hair was cut short. Sand covered tables and beds with a thin film at all times, and it made food gritty to eat. But when the Khamsin – a fierce wind from the south – blew, everyone had to move quickly. It whipped up spirals of whirling dust that obscured the sun and blotted out daylight; it swished under tents and blankets. 'We had to rush round covering patients with sheets and mosquito nets. Everything had to be made secure – guy ropes, pegs and tent flaps, for on a few occasions the tent roofs were blown away,' said Marjorie Bennett.

But, like the men, the nurses got used to the sand. They could live with it; they became accustomed to shaking it out of their shoes, out of their clothes, beating it out of their shirts when they dressed in the morning; they learnt how to skim it off their mugs of coffee, and they accepted it as part of the daily routine. But they could never accept the flies.

Flies were something different.

From first light they came, singly at first and then in ever-increasing numbers, buzzing and prying with persistent malignity, settling on eyes and lips, clustering in clumps round the rim of a mug and following it up to the mouth. They swarmed onto food, refusing to budge for the wafting of a hand until the last moment as a forkful approached the mouth and sometimes not even then, so that a half-chewed mouthful had to be spat out. They landed on perspiring bare flesh of arms, neck and face, scurrying aimlessly about, irritating almost beyond endurance. They grew fat on the dirt and debris from the battlefield, crawled over mouldering corpses, flew into primitive latrines and landed on any open wounds they could find. They would not leave them alone, clustering on grazed knees or knuckles, sipping and nuzzling at pus ooozing from beneath the hard scabs of desert sores, infecting them still further.

'Flies were,' said Marjorie Bennett, 'the worst plague of all. They were with us every day in their hundreds and thousands. Even when you spoke, flies entered your mouth, and now you know why Middle Eastern Moslem women wear a yashmak. Flies were a great source of infection. When on our dressing rounds we would take Italian prisoners of war, who worked as orderlies, and excellent fellows they were too, and they would stand at either side of the bed with fly swats waving them to and fro whilst we removed the dressings beneath, otherwise flies would swarm onto the wounds, causing sepsis.'

The flies infected the food with their filth, to give everyone at some time or other the dreaded dysentery. The cork-screwing pain that came with it and the equally distressing weakness that followed could cause greater havoc amongst the nursing staff of hospitals than the most accurate shelling or bombing. No matter how careful they were, no matter what medical precautions were taken, no matter how desert-hardened the nurses were, inevitably they would be struck down.

What else was there for these women to endure?

There were snakes, scorpions, bugs, desert rats and kite birds [recalls Marjorie Bennett]. Kite birds were a type of vulture with a three-foot wing span, and they were crafty. Around noon they would gather and perch on the kitchen roof. The hospital meals were cooked in a field kitchen away from the wards, and when the bugle sounded at mid-day – 'Come to the cookhouse door, boys, come to the cookhouse door', off would go the orderlies and a few of the 'up patients' to deliver the grub to the wards. So, when the food was dished up and taken to the patients on trays, those darned kite birds would swoop down and the poor orderlies would drop the lot. Now food, like water, was in short supply, and we too became quite crafty. Just before noon we would send two POWs with garbage pails to the refuse pit. The kite birds would follow and rummage around whilst we quickly dished up the dinners before the birds got back to the kitchen roof.

Such was the varied and difficult life in the tented desert hospitals.

Servicing those hospitals were women of the 5-0-2 Motor Ambulance Company. We have already seen how this company escaped from the Germans in 1940, by means of a bit of smart manoeuvring at the crossroads on the way to Dunkirk (p.49). After re-forming in Britain they eventually embarked for the Middle East on the long voyage round the Cape and months later arrived at Alexandria. They were soon to find that the Middle East did not yet cater adequately for the needs of women. On disembarking at the docks they formed up on the road, an impressive convoy of twenty-six American Dodge ambulances and four Fords, with two women drivers to most vehicles. They were tremendously excited as they drove down the eighty miles of desert road to Cairo. Soon, though, they became aware of other feelings, urgent physical ones. They would have to stop, and it was therefore a relief to come upon 'Halfway House'. They drew into the forecourt, parked their ambulances neatly and walked to the loo. But, as Pat Hall recalls, "Halfway House" was not used to women's convoys, for the "ladies" was found to be locked. It was alleged and widely believed that Maria, the tomboy of the group, undaunted, whipped out her revolver and shot the lock away'.[3]

Refreshed, some little time later they swept into their destination at the Helmieh barracks to be greeted by the garrison adjutant, who clapped his hand to his head and said, 'Good God, no one told me you were women!'

Accommodating women was far too big a problem for him to handle. Why, they would need separate places for washing, eating and sleeping. It could create all kinds of difficulties, and what would happen when women moved into a camp full of men?

Without wasting any more time on the perplexed adjutant, the ambulance company moved into the Heliopolis Palace Hotel – or 'Hell House', as it was commonly known to those officers who had enough cash to patronize it.

From that evening on, the unit was kept very busy. They learnt as they went along. They learnt that if they drove too slowly, the 'blanket-snatchers' would get them. Pat Hall experienced what thousands of other servicewomen from Alexandria to Algiers experienced – the kit-snatching ploy. A small boy would stagger across the road and fall in the path of an oncoming truck. Naturally the driver would brake suddenly and it was then that two other boys would leap over the tailboard and open the doors and throw any kit or blankets out into the road where others of the gang would pick them up and run. 'There was nothing the driver could do short of running over the fall-guy, which was hardly practicable,' said Pat Hall.

However, there was something the cheery fighting men from Nepal, the Gurkhas, could do about it, and the message quickly got home, so that their trucks were rarely touched and then only by those too stupid to be able to identify the sign of the 4th Indian Division. These happy warriors, who went into battle with their razor-sharp kukris drawn, would hide behind the tarpaulin and the tailboard and have a go with those same knives at the thieving fingertips as they appeared over the top.

The MT women were quickly to learn from all their experiences, including the lesson of the 'Halfway House' and its closed loo: Like ATS convoy drivers in the Western desert they developed a sixth sense for places along the road which afforded cover for those needing a 'comfort break'. 'It was extraordinary,' said Pat, 'how any stop for this purpose seemed to bring a rush of traffic along a normally empty road.'

They also learnt something which is only now being truly appreciated: that sunbathing can be dangerous. At first, when they were off duty and at week-ends and were able to drive to a beach for a picnic and swim, they would all, almost without exception, misjudge the heat of the sun and suffer from raw shoulders and faces the next day. All pretended there was nothing amiss, however, for sunburn sores amounted to a self-inflicted wound (like shooting yourself through your foot) 'incapacitating oneself through carelessness', and as such were a military crime that could be tried by court-martial.

Of course, being so few women amongst so many men, they all had to learn how to deal with the different approaches of men. Dorothy Calvert remembers how, 'After a few good dates some men caught a dreadful complaint, "the wandering hand disease". Some would respond to the old medicine of a good slap in the face or, if they were incorrigibly "fruity", there was no help for them at all, so sadly we bade them a soldier's farewell. Then there was always the man who assumed immediate familiarity with some questionable jokes – testing the water, as it were – and the answer to that was a frigid reception, leaving the chap with an expression on his face like a bewildered puppy that gets beaten when it thought it was at play.'

The ambulance women had a name for such men and a way of treating them. 'They were just like a dangerous corner, so obvious that you went slowly,' said Pat Hall.

There was indeed much to learn when it came to entering a man's world, especially one in the desert. These women soon saw the writing on the wall, as had others in various branches of the women's Services, and as they still continue to see – that it is never enough for women to show themselves equally good at the job: they have to show themselves to be better. Pat Hall explained what her drivers were up against with men in the Royal Army Service: 'Errors which would pass in a man's unit with little more than a mild reprimand would be classed as crimes with us and greeted with snorts of "Women!" '

Facing such a situation forced the women drivers to prove they were more than a match for the men, and their commanding officer, Brigadier J. Clynton Reed, CBE, in spite of his initial reservations, was later to write:

I am happy to say they were an unqualified success; an intelligent highly responsible and thoroughly reliable group of girls. Incidentally their presence had an elevating effect on our general behaviour and turn-out.

Brigadier Reed also found that a sense of 'competing developed and that the high standards of motor transport maintenance achieved by the women soon forced the men to look to their laurels. 'On the medical side,' he added, 'the effect on morale of battle-weary patients who found themselves in feminine care for the last lap of their journey to hospital, could not be over-emphasised.'[4]

By the summer of 1942, then, the women of 5-0-2 Company Motor Ambulance Convoy had learnt a lot about survival in its many forms. It was just as well they had, for in that hot, stinking summer there was a real flap on in Cairo. The German-Italian Army of Field Marshal Erwin Rommel was but a morning's drive from Egypt's capital. The great offensive into Libya which the British Eighth Army had launched so promisingly in the winter months had disastrously misfired, and its troops had been driven back towards the Nile, their armoured vehicles and tanks decimated. At 'Knightsbridge', British tank formations had fallen into a trap: 200 out of the 300 there were destroyed or captured. Casualties were high. Ambulance companies such as 5-0-2 drove from dawn to dusk carrying wounded to base hospitals.

The situation was grim.

On 16 June German radio announced that Rommel had won the desert battle and that all British forces had been wiped out. The Afrika Korps was now massing 3000 tanks close to the Egyptian border ready for the final battle.

To the British women based in Egypt, special instructions were sent. The 'Flap' was on. Every woman had to have a bag packed ready to embark at a moment's notice. On 29 June the Wrens were evacuated. Orders came through confining to barracks all troops not actively engaged. The fleet left harbour, and even the old *Queen Elizabeth* troop ship picked up her skirts and ran. Outgoing trains from Cairo and Alexandria were crammed to overflowing with people sitting on the bumpers and on the roofs of carriages and standing on carriage steps.

From the tops of buildings in Cairo and Alexandria British flags were hastily torn down by Egyptians and replaced with Nazi and Italian ones. Sister Marjorie Bennett recalls how she met a chanting crowd marching down one of the main streets shouting in a curious mixture of Arabic and broken English: 'We want Rommel! English go now! Down with British! We want Rommel!'

At any moment, it seemed to the women of the medical and ambulance service, they would receive instructions to embark. But suddenly instructions came to the contrary. The Director of Medical Services, Middle East, wrote to all units saying that rumours that women were to be evacuated should be disregarded as without foundation and that he was adamant that '... women drivers who knew the area and the ways of hospitals were irreplaceable and furthermore it was the opinion of the Area Commander that "they were good for morale".'

Women were helping with another big problem too – water. As Captain R.M. Nichols of the ATS explained: 'I was then driving a 15-cwt water truck in the dusty convoys down the desert track. It was hot and thirsty work. We were kept on a tight ration for water ourselves, for water was the life line of the army. We each had a jerry can of local water – about three and a half gallons – to last us a week. We used to make a desert fire in the evening by pouring petrol onto a tinful of sand, we warmed the water for a good wash, used it again in the morning, at lunchtime and tea-time as well and then threw it away!'[5]

In July 1942 the two desert armies faced each other across a battlefield bounded on the north by the sea and on the south by the Quattara Depression – the place was indicated by an insignificant little railway station whose name would go down in history, El Alamein. There, both armies, plagued by heat, flies and thirst, waited for what they knew would be the signal for Rommel to launch his last bid for Egypt – the August moon.

The ex-patriate upper-crust British in Cairo and Alexandria seemed incredibly unaware of this. As Noël Coward reported in his diary:

The restrictions of wartime were unknown, people sat there sipping gin-slings and cocktails and chatting and gossiping, waiters glided wearing fezzes and inscrutable Egyptian expressions. There were uniforms everywhere of all ranks of the Services and of all nationalities. Constance Carpenter, in a natty shark-skin two-piece with ENSA on her epaulettes. These uniforms indicated that perhaps somewhere in the vague outside world there might be a war of some sorts going on. All the fripperies of pre-war luxury living were still in existence here: rich people, idle people, cocktail parties, dinner parties, jewels and evening dress. Rolls Royces came purring up to the terrace steps; the same age-old Arabs sold the same age-old carpets and junk; scruffy little boys darted in between the tables shouting 'Bourse! Bourse! which when translated means 'Times'. Here they had all stayed, floating about lazily in this humid backwater.[6]

All this was certainly an eye-opener for most of the servicewomen, whose social life had hitherto gone scarcely beyond the NAAFI canteens.

To Noël Coward the NAAFI was a nightmare. He visited one in Cairo and attempted to give one of his sophisticated concert appearances there. 'It's Hell in there,' he said, 'a vast cavern of a place crowded with troops and there was no "mike". I tried to make myself heard but without much success so I quickly sang some popular choruses and they all joined in and everything was all right.'

And so life, shot through with such paradoxes, went on its peculiar hot-season way. The humidity was high, tempers were short, the Nile was in flood, and mail was long delayed. When, after a long wait, the first batch did arrive, it did nothing for Pat Hall's morale. The first letter she opened was a demand for an income tax return, and because of this she now has a record of what she was earning then as a sergeant – £94 a year, made up of 4 shillings a day basic pay plus 8 pence war pay, plus 6 pence colonial allowance and 3 pence cleaning allowance. From this, barrack damages and 6 pence mess money were deducted.

But pay was the least of worries for the servicewoman in Cairo then. Rommel made his last offensive and failed. Now things really began to move.

More and more troops poured into Egypt, and then, on the night of 23 October 1942, there came to the ears of those in Alexandria the rumble of Montgomery's thousand guns heralding the Eighth Army's attack at El Alamein. It meant also that the ATS drivers, FANY and nurses would be on the move again. On the afternoon of 4 November, Rommel ordered his forces to retreat. The second battle of El Alamein was over. The Eighth Army had utterly defeated the Afrika Korps and put it to flight.

But casualties were high. 13,500 British and Commonwealth troops were killed.

Amongst them was Captain Etienne Szabo. He had heard just before the battle that his wife, Violette, had given birth to a daughter, Tania, and he looked forward to going home on leave after the campaign in the desert was over. His death greatly affected Violette. At first she was grief-stricken, and then she was roused to a fury. 'I want to do something in this war,' she cried, 'I want to fight with a gun in my hand.'[7] So it was that the El Alamein battle, said to be the turning-point in the Second World War, became the turning-point in the short life of Violette Szabo. She was shortly to be given the opportunity of fighting with a gun in her hand.

Meanwhile, in the Western Desert the war raced ahead, and as the front advanced, so also did the tented hospitals, their nurses and the ambulance units. Lillie Muff, now Mrs Saxton, was then a lieutenant in the Queen Alexandra's Imperial Nursing Service with one of those hospitals and found her experiences described in the *Egyptian Mail* under the headline: 'BRITISH NURSES ARE ON THE FRONT LINE'. The article read:

Only a few miles behind the forward most troops of the advancing Eighth Army during their fifteen hundred miles chase from Alamein to Tripoli travelled British nurses. Twenty-four hours after Tripoli fell, a travelled-stained column of motor ambulances and medical store lorries rolled into one of the main squares, halted, and from the front seats jumped down nine nursing sisters – the first British women in the city. They gathered together gazing round at Mussolini's 'Jewel of Africa', patted their hair into place, and then briskly set about getting into operation their mobile hospital.

'Blimey, Nurses!' said Jock, Tommy and Kiwi alike, gazing at the trim battle-dressed figures of the sisters.

And 'Blimey, Nurses!' has been the expression of amazement of all our wounded all along the way – amazement at finding nurses up with the most forward Casualty Clearing Stations, amazement at finding only a short ambulance ride from the 'Front Line' the gentle hands and soothing words of nursing sisters.

'There is an amazing change when you have women about,' said the Colonel of an Advanced Casualty Station to a military observer. 'Usually the lads have been prepared to have a fairly roughish time after they have been wounded until they get into a General Hospital, but now with these girls right up at the casualty clearing stations you can see the difference. The best male orderly is not a patch on a woman. The atmosphere is different. Even the hospital tents don't look the same. You can always tell the touch of a woman. In the most desolate spots sometimes they have managed to find a few flowers. It is surprising to see how our boys appreciate it too. When they are wounded they are amazed to find nurses so near the battle and they seem quite content when they find themselves in women's hands.

Bombed, shelled, machine-gunned, some of the nursing sisters have been under all sorts of fire. Sitting in the front of the ambulances and lorries, muffled up to keep out the biting wind and rain, they have bumped over mile after mile of the world's worst gunge and been ready at a moment's notice to halt, set up the tents and carry on dealing with the wounded. The way they work is in the smooth calm way as if they were in the ward of a London hospital. But we've enjoyed every minute of it,' said the trim, dark-haired Miss C.M. Butland of Spencer Avenue, Coventry, the Sister-in-Charge of the Mobile Hospital. 'We've had to rough it. Bully beef and biscuits, sleeping on the ground, and very little water, but every one of us here would do it again like a shot. But I'm sure the matron of the hospital where I trained would have a fit if she saw us now,' she said, gazing down at her battle-dress blouse and khaki trousers. 'But we've been glad of these in the cold. And what do you think of the cap?' she asked, patting a khaki handkerchief tied round her head. 'Half a gallon of water a day doesn't give you much chance to keep white caps clean. Thank the Lord we're in Tripoli, we'll be able to get a bit of washing done.'

The Chief Principal Matron of the Middle East, Miss P. Sowter, told how her nurses had even decorated make-shift wards in Tobruk at Christmas. 'They used blue paper from bandages and silver paper from cigarette packets and they even managed to get flowers from somewhere. They are all immensely cheerful and I try to help them by sending off parcels now and then.'

And what was in those packages? '*Tinned sausages and face powder!*'[8]

Now, with the Desert Fox, Rommel, and his Afrika Korps in full retreat, more and more women were needed for service in the Middle East. Jacky Burgess recalls how,

One freezing and damp winter's morning our unit was paraded in front of a visiting ATS officer who asked for volunteers for overseas, probably the Middle East. With the wind howling in Hertfordshire and snow beginning to fall, it seemed a delightful prospect. No more Arctic working conditions, no more of those early morning runs and PT with goose pimples beneath our shorts and shirts (Anyone cold? Right, we'll do it again then), just blissful warmth. Ninety per cent of the hands went up, mine included.

Prior to embarkation we were sent to a holding unit in Sussex Gardens, London. We had plenty of free time although we had to report to the unit orderly room every four hours. Each night we had a special parade followed by a march around the block with full kit; one kitbag on the shoulder, another in the hand, water bottle, haversack and various other impediments slung around our necks – one girl even had a violin! It was after one of these parades that we came back to find a sergeant waiting by each letter-box who told us: 'No more letter-writing. Go and get your bacon-and-egg supper. You're off!'

After we had eaten, we were given a pack of sandwiches, driven to the railway station in the dark and travelled all through the night until we eventually pulled into a dock siding. We were all aboard before first light but shortly afterwards one of the Scouses in our party let out a whoop of surprise: 'Look at that,' she cried. 'The Liver Buildings! We're in Liverpool!'

Six girls were crammed into cabins meant for two. There were two three-tiered bunks, and we drew lots for them. The top one was favoured because there was more air space, but it was not easy to climb into it, especially when the ship was rolling and pitching. Those in the bottom bunk, though, had to face the hazards of having a foot in the face or of someone above being sick. I had a bottom bunk.[9]

The first surprise came at breakfast. The women were queuing up outside the ship's dining-room with their mugs and eating-irons when they heard the tannoy telling them to go right in and sit at the tables. 'The tables were all laid with cups and saucers, and it was just like being on a cruise. The next night, as I looked through the porthole at the red sky over the city, I suddenly noticed we were moving. The Liver Buildings were receding. I have never known such panic as I felt then. Would I ever be seeing Britain and my folks again? That night there was dead silence in the cabin.'

Any feelings those women might have had of being on a cruise rapidly disappeared during the next few days as they zigzagged in a convoy in a north-westerly direction towards Greenland. Where on earth were they going? It seemed a funny way of sailing to the sunny Middle East. The weather grew colder, the sea greyer and rougher. On the first night the alarm bells rang about midnight. All the women rushed up on deck for life-boat drill and stood there petrified, shivering in their odd assortment of dress and looking at the black, swirling water below. This was the real thing. After that they made sure that their 'Mae West' life-jackets were handy at all times, their water bottles full, and 'panic' bags of emergency rations – ship's biscuits and a big block of chocolate – ready.

Soon the Atlantic swell began to take its toll. Nearly everyone was seasick, for it was the season of the equinoctial gales. 'Our Steward, whose name was Joe, was a young chap who actually seemed to enjoy his job, and he made a bet with the six of us that he would take us all out to dinner in Cape Town if we did not miss a meal. Despite our determination though, the ship's dining-room became more and more empty with each succeeding meal. One of the girls who had dashed out after starting her dinner eventually came back to find that all the food had been cleared away, so she asked for another dinner, saying, "I've got rid of the last one. Can I have another please?" '

Each Sunday, as was the custom in those war-time days, there was a Church Parade. It was held on the well deck. Afterwards the girls would go to the library, which was much lower down in the hold, where the troops were crowded together in their swaying hammocks. 'We felt sorry for them with that awful oil smell all the time, and we were not surprised at their being more seasick even than we were.'

They were not particularly surprised therefore by what happened on Easter Sunday. Mutiny.

There were on the ship 2,000 men and 200 women, and it was decreed by the Officer in Charge of Troops that there would be no fraternizing between the servicemen and the women, though the 'other ranks' ATS could, if they wished, chat to the officers on the boat deck. The girls did not think this at all fair. 'After all,' said Jacky, 'we were all in the war together, we thought, and so we did talk to the men through portholes, and some of the girls did their mending and darned their socks. However, on this particular Easter Sunday some of the men got very drunk and threatened to break into our cabins. Razors came out; there was a lot of shouting and fighting. We hurriedly barricaded and locked our doors. One girl held a chamber pot aloft, threatening to bash the first head that came through the door. Eventually the riot was quelled. The men involved were taken off under arrest at Durban. Later we heard they had only recently been released from Exeter gaol.'

Once the ship began to steam in a more southerly direction, the days became more exciting, in more ways than one.

'Our Commanding Officer decided that it was not good for us to loll about all day enjoying ourselves with ship's concerts, dances and deck quoits, so she arranged for us to do duty as submarine spotters. Four of us at a time had to stand on the boat deck, one facing in each direction. If anything was sighted we had to shout: "Ahoy there, starboard bow, starboard beam, port beam" and so on, depending on where the thing was seen. We were all very conscientious about this, I for one believing that the whole future of the war at sea depended upon my efforts and hoping that I would not get my "beams" and "bows" mixed up when the time came.'

As was the tradition in peace-time, so in war-time, when 'The Line' was crossed everyone got a ducking as a prelude to receiving a certificate saying that they had invaded King Neptune's territory. 'We were all soaking and very happy. The war seemed a long way away. The OC Troops joined in the fun. It must have been too much of a strain for him. The next day he collapsed and died while making an after-dinner speech. We had the service and burial the next morning, standing on the deck while the body was piped overboard. The convoy slowed down with flags at half mast and we sang, "Eternal Father, strong to save". I cried.'

And so the long sea voyage went on. After six weeks they reached

Durban, where they disembarked before tackling the next stage of the journey to Cairo.*

Steaming up the African coast was an ordeal that everyone had to suffer. The intense heat became almost unbearable, and each man and woman had to take two salt tablets a day to prevent heat exhaustion. Furthermore it was made clear to everyone that to go down with heat exhaustion would be treated as a self-inflicted wound, and the sufferer would be charged accordingly. 'Most of us put all our salt tablets in one lot of soup to avoid ruining every meal. In spite of this, some of our girls did get heat exhaustion, also prickly heat and other discomforts,' said Jacky Burgess.

The great thrill that came with arriving at Cairo was not the sight of the noisy, dusty city but the pile of mail that was waiting, from home. For Jacky Burgess and her friends, though, the journey was not yet over. There was still a hundred miles for them to travel to their camp, and rail journeys were not in cruise-style luxury, as Mary Hughes, an RAMC medical officer said:

At noon, with the English sisters, I was put on a train and, although it was not due to leave until five, told to stay there. Iron rations – bully beef and biscuits – were washed down by the tea I had scrounged, but at six o'clock the train was still sitting there like a broody hen trying to hatch out a door knob, so a few of us climbed out on the line and went in search of more tea. No luck! But we stretched our legs and met some sights and smells-dirty flat houses of cracked mud bricks, shy veiled women, carrying babies with sticky eyes, while their black gowns were clutched by little dark boys and girls in ankle-length gowns. Their lords drank coffee in outdoor cafés to the accompaniment of plaintive Egyptian music, going up and down the scale of five notes, all minor.

Suddenly came a transformation. The air-raid siren howled shrilly, and great was the scatter. Men and women looked like beetles on the wing, their black cloaks billowing as they raced to the shelters. What a contrast to the unhurried processions in London's streets under similar conditions! 'Here come the Jerries again! I suppose we had better get down to the shelter.'[10]

When Jacky Burgess and her ATS friends eventually reached camp, they found it to be near the sea – but it was far from being a holiday camp. There were too many unwelcome guests trying to get into their beds.

'There were three beds in each tent, and we noticed that all the legs of the bed stood in tins full of paraffin. This was to discourage the bugs. They were there in their thousands. We also had mosquito nets, which

* Few people today realize that such a trip would take ten weeks and would cover 11,500 miles or more according to evasive action taken.

gave one a feeling of privacy until you found that a mosquito or fly had somehow got inside during the day. Other frequent and unwelcome guests were the sand lizards, as well as numerous unnamed creepy-crawlies,' recalled Jacky.

Then there were always the silent Arabs who suddenly appeared ghostlike and without warning. They wore red tarbushes or dirty headdresses worn turban-wise, their dark bodies covered by bedraggled, long, very off-white gowns and torn European coats. They could rifle a tent whilst the occupants were asleep even remove wallets and purses from under the sleeper's pillow. Great care indeed had to be taken over one's belongings.

Equal care had to be taken with food and drink. Everyone was warned not to eat or drink anything that had not been prepared on the camp or in a Service club. One woman Jacky Burgess knew disregarded the warnings, caught typhoid and nearly died. 'She had bought a bottle of ginger beer from an Arab on the beach whilst she was on leave in Palestine. It was three months before she came back to us from hospital, a pale wraith of her former self with all her hair cropped short.'

Naturally overseas service provided unparalleled opportunities for leave in exotic places, and this gave a new dimension to their lives. Palestine was a much-favoured though sometimes hazardous location. Mary Hughes told of how she went shopping to Haifa in an Arab bus:

> We proceeded in an uproar of chatter and gesticulation. The driver frequently had both hands off the wheel, flapping them overhead. We tore round the bends through the hills between Haifa and Nazareth in a terrifying way. To Arabs a car or bus is a thing to be put in top gear and sent headlong at maximum speed, irrespective of what might be round the next bend.
>
> Coming home from Jerusalem one night, through the mountains of Samaria, it terrified me to look over the precipices that were rushing past. I said to the driver: 'Surely it is dangerous to drive like this,' as I gripped hard on the seat. 'Yes, Madame,' he agreed, 'it is dangerous, but Allah is good!'[10]

Jacky Burgess and her friends had a memorable holiday in Palestine too. They had saved up their leave to spend two weeks together at a military holiday camp, Nathaniya, on the Palestinian coast, but then changed their minds in order to have a little more luxury by booking in at the YWCA in Jerusalem. The journey, though, almost spoilt the holiday: 'It took twenty-four hours and we were packed like sardines, sitting on kitbags, sprawling over the windows, dozing against each other. I found myself a place in the corridor and stretched out along the floor, among the feet, as it was more comfortable. When we arrived at Jerusalem the next day, I was covered from head to foot with bug bites and had to spend the whole holiday covered up. I should have known better, for at work we knew that if we leant our arms on the tables they would be covered with bites. It was policy to squash as many bugs as possible at the beginning of each watch.'

The much-bitten young woman and her friends also had a hair-raising ride on a bus that took them through the Biblical Wilderness of Judea to Jericho and the Dead Sea, more than a thousand feet below sea-level. 'It was too salty for swimming, so we just sat and paddled in it, knowing we were unsinkable. At a Bedouin camp near Bethlehem an Arab sheik invited my friend and me into his tent for coffee. I was afraid it might be drugged but my friend with the Baedeker Guide quoted something about never refusing Arab hospitality and that it would be an interesting experience. It was!'

Returning to camp from leave spent in one of the Service holiday centres was an experience of a totally different kind, one that always came as something of a shock to women – having to get used to primitive latrines after hotel toilets. Frequently women suffered from 'Gippy Tummy', as we have already seen, and it became a real problem in a tented camp, as Jacky Burgess can recall:

The latrines were a long way from our tents (they needed to be) and consisted of long pole and canvas screen affairs. Inside were long pieces of wood with holes, and buckets underneath. For obvious reasons the canvas did not reach the ground, as each morning the 'dung carts' drawn by mules came round and the buckets were emptied into them. This did nothing to decrease the fly population. The Egyptians seemed fascinated by us and, as the canvas structure was open to the sky, it was nothing to look up and see a hand, or a face looking at you. One day my friend, having felt something, looked down to see a hand removing the bucket from under her. For toilet paper we had torn-up books. Some of the pages were very thick, almost like cardboard, but the stories were interesting enough sometimes to make us forget the smell. Invariably, though, a page was missing just when they were getting exciting.

The cure for 'Gippy Tummy' was to take some foul-tasting purgative from sick-quarters and then eat hard-boiled eggs for a week.

Eggs came from swopping tea with Arabs who had eggs tucked in their capacious pockets. Sometimes the troops would dry the infused tea leaves, rub them on the outside of the smoke-blackened brew cans and take pleasure in putting one over the crafty Arabs for a change.

Anyone who had ever suffered from 'Gippy Tummy' was always extra careful about food thereafter. When Jacky Burgess first arrived in Egypt, she was advised on many precautions, including never to eat the top slice of bread on a plate because that was the one which had the most flies on. 'We used to hold each slice of bread up to the light too, so we could see the weevils and pick them out before eating. In the same talk, given soon after our arrival, we were told to try to forget the flies, otherwise they would drive us mad.'

They did their best to forget, doing the job in hand and trying not to worry too much about what came next. Not only did they do their job well but they contributed in many incalculable ways to the morale of the British Army which was fighting alone as an entity for the last time. Three years of fluctuating fortune were coming to an end but now morale – the factor in war which Napoleon considered three-quarters of the game – was high. Furthermore, the Eighth Army was now no longer alone with the enemy in North Africa.

On 8 November 1942, four days after Rommel's retreat from El Alamein, the biggest invasion fleet the world has ever known landed assault troops at several points along the French North African coast between Casablanca and Algiers. The Commander-in-Chief of that Anglo-American Force was General Dwight D. Eisenhower.

Waiting eagerly in Britain for her embarkation to join the General was his FANY driver, Kay Summersby, but she, like many other servicewomen then in overseas holding units, was having to be patient. Things were not going according to plan. The troops who had landed so boldly two months earlier had finally come to a halt. The mud, the mountains and the Germans had stopped them.

Someone had blundered. The Allies had made the classic military error of making war in petty packets for, despite the size of the invasion convoy, the number of fighting troops actually available at the front was pitifully small. What the Allies had not foreseen was how easy it was for the Germans and Italians to rush reinforcements of men, tanks, guns and planes across the sixty-mile strait from Sicily every night in troop-carrying planes and small ships loaded with weaponry and tanks.

Consequently, whilst servicewomen in Britain earmarked for North Africa waited impatiently for movement orders, the fighting troops on the battle front there were taking a terrible mauling. Virtually every infantry battalion which had landed with the invasion was down to half strength. The Hampshire Regiment, for instance, had gone into action 800 men strong but was now down to exactly six officers and 194 men.

To deal with casualties on such a scale, nurses were desperately needed. Many had already been in action in the opening stages of the assault landings – they had picked up casualties from the dockside whilst under fire from the Vichy French and had saved countless lives of men from the HMS *Partridge*. Now base hospitals were urgently needed.

So it was that at the end of November 1942 the troopship *Strathallen* sailed from the Clyde with the nursing staff of a general hospital under its principal matron, Miss Lucy Wane. Amongst this draft of nurses, troops and other servicewomen was General Eisenhower's driver, Kay

Summersby. By this time, though, it might be truer to say that she was something more than just his driver: she was his secretary, his confidante – his ... mistress perhaps? As Kay herself was later to confess,[11] she felt at times like the girl in the hair-colouring advertisement of whom people were asking: 'Does she ... or doesn't she ...?' But in her case they were not speculating about her hair colour.

Shortly before General Eisenhower set sail for North Africa, he took Kay into the garden of his retreat at Telegraph Cottage, Kingston, and from his pocket pulled a small Beretta pistol, saying: 'When we are overseas you never know what might happen, I'd prefer to see you dead rather than a prisoner of the Germans!' Such was the intensity of his feeling.

The pistol went in Kay's 'torpedo bag' aboard the *Strathallen*. This survival kit was an odd mixture, for, as well as the usual medication, emergency rations and warm clothing, there were a few frivolous items: cosmetics and a silk trousseau – for she was engaged to be married to a British Army colonel then serving with the First Army in North Africa.

Right from the moment they left the quayside it was a rough trip, but once the ship entered the Mediterranean, calm prevailed, blue skies and serenity. So came the last night of the voyage. There were farewell parties to attend, kit to be sorted and 'torpedo bags' to be unpacked. In twenty-four hours they would land. Kay and her friends were just getting their khaki uniforms ready for the morning's disembarkation when it happened – 'A tremendous explosion,' Kay remembered vividly. 'It threw me off the bunk. Then the lights flickered and went out. The ship was shivering as if it had a monstrous chill and then began rocking ominously back and forth. "This is it!" a girl shouted, "Let's get going!"'

Clutching shoes, handbag, life-preserver and whatever else came immediately to hand, the women dashed onto the boat deck and clambered into a lifeboat. Within minutes they were adrift on the moonlit Mediterranean. But, as Kay was to write later, 'It was not as romantic as it sounds. Not romantic at all when the sea around you is filled with soldiers and nurses swimming about trying to find somewhere to hang on to. Not every group had been as fortunate as we had. Several lifeboats had capsized. We pulled a good number of people into our boat; several had broken legs and arms. The boat was bobbing madly about as depth charges exploded far below. We could see the convoy silhouetted against the sky, our sister ship went steaming past seemingly aloof and uncaring. The *Strathallen* was in the distance now settling lower and lower in the water. Very soon, I thought, it's all going to be at the bottom of the sea. My little trousseau, the precious diamond earrings ...'

The stricken *Strathallen* was not only settling (a torpedo had gone clean through her engine room) but burning fiercely, with flames spouting from her side. Soon, far more than a silk trousseau was going to be lost. On board still were two QAs, Sisters Olive Stewardson and Julie Kerr, looking after a score of the ship's company. When the ship was first hit, they had rushed down to the sick-bay, where five badly wounded soldiers lay helpless. Hastily the two women bandaged and strapped them for despatch. They were just about to leave when several badly burnt men from the engine room were carried in for treatment. Without a thought for their own safety, these nurses, now helped by two American WAACs and a British nurse, Judith Baskott, worked right through that night treating a constant stream of other severely burnt seamen.

When dawn came, the doomed ship was listing at such an angle that the deck and rail were awash. It was then that a destroyer came alongside and lifted off all survivors. Except the unlucky ones.

Five nurses lost their lives.

Not far away another destroyer was carrying out a similar rescue operation: rope ladders were thrown down into Kay Summersby's lifeboat and to those still clinging on to its sides. Soon they were all steaming towards Oran.

That afternoon a dishevelled Kay Summersby was standing in the hallway of the Oran Garrison Headquarters trying to convince a junior officer that she must see her fiancé, Colonel Richard Arnold, and also that she must speak on the telephone to the Commander-in-Chief, General Eisenhower. This was just a little too much for the junior officer. He passed the can upwards. It went through several hands before eventually someone was senior enough to make decisions. Then, in front of many raised eyebrows and incredulous eyes, Kay telephoned her boss. Much to everyone's surprise, there was to be a special plane sent for her the next day.

In story-book style Kay turned away from the telephone and there in the office doorway stood her fiancé. In no time at all she was soaking in a hot bath in his apartment, and telling him how she had packed her trousseau so that they could get married in North Africa, but that it was now at the bottom of the sea.

As Kay Summersby fell asleep that night in Dick's bed, knowing that he was sleeping next door, she must have felt serenely happy about the future. It was fortunate that she could not see then what the coming months would bring.

The next morning, as promised, General Eisenhower's B17 plane took her to his headquarters at Algiers. The General, though, had left for the front to spend Christmas with his troops. Consequently Kay was free to go shopping with her friend Ethel – one of the nurses from the *Strathallen* – to replace clothing lost at sea.

On that pre-Christmas shopping spree one could imagine her buying warm underclothing and protective kit to keep out the cold when driving her boss through the freezing grey drizzle that was then shrouding the Tunisian hills making them look more like Scotland in winter than Africa. But what did she buy? In her own words: 'Underwear that had obviously been made for ladies of a certain calling. Panties of black mesh with a satin vine leaf strategically placed, black satin brassières, cut out at the nipple, which were definitely not for nursing mothers.'

When she did drive General Eisenhower to visit his front-line troops, which he often liked to do – making up perhaps for the fact that in the whole of his thirty years of service he had never once been in action or shot at – Kay made sure she was well wrapped up, with fur-lined boots, an old Air Corps flying-jacket over a man's battle blouse and, of course a sleeping-bag just in case they had to spend the night out.

Those overnight stops did not go unnoticed, and people began to talk. Indeed, after one such night, Eisenhower's personal aide, Tex, took Kay aside and said: 'I think you ought to know, Kay, that there's a lot of gossip about you and the Boss. People are saying that you … uh … uh …' He stopped, embarrassed.

'That we what?' Kay asked.

'That you … uh … well that you slept together when you went on trips.'

She stared at him, then burst out laughing, saying, 'We did, Tex, we did!'

When Matron Lucy Wane caught her first glimpse of the magnificent hospital which was to be her domain in Algiers, she must have been more than impressed. It stood high above the city, on a hill-top, and it was set in the most beautiful residential area at the end of the Rue Michelet. When the wounded soldiers saw the hospital, they surely thought it was heaven, after what they had been through. Most of the casualties had been carried from front-line foxholes high on the 'bloody Djebels' lashed to the sides of swaying pack-mule saddles, then in jeeps which slid around muddy, precipitous, hair-pin bends and finally in motor ambulance convoys over shellholed roads at high speeds on the dangerous stretches exposed to shelling where warning signs spelt out the drill to men and women drivers in no uncertain terms: 'DON'T SIT AND DIE – JUMP AND RUN AND IF IN DOUBT – GET OUT.'

To find themselves at last safe and snugly tucked up in crisp white sheets and baby-blue blankets was marvellous, but to be looked after by women nurses into the bargain was absolute heavenly bliss.

The nurses enjoyed Algiers' hospital too. They were rushed off their feel until other hospitals opened at Bone, Philippeville and Constantine, but when they did have time off duty, there was much to see and do. Sister Vivienne Templeton recalled how exciting the city was:

'Algiers was not just the headquarters town: it was also "leave town", glamorous, noisy, sordid, crowded, glittering and exciting. It was full of so many different sounds, sights and mysterious smells, in which garlic predominated. In the modern part of the town there were high-speed three-car trams, festooned with Arabs clinging on to the outside, and they clanged straight through the teeming crowds and traffic. Buildings of all shapes and sizes rose in tiers right up the hill from the port; warehouses, shops, offices gave way to red-roofed houses at the top, and somewhere in the middle of it all was the kasbah which was definitely and clearly signed "OUT OF BOUNDS".'

Off-duty hours for the nurses were strictly controlled. One can well imagine what it must have been like to serve under a traditional martinet of a matron who, even in the lifeboat after the *Strathallen* was torpedoed, behaved more like a sergeant major of the Grenadier Guards – as Brenda McBryde reported: 'Everything was ship shape, however, in the lifeboats where sat the Principal Matron Designate for Algiers, Lucy Wane. In gloves and crisp, white blouse over neatly pressed slacks, she regarded her party of sisters with some disapproval. One in particular, who was hanging miserably over the back of the boat, came in for a sharp rebuke. "This is no time to be sick, Sister!" Miss Wane passed her comb around the bedraggled company. "For God's sake," she said witheringly, "there's no need to look like survivors".'[12]

Though today it is common practice for films and the media to poke gentle fun at these 'old-school' matrons, there is no doubt that thousands of servicemen owed their lives to the work done by such matrons, and to their nurses, in those North African hospitals.

One memorable morning in April 1943, when the fighting in Tunisia was at its bloodiest, with the armies battling for possession of Longstop Hill and casualties overflowing into officers' mess tents, there walked into one of the surgical wards of the 98th British General Hospital a most oddly dressed man in his early sixties. He wore a panama hat and long khaki issue shorts which almost covered his white knees. His name then meant nothing to most of the nurses there, but today it would be given with little difficulty by most competitors in a children's quiz competition. The stranger was Professor Alexander Fleming. He had arrived to supervise personally the administering of his new drug – penicillin.*

Soldiers with repulsive wounds infected with gas gangrene were selected, for patients at that advanced stage rarely survived. And then before the marvelling eyes of all the hospital staff involved, these

---

* Though the drug was discovered in 1929 by the British bacteriologist, it was not yet being used for septic wounds; four-hourly hot fomentation was still the standard treatment. Commercial production of this 'wonder' drug was developed by Ernest Chain and Howard Florey, and all three men shared the 1945 Nobel Prize for Medicine awarded in recognition of this work.

critically ill patients began to recover. The new yellow powder smelling of 'old hay' had revolutionized the treatment of wounds. Death from sepsis was reduced to a hitherto unknown low level.[13]

Nurses working with this new drug, penicillin, during the next few weeks as casualties poured into the hospitals, had the satisfaction of seeing for themselves the tremendous effect it had on the death and disability rate, a boost to morale in those overcrowded hospitals, with hot, tiring work for long hours at a time.

However, on 13 May 1943 it all came to an end. The German Commander-in-Chief, von Arnim, left his rear headquarters and drove all day along the hundred miles and more of dusty roads, all the while seeing his men laying down their weapons by the thousand. Into the prisoner-of-war cages walked 248,000 German and Italian soldiers; 50,000 men of his Army had been killed. Tunisia had cost the enemy the Stalingrad figure of 300,000 men.

That night, as von Arnim sat eating bread and jam outside his tent by the prisoner-of-war cage, there was on his face, under the flaunting eagle of his general's hat, a grey tiredness, and he was perhaps ruminating: 'What now …?'

That was the question women were also asking themselves. Vivienne Templeton remembers the night well, sitting outside the nurses' mess drinking a little whisky and water, speculating with her friends the inevitable moves that would lie ahead: 'You got used to a place, no matter how bad it was. No one liked moving. Moving meant leaving familiar faces and places.'

In Algiers, now that the campaign in Tunisia was over, Kay Summersby could contemplate in greater detail her forthcoming marriage to Colonel Dick Arnold. She had, of course, explained her teasing remark to Eisenhower's aide, Tex, about sleeping with the General: they had used the same tent only one night, in an emergency, and even then with separate folding camp beds and separate sleeping-bags. Now, with her divorce papers having safely arrived, there was nothing to hold up the wedding. It was a warm comforting, warm prospect for her to contemplate. She enjoyed the feeling of utter relaxation, talking idly with her women friends from Allied Force Headquarters, riding and playing bridge in the evenings. She was therefore completely unprepared for the blow that fell one evening shortly after hostilities ended.

She had driven General Eisenhower back to his villa. Throughout the journey he had sat slumped in the back, saying nothing, and when they arrived he got out like an old man and said: 'Kay, come in here. Make us both a drink … Kay … I'm going to give this to you straight. Dick has been killed.'[14]

He had been inspecting a minefield with another man who had

stumbled and caught his foot in the tripwire. The other man had been badly wounded. Dick was dead.

Kay Summersby was left wondering, 'What now ...?'

Fifteen hundred miles to the east, Sister Marjorie Bennett had found the answer to that same question – 'What now?' – which had been troubling her too. The tented hospital she was in had been left far behind the advancing troops, and she felt she was in something of a backwater. Consequently, when volunteers for duty with forward troops were called for, she put her name down straight away. Soon afterwards she boarded a ship in Alexandria and sailed to join the 33rd General Hospital in Malta.

Sister Bennett had heard that Malta had been so heavily raided in 1940 and 1941 that it had been awarded the George Cross for national bravery, but she was totally unprepared for what she saw when her ship nosed into the Grand Harbour. There, where Phoenician galleons had anchored and proudly paid their taxes with bags of soil to improve the fertility of the island, a scene of utter devastation met her eyes. The mighty ramparts and fine buildings above the harbour were pierced with gaping holes, the dockyard was a mass of tangled, twisted cranes, and the harbour itself was little more than a graveyard of sunken ships.

In Hitler's desperate attempt to subdue and conquer the island in 1942, he had stepped up the bombing raids to a vicious stream that went on night and day, week after week, month after month. Beleaguered, hungry, cold, dirty and dog-tired, the defenders had stuck it out. For months no convoys had got through. Starvation was a reality for everyone, from the Governor, who shared the privations of his people, down to the lowliest aircraftsman.

They were unconquered but losses had been appalling. Now the hospital ships were arriving – but these days without meeting a deluge of bombs – to take away the wounded soldiers, sailors, airmen and many nurses to Egypt, where they could be nursed back to health.

When all the wounded had been evacuated, Sister Bennett returned to Valetta, where she, along with her colleagues, occupied a lovely tented compound to the north of the town. There they received an order that was exciting in more ways than one. They were to report to the neighbouring commando unit for intensive swimming instruction. Every nurse had to be able to swim at least 100 yards. They did not have to cogitate long before they realized what was afoot. They were going to take part in the next landing.

'We were told,' said Marjorie Bennett, 'that if we were attacked at sea and the ship was hit, it would be "every man for himself", and so we had better be ready.'

Commando officers proved to be admirable instructors. The nurses enjoyed the lessons very much.

But that was not the only excitement the island held for them in those next few weeks. Malta proved to have much to offer, as Marjorie Bennett recalled:

It happened in this way [said Marjorie]. At this time there was a shortage of food and water on the island. The meals in our mess were pretty grim. Mid-day meal, for instance, was usually hard cheese, dates and Army biscuits with a mug of tea. Not far away, though, was an American unit, and their food was much superior. We were therefore always pleased to accept an invitation to their mess for an evening meal and dance afterwards. On the night I am talking about, the weather was particularly hot and clammy. It was made worse by the fact that all shutters on the windows were tightly closed because of the strict black-out regulations. There were in that crowded room between thirty and forty American officers and about twenty nursing sisters, and so when the dancing began we were all kept busy.

Quite early on in the evening a tall, handsome officer with a trim black moustache asked me to dance. He held me tightly and we danced cheek to cheek. He was sweating profusely but he was a very good dancer. When the music stopped, I went back to our group of dancers, and then I looked down at my uniform and felt all embarrassed. On my white dress just above my boobs there were two enormous sweaty marks. I was furious! And when the music started up again and this officer came again to ask me to dance, I refused. It was only later I learnt the name of that officer – Clark Gable – the rugged, romantic movie hero of the 1939 film *Gone with the Wind*, who had joined the US Army Air Corps for the duration.*

My daughter delights in telling her friends: 'My mother danced with Clark Gable and refused to dance with him again.'

After four weeks on Malta the nurses were warned to be ready for embarkation at an hour's notice. Soon they would know what all the swimming instructions had been about.

---

* In later years former Lieutenant Clark Gable USAAF rarely spoke about his Service life. He was stationed most of the time in Lincolnshire, completing thirty operational missions in Flying Fortresses – missions which RAF Wing Commander Winfield, with 120 missions to his credit, found terrifying. He met 'Lootenant' Gable at Bassingbourn with 7th Bomber Group USAAF. For an interesting account of this meeting see pages 154-7 of *The Sky Belongs to Them* (Kimber, 1976).

6   Where Do We Go From Here?

And something happens to me inside
That is deeper than grief, greater than pride,
And though there is nothing I can say
I always look up as they go their way.

Sarah Churchill*

1943-4

Fifteen hundred miles to the north of Algiers that May of 1943, another young woman in the uniform of the FANY was feeling more than a little apprehensive about her future too.

Her name was Violette Szabo, and early one evening she was sitting in the front room of her home, a terraced house in Burnley Road, Brixton, while her father, Charles Bushell, was asking far more questions than she wanted to answer.

'If you're not careful, my girl, you'll come to a bad end,' he said, never imagining for one moment just how soon and how gruesome that end would be. 'I know you're twenty-two, a mother yourself and with a baby girl to look after, but your Mam and I are worried. All this coming and going. Not knowing where you are. Why don't you come home and get some real war work in the aircraft factory again?'

The ex-army sergeant of World War I could tell there was something not quite as it seemed to be by the evasive way his daughter was answering his questions. Why had she come hobbling home with her ankle in plaster? But he was still no nearer the truth, and he knew it.

'At least, when you were in the Ack-Ack battery in Liverpool we knew where you were, bombs or no bombs ...' He seemed to lose the last shred of his patience. He suddenly stopped and raised his arms in a gesture of despair before adding faintly, 'But now ...'

Violette came to a decision and turned to face him, saying: 'I can't tell you anything. I'm under oath.'

It is not surprising she could not talk – even to her father. She was a member of Britain's 'secret army', the organization formed almost as

---

* Sarah Churchill, daughter of Prime Minister Winston Churchill, forsook a career on the stage to join the WAAF. These lines are taken from her poem 'The Bombers' in *Chaos of the Night*, ed. Catherine Reilly.

soon as the last of the British soldiers were wading off the bomb-blasted beaches of Dunkirk. Then, with Britain under threat of invasion and standing alone against the victorious might of Germany, Churchill had hurled defiance at Hitler, scorned his peace proposals and issued his famous directive to set up an organization to harass the German war effort at every possible point by sabotage and subversion; in fact, as he put it: 'to set Europe ablaze!'[1]

It was perhaps ironic that, while Churchill and his chiefs of staff were hastily putting together an organization to implement this directive, London was being set ablaze by the Blitz of the German Luftwaffe. Nevertheless, though forced to move its headquarters from time to time as bombs demolished buildings, the new organization, called Special Operations Executive, grew into a formidable force which eventually – according to Supreme Allied Commander Eisenhower – shortened the war by six months.[2]

History records quite objectively that the aims of SOE[3] were to bring about Germany's downfall by nurturing the seeds of revolt within the conquered territories, to establish intimate contacts with local people, to plant agents, to organize scientific sabotage of industries and all methods of communication, to boost the morale of the faint-hearted and to co-ordinate the efforts of the most ardent resistance groups. Ultimately the object of the whole scheme was to recruit and train a gigantic force of patriots who would be secretly armed and ready to launch attacks against the German Army at the precise moment ordered by Allied High Command when the armies of liberation invaded Europe. By May 1943 that day was rapidly approaching.

For the success of such an invasion, France was strategically vital; it was close to Britain, and a well-organized resistance movement could, it was said, pin down German divisions in out-of-the-way corners and so give assault troops a better chance of gaining a good foothold. However, in the immediate post-Dunkirk days the suggestion of such a highly organized resistance seemed more like 'pie in the sky', for the demoralized remnants of the French Army were already mingling with the columns of panicking refugees fleeing before the advancing German armour. But the planners had faith. They knew that in time the stunned French people would begin to fight back. They would need more than encouragement, though; they would need close links with Britain for supplies of arms and ammunition, and they would need a central control to co-ordinate their efforts.

Nobody thought it was going to be an easy task. 'You had only to walk through the fashionable parts of Paris to see that,' recalled Madame Joanne Duprés to the writer forty odd years later. 'At the pavement tables outside the Brassérie Georges V on the Champs Elysées you would often see noisy groups of well-heeled French profiteers drinking with German officers, currying favour for contracts. They were doing very nicely out of the occupation, and they did not care who knew it. Even small shopkeepers often kept scarce goods out of sight to sell to German troops for a higher price.'

True, the situation did not seem conducive to organized resistance. Fortunately Churchill and the arrogant and newly promoted Charles de Gaulle thought otherwise. Events were soon to prove them right.

Why were women needed for this formidable task? Because they were in many ways better than men for a number of reasons. They could move about occupied France more easily than men, for most of them had genuine reasons for travelling: they were going to join their husbands who had been moved to munitions factories, to visit their parents, to look after their families – and many other very plausible reasons. Men, on the other hand, were more static, because of their work and home. Furthermore, men were much more suspect than women, and when they travelled by train or road the Gestapo or Vichy police checked their papers more meticulously. Rarely were women given the rigorous routine questioning that men had to endure, and men certainly did not have the talent to charm and disarm with a flutter of eyelashes and coy smile!

The logic behind the recruitment of women can be seen quite easily but not why so many women volunteered for this role – one of the most dangerous of all jobs created by modern warfare, certainly the one with the highest casualty figures amongst all the women who went to war. Tremendous courage was needed, for they worked in almost complete isolation. As Military Intelligence historian R.V. Jones was to write, 'Courage in battle is at least helped by the presence of others, and perhaps the fear of shaming oneself in front of them; and it may be summoned by the sight of a comrade in need of rescue. But the Resistance men and women were for much of the time alone with their fears, often in the hands of their perverted enemies. That is when character is most severely tested and we who have not experienced it can only imagine how great the strain can be.'[4] There was the strain of pretending to be one person whilst in fact being another, the strain of curbing one's tongue when provoked, of waiting for the appointed hour of action, of knowing all the time that one could never relax.

Most agents lived 'in a state of perpetual terror', wrote SOE's official historian.[5] They had to be tireless, constantly on guard, knowing all the time that someone close by might betray them for money or favours.

All this was made known to the women before their training finished, and even at the last moment before departure they were always given the opportunity of withdrawing without loss of regard. Yet these gallant women went on. Why?

Certainly, with all these women, patriotism had something to do with their motivation, a virtue prized more highly then than it is today. They knew they had something worthwhile to offer – specialist knowledge and experience – and were determined to see it employed. And with all of them there emerges evidence of a hatred of the evil that Nazi Germany stood for and determination to see it crushed. Naturally, too, there was bound to be a mixture of other motivating factors that cannot be altogether discounted: for some, SOE work satisfied a zest for adventure, a buccaneering spirit, a way of proving themselves; for others, SOE provided the opportunity for working alone, not being ordered about by stupid commanders.

Whatever the motivation might have been, one thing is sure: they were amazingly courageous people, for, as one former SOE member, Baroness Ryder, recently said: 'They were all under sentence of death.'[6] And it was not just the German Army and the Gestapo who posed this threat to their lives: many civilians hated SOE agents and Resistance groups because their activities brought savage reprisals upon innocent people in towns and villages all over the country. It is no wonder then, that the stories of the women in SOE make probably the most moving narratives of all war memoirs. It is not within the scope of this book to offer a comprehensive appreciation of what they all did, but one can gain an insight into their magnificent work from looking at what happened to just a few of them, such as Violette Szabo, Diana Rowden and Vera Leigh, all of whom gave their lives yet never really received the public acclaim they deserved.

Violette Szabo had never even heard of Special Operations Executive during the whole of her service in the ATS, which ended when she left her mixed anti-aircraft battery to have her baby, Tania, but then, shortly after being notified of her husband's death at El Alamein, she received a mysterious letter.

It might have been merely coincidence or it could have been a well-chosen moment for those who were on the look-out for women like Violette Szabo, with her French background, to write to her.

It was a strange letter, inviting her to an address in Sanctuary Buildings, Westminster. Eager to know what it was all about, she went, and there she was introduced to Britain's 'phantom army' – the secret army of the French Section and its most irregular regulars, the women and men who were to write one of military history's most bizarre chapters.

After a thorough grilling and psychological questioning in more than one interview, Violette Szabo was accepted for service with Special Operations Executive, French Section. It was, however, one thing to be selected for SOE, quite another to complete the training. For, just as the selection board was prepared to accept women on a perfect equality with men – far in advance of current practice, so also were the instructors at the training camps. The women were treated exactly like men.

The training was really tough. As one chief training officer said, addressing a new intake of women: 'You will work hard and I think I should warn you that all your reactions during the course will be carefully noted. It is for a tough, solitary life you have volunteered, and security is high. Not only will your lives depend on these qualifications but also the lives of your comrades in the same group.'[7]

There was a lot to learn, and the women realized how much only as they passed from one super-secret training school to another, for by that time SOE had assembled experts to cover every possible contingency. Violette was soon shooting at moving pieces of cardboard with all kinds of automatic weapons, crawling across countryside to blow up mock targets, tapping out messages in morse on a dummy key, handling 'time pencils', 'instantaneous fuses' and 'pull and press' switches, and acquiring the 'know-how' of exploding high-power charges. These women had to be proficient 'all-rounders', fit to take charge of a small army if necessary, as indeed one of them, Pearl Witherington, did, commanding 2,000 Maquis.[8]

In those days, men on similar courses rubbed their hands in gleeful anticipation of the howls of fear and dismay that would come when the women were faced with the tougher parts of the course. But they were to be denied this pleasure, for the women came through it all just as well as the men. They covered twenty-five-mile treks over mountains, took the rough and tumble of unarmed combat and completed the rigorous early morning PT sessions without any more grumbling than the men.

They never thought about it then, but what they were doing was breaking down the convention barriers of centuries.

At the Security School they became adept at picking locks, code and cypher techniques and the art of disguise. And during all this, tension grew and the sense of looming perils developed.

Eventually came the time for parachute training at RAF Ringway, Manchester, and it was more frightening then than now – only one parachute, no second chest parachute, no doorway to jump from.

Dropping through a small hole in the fuselage at 100 mph can be a dicey business [said former SOE member Brenda Weeks]. You had to sit down on the floor near the hole and then when the red light came on shuffle along on your bottom until you were sitting with your bum and your legs just alongside the gaping hole, so that when the green light flashed, four things could happen at once. You swung your legs over the hole and dropped into a rigid straight-up position of attention as the instructor shouted 'Go' and gave you an 'encouraging' nudge with his leg. That was the theory. In practice, if the instructor was too keen and pushed hard, you broke your nose on the opposite side of the hole, and if you went out too slowly, you banged the back of your head on the other side of the hole. Added to these hazards was the one that, if you did not get properly into a straight position, you stood a good chance of getting caught up in the shroud lines and falling like a badly tied parcel or, worse still, being towed along behind the aircraft by your static line.

When we first started the parachute training at Ringway, we had to learn the falls and rolls by jumping off a vaulting box onto a coconut mat – doing a 'side right' or a 'side left' or a 'backward roll', to transfer the shock of landing along a rolling line from the side of the legs, thigh, shoulder and back, keeping the head well tucked in, chin on the chest. But most of us novices made the 'classic' landing – feet, bottom, head. Even in daylight it's hard to judge which way you're drifting, and you're so relieved that the parachute's open, you don't really care anyway.

The most frightening part of the training I found was the jump from a balloon. It was so eerie and quiet as you rose in a metal basket-type box suspended from a kind of barrage balloon to about 800 feet with only a thin iron bar as a door. You clipped your static line to a hook in the framework above your head. I was the first to jump out. I've never forgotten the first feelings as I stepped out into nothing. 'What have I done? Oh God' The wind rushed up my nose, and I was gasped for breath. Then I felt a tug, and I was swinging from side to side under the parachute canopy. And I was dimly aware of some idiot shouting through a megaphone down below. He was shouting at me: 'Adopt a correct landing position!' And then, 'Put your bloody feet together!' Thump, bump, bang. I was down. It was over.

It was a similar kind of bad landing, with one foot hitting the ground before the other, that had torn the ligaments in Violette Szabo's ankle and put her in plaster. A fortunate accident! She was to have gone to Rouen to organize a Resistance group in readiness for D-Day, in the area immediately behind the German defences of the Atlantic Wall – a forbidden zone, totally barred to everyone except those who lived there. But just after the day she would have set off there came a message from an SOE agent then in the south of France: 'For God's sake, don't come. The Nazis are waiting for you.'

Now, in the summer of 1943, Violette was waiting for her ankle to heal and for whatever future orders might bring.

In that summer of decision, 1943, training was stepped up considerably; the period of waiting seemed to be drawing to a close. Conscription had swollen the ranks of all three Services to new peaks; in the midsummer of 1943 there were, for example, 209,877 women in the ATS. Not all were volunteers by any means. Not all were happy to be in uniform, but they had to be trained nevertheless. In some trades the shortage of trained ATS personnel was greater than others.

There was such a great demand for drivers in the ATS, for example, that privates were being posted to units before finishing their training and before having taken their driving tests. Many of these young women were very far from being 'affable' colleagues, having been conscripted into the ATS as the last thing they wanted, and this could lead to difficult and frightening situations, as driving instructor Vera Cole recalled:

I remember one incident today with the same dread as at that time. The girls I had to deal with were rebellious, loud-mouthed, tough types who had no intention of 'toeing the line'. On this particular day I collected the utility truck plus three girls and, telling one of them to take the wheel – a common enough way of speaking amongst the drivers then, I got back: "'ere, where shall I take it to?' But I knew better than to rise to that bait and so just suggested that we got going because of the time. The girl drove well enough but, being new to the area, it was necessary for me to give her directions, and at each instruction she endeavoured to do just the opposite or go another way. Trying hard to keep my cool, we went along until a roundabout came into view and, knowing that we had to continue on the same road, I said to her, 'Straight over the roundabout', meaning, of course, bear to the left and then round to the right and continue on the same road. However, that girl took me exactly at my word: without slowing down at all, she bumped up onto the roundabout, over it and off on the other side. I ordered her to stop, and I was just about to say something to her when out came the words, 'You told me to go straight over the bleedin' roundabout.' That was enough of her. The other two proved no better. I'm given to attacks of migraine, and that afternoon's experience resulted in a very bad one.

MT drivers were called upon for some strange jobs at all times of the day and night, some funny, some frightening. Ada Ryder was stationed at RAF Manby in Lincolnshire when 'Ivan the Terrible', her CO, who did not like women on his station, called for her to do a special job. She had to go to his big private house and service his own car. 'It was a Riley 9 in the garage, so I started by lifting the bonnet. Just then a sergeant who was nearby said: "The Group Captain wants you to start on the interior first. He wants all under the seats cleaning, so lift them out first." Well, I only just got started with my hands on the seat which I had hardly moved when thousands of mice jumped out over my arms, onto my legs, from all directions. I just flew and never stopped running until I reached the MT yard. That car had been standing there untouched since 1939. The old devil had been watching me all the time too.'

There were other occasions which were terrifying and terrible in a different way: 'We used to watch the Lancaster bombers go up on their big raids in the months before D-Day, a wonderful sight, but then, occasionally, we would get a telephone call from the local police station saying that some airmen had been washed up on the beach at Mablethorpe. Sometimes this would be at two or three in the morning, and we would have to drive out in the half light with the ambulances to pick them up. It was awful. Usually about five or six airmen, all nationalities, still with their Mae Wests on, and they had no eyes or nose

– the fish had eaten them. The bodies were all swollen up with gas and water, and we had to lift them into the ambulances and take them to Manby. There the medical officer identified them by their discs. I was only twenty-one at the time and it haunts me to this day, and if anyone mentions Mablethorpe as a holiday resort, I go all funny.'

During those long weeks of training and waiting for something to happen in the war situation, the Government was very conscious of doing what they could to maintain morale, and quite often the assistance of the royal family was enlisted. Vera Cole's unit came in for its fair share of visits.

We were told that the Princess Royal was coming to inspect us, which meant more spit and polish. I could never understand why all this was necessary. Surely it would have been more realistic to see us in working order. However, like all the rest, I obeyed instructions and made a show. I put a clean bit of blotting-paper on my desk and hid all the papers out of sight. Outside the soldiers whitewashed all the boulders which were placed down the drive to keep vehicles off the grass lawns. They whitewashed lines around all the huts and we used to say, 'Keep moving or you'll be whitewashed.'

The visit got under way, and it's strange how just one person can get things wrong just at the wrong moment, because at the top of the stairs were a couple of toilets and there an orderly, completely unaware of what was going on below, was busily scrubbing a lavatory seat, singing at the top of her voice the popular song of the time: 'You would reign all alone, like a queen on a throne, if I had my way.' Imagine her surprise when, turning round, she came face to face with the royal visitor who, fortunately for her, was quite amused.

What questions did such royal personages ask the humble privates? And did they ever listen to the answers? Joyce Taylor, a former WAAF stationed at RAF Wittering, was visited by the Duchess of Gloucester and was asked various questions. Ten minutes later, Joyce reported for lunchtime typing duty at headquarters, and in walked the Duchess once again. 'Everyone else was at lunch, so I got the questions. The Duchess seemed quite amused at receiving the same answers.'

Commanders from the very top to the most junior section officer were made aware of the importance of morale not only in lectures at OCTU but by means of frequent reminders in routine orders. In the words of General Montgomery they were told that, 'In men and women there are great emotional forces bottled up which have to be given an outlet in a way which is positive and constructive, and which warms the heart and excites the imagination.'[9]

Various methods were tried to 'warm the heart and excite the imagination'. When all else failed, there was always the route march. But even that could be funny. Vera Cole remembers one in particular: 'The sergeant over us had a kind of lilting walk in as much as she seemed to sway or swing her right shoulder at a strange angle, and this amused quite a number of us. Whilst out on a very long route march one day, we imitated her, complete with a fit of the giggles – very unbecoming of us as corporals, but it eased the boredom of the day.'

The boredom of the night was sometimes relieved by dances if anyone could be found to organize one. This task fell to Vera Cole.

It sounded easy enough, so I volunteered to run the evening and, after giving me a rather old-fashioned look, my officer agreed to let me have a go. She handed me a small amount of money, and off I went down to the village shop, to buy a few spot prizes, and then returned to sort out the very few old 78 records and made a rough programme. The evening began with a very worn Victor Sylvester record in place, and I brought the room to a complete state of silence when I called out: 'Ladies and Gentlemen, please take your partners for a waltz.' We went on to quicksteps, with 'Run Rabbit, Run Rabbit, Run, Run, Run' and all the other popular tunes of that era. The beer was on the house, courtesy of the officers, and the evening was a great success. Just to make sure that nothing spoilt it, the officer, Junior Commander Brown, went round all the huts and buildings with a torch afterwards to check that none of us was doing anything likely to cause us to be dismissed from the Services.

Discipline was good, for most of the time and with most of the women, but those who were bad were, like the girl in the nursery rhyme, very bad.

What could they do with really bad girls in 1943? Very little. Under the new disciplinary code, the girls definitely got off more lightly than the men. In cases where a solider was liable to trial by court martial with a sentence of anything up to two years' detention, the ATS girl, if a private, could not even be brought before a court martial – unless she chose to appear of her own accord. Even then, the punishment for women was restricted to confinement to camp or forfeiture of pay. It was a fact that no auxiliary could be locked up 'except in her own defence'. Once a woman decided that she had had as much as she could take of the Service life, there was a well-known way of bringing it all to an end. Going absent.

As the official history was later to report: 'The easiest way to get out of the Service was to get a bad name as a continual absentee as, although they could now legally be held to serve, no sentence could be awarded involving restraint of liberty and it was often a matter of considerable difficulty to hold offenders. The only alternative still was to discharge the auxiliary, and this constituted a sign of weakness and was often pandering to the wishes of the offender.'[10]

True, some unit commanders did try to hold their defaulters by various ways and means but, as the official history records, the cunning ones 'often managed to escape, without uniform or shoes, squeezing through lavatory windows that looked far too small for anything bigger than a cat to get through.'

But others who decided to stay with their free board and lodging were really a bigger problem than those who escaped. They were, at times, uncontrollable, refusing to obey orders and deliberately vandalizing any government property they could get hold of. They were a menace to military discipline. Three recruits made history when, amongst other exploits and clad only in pyjamas, they mobbed a male Regimental Sergeant Major on parade, after which they were, contrary to all orders, placed under lock and key. Authority was obtained for their discharge that afternoon but not before they had torn down the walls separating the three cells, partitions which had proved strong enough to restrain generations of male offenders.

The Air Force had similar problems. By 1943, the Air Officers Commanding were definitely of the opinion that the disciplinary code for WAAF personnel needed strengthening. Some suggested that persistent offenders be dealt with by civil courts, but that would mean that airwomen would be sent to a civil prison, which would give them a 'record', whilst for the same offence an airman would go to a detention centre and thus have no prison record when he returned to civil life.

Others advocated a detention centre to be run on the lines of those set up for military personnel. The Director of the WAAF thought that detention barracks should be used only for the 'really tough airwomen' and that no attempt should be made to mix that type of airwoman with those merely in need of 'reform'.[11]

Shortly after writing this memo, the Director of the WAAF asked for a team to report on what a detention centre was really like. After reading this* and making further enquiries, she wrote in no uncertain terms that she would not support any scheme whatsoever for the setting up of a detention centre. And no wonder. At that time the inmates of military detention centres were subjected to brutal treatment. A captain and former inmate wrote: 'When a prisoner passes the iron gate he is treated with total contempt for his identity as a man. He is made to strip naked and double mark time with knees up, arms held high above his head while the sergeants watch, smoking cigarettes and yelling orders or abuse. Had not the material of these men been stronger than their tormentors they might have succeeded in bestialising them. They were mainly average disciplined young civilian soldiers who had not committed a crime, their chief fault was overstaying their leave.'[12]

Naturally the Director of the WAAF would not see what was really going on but she formed an accurate enough opinion, and this would be

* See Appendix C.

reinforced not many months later when a frightening account emerged through a famous court case over a forty-year-old soldier under sentence being brutally attacked and killed by two staff NCOs at Fort Darland Detention Centre.

After the man had been knocked out cold, striking his head on the ground, RSM Culliney, who had lost his temper and struck the soldier, ordered that he be conveyed to the sick-quarters on a handcart. On the way the cart was stopped by CSM Leslie Salter. He was not going to allow Clayton to be 'driven' to the sickbay. He tipped over the cart, and the private soldier fell onto hard concrete, cracking the back of his head once again. Now the CSM got worried. Clayton had gone strangely limp. The CSM ordered a bucket of water brought up and thrown over the soldier. Clayton lay motionless. He was dead.

A subsequent post mortem recorded that Private Clarence Clayton died as a result of 'tuberculosis accelerated by violence'.[13] Both NCOs were court-martialled and stripped of their rank. Culliney got eighteen months and Salter twelve. Did they spend it in the glasshouse? One wonders.

If such draconian establishments were not to be used in the WAAF, what were station commanders to do with their difficult women? They were worried about the effect such women would have on the rest of the station, who could see them flouting authority. 'A woman with a really bad streak in her will not listen to reason,' wrote the commanding officer of Spittalgate.[14] A group commander wrote: 'Recently at a station in this Group, an airwoman who had been recommended for discharge for misconduct deliberately set out to get her own back on any woman who had anything to do with the charges preferred against her, by assaulting her. The difficulty in finding volunteers for escort duty in such cases is obvious.'[15]

The problem was never really solved other than by discharge. Women were then directed by the Ministry of Labour to factories, and breaches of discipline then became breaches of civil law and, where appropriate, punished by prison sentences. For the women's Services, punishment remained adequate for those who transgressed in a minor way and ineffective for the hard cases. In May 1943 a letter went to all unit commanders saying: 'The War Office is not convinced that there is any real need at the moment to introduce a more drastic code of discipline with severe penalties.'[16]

So, in that summer of decision, the Services got on with their main task: training for the day when the invasion of Europe would be possible.

In one part of Britain, however, an invasion of a far different nature had already begun, and it was to have tremendous impact upon servicewomen there ...

*

In the compact east Suffolk village of Grundisburgh (if you lived there long enough, you called it 'Grunsbra'), there was a growing fever of excitement. The calm of this picturesque collection of ancient cottages with a church, a general store, post office and public house called 'The Dog', all surrounding a triangular green, was to have a new experience.

The American invasion of Britain was about to begin.

Seven GIs stood for a few moments in the doorway of 'The Dog'. They looked into the room with the dartboard, into another with an antique upright piano, and finally they approached the small bar and ordered beer.

The news soon spread: 'The Yanks are in "The Dog".' The natives began to arrive. In ones and twos they came and sat themselves down in their accustomed seats. That Saturday night people flocked into the pub from all the farms and cottages and filled the place with a carnival spirit. 'The work on our aerodrome is going to begin at last!' they cried. 'We're going to have a great new bomber aerodrome with thousands of American soldiers and airmen. And bombers flying right over Berlin to pay those Jerries back.' The word 'Yanks' was on everybody's lips. The last round they bought that evening was for forty-seven drinks. There had never been anything like it before in the long history of 'The Dog'.[20]

Grundisburgh was witnessing something villages, towns and cities the length and breadth of Western Europe would witness before the war's end; something which can never be denied, a feature of the American character deeply ingrained – generosity. They were not only generous in buying drinks and presents, giving cigarettes and chocolate to all who asked: they even gave food off their plates, as Joyce Taylor remembers. When a draft of American airmen were posted to RAF Wittering to share the station with British squadrons, 'We used the same mess and we were soon aware that their standard of meals was superior to ours (though we had no complaints as we fared better than folk at home). I remember passing one airman on my way back to the table. He had two large sausages, rather over-done sausages, on his plate and he lifted a luscious-looking leg of chicken from his plate and put it onto mine, hurrying away before I could thank him. What a kind thing to do!'

Former WAAF D/F Operator M.J. Edge, also at Wittering, recalls similar feelings of admiration and affection for the American airmen there: 'Having seen so many casualties lifted from their B17s, I have always had a tremendous admiration for those aircrew who did those day-time low-level raids. They were always badly shot up. I hardly ever went on duty without having a "Mayday" or "Darky" call. We had hundreds of GIs on the station, and they made life bearable with turkey legs from their marvellous "chow". Our food was horrible.'

It was not long before servicewomen were enjoying the new experience of being looked after attentively by smartly dressed, rich GIs

Margaret Taylor's minewatchers, Richmond, Surrey

'Stretch up!' Barefoot PT for the ATS

Members of the Motor Transport Corps, FANY, training to go to Africa, learn how to move an ambulance bogged down in mud or sand

One Horse Power. ATS hay-making

ATS and the nation's food effort. Sergeant I. Ward helped to run a miniature farm on an ATS camp. Ducks, chickens and rabbits were kept on the farm with waste from the dining-halls. Pens and hen-houses were made up from odds and ends 'found' around the camp

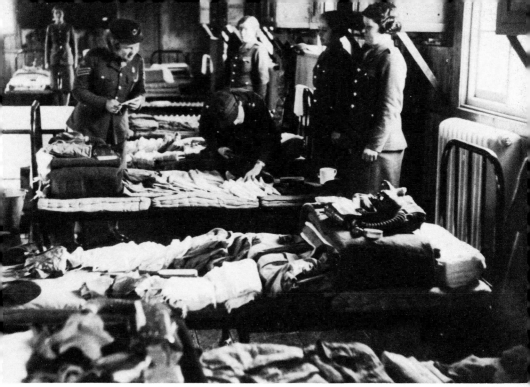

'Stand by your beds!' The dreaded kit inspection, ATS style

Grub up. Mugs and mess tins at the ready, women stand in line with the men

Nursing sister outside the ward
of a tented desert hospital,
Western Desert

Base Hospital in the Libyan Desert. Note the nurse walking near the stunted
trees between the huts

Radio operators on secret work, often with the Special Operations Executive

The Old Rectory, near Whitchurch, Shropshire, which housed the secret radio operators

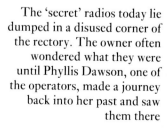

The 'secret' radios today lie dumped in a disused corner of the rectory. The owner often wondered what they were until Phyllis Dawson, one of the operators, made a journey back into her past and saw them there

Wrens training for boat crew. They handled many kinds of small craft in harbours

Wrens getting a torpedo ready for loading onto a submarine

'Come in Number One.' An aircraftwoman of RAF Coastal Command attending
RAF Flying Boats, 1943

Off-duty Service women had plenty of scope for hobbies and recreational activities. Here Phyllis Linsdell (*right*) watches a pottery instructor

Wrens of Ormonde Lodge, Richmond prepare for a concert

Anti-aircraft women of 137 battery occupy their evenings before Christmas making toys

in pubs all over East Anglia. Betty Davenport, who worked as a cook in the sergeants' mess at Martlesham, remembered being taken to 'The Red Lion' there, to 'The Bull' at Long Melford, the Lavenham 'Swan', the Thetford 'Bell', the 'Angel' at Bury St Edmunds and the 'Crown' at Woodbridge. 'It was such good innocent fun. I know my parents weren't keen, for they thought dreadful things happened to girls who went out with "Yanks" but it wasn't like that at all – they treated us as "ladies". Under low-beamed pub ceilings and in front of roaring red fires we laughed at their jokes, listened to their stories and we cried when their "Flying Fortresses" failed to return from a mission.'

On those big US bomber bases, social evenings and dances were a regular feature of their lives, for British servicewomen received block invitations through their unit adjutant. 'I've never danced so much in my life,' said Eileen Kisby.

Dancing was a great outlet for anyone bored with humdrum routine. It released pent-up tension, soothed frayed nerves and made people forget the war for a few hours. At this time, when for most people in Britain it was neither peace-time nor war, there was a tendency for Service personnel to feel – as the Elizabethans put it – like chimneys in summer. And there was no doubt that at times servicewomen as well as servicemen began to wonder just what they were supposed to be doing. Dancing counteracted the feeling of being useless and bored.

In fact, the country as a whole was dancing. People danced at lunchtimes in canteens; they danced to Victor Sylvester's lessons on the radio; they danced in village halls, town halls, Army, Navy and Air Force camps and clubs and in the big dance halls like the Hammersmith Palais, the Manchester Ritz and the Blackpool Palace Ballroom.

Gradually the form that dance music took began to change. In the 1930s there had been mainly swing and crooning – the most celebrated crooner being Bing Crosby, who, it is said, sang in that way because of a defect in his vocal chords – and every band was expected to keep a crooner huddled up to the microphone swaying and twisting voluptuously, grimacing and breathing out a syrupy wail.

By the summer of 1943 the big bands had really come into their own. To rival the pre-war bands of Ambrose, Joe Loss, Jack Hylton, Roy Fox and, of course, Victor Sylvester's strict-tempo dance band, there came onto the scene a new breed of Service dance band: the Navy's 'Blue Mariners', the Army's 'Blue Rockets', the RAF 'Squadronaires' and, naturally, the US Army Air Force band of Glen Miller. The latter delighted crowds of servicewomen and men for six months before he took off on his fatal flight to Paris.

With the new bands there came also a far more ecstatic mode of dancing – the jive and jitterbug. In this, the partners could perform any tap or acrobatic feat they wished, provided they kept in time with each other. Jitterbug competitions became popular, and some servicewomen were well-known for their prowess. Often the dance floor would clear to leave a large circle in which exponents could have freedom and space to move in order to display their remarkable agility and talent in the dance.

At other times it could become a frightening and rather unnerving experience for a young woman to find herself being led by one of these experts. Joyce Taylor, then a WAAF corporal at RAF Wittering, found herself in such a situation: 'The loose-limbed American kept grabbing my hand and flinging me diagonally past him, yelling, "Loosen up!" I was only at the stage of dancing the basic first steps of the slow waltz. I was shaken and shocked but nevertheless pleasurably excited by the experience.'

The Americans had to do their share of learning too, for there were new dances sweeping the country from the British stage. From the musical *Me and My Girl* came a song called 'The Lambeth Walk', sung by Lupino Lane, which became so popular that a dance was invented to suit it:

Any time you're Lambeth Way
Any evening any day,
You'll find them all doin' the Lambeth Walk.
Every little Lambeth gal,
With her little Lambeth pal,
You'll find 'em all doin' the Lambeth Walk.

Ev'rything free and easy,
Do as you darn well pleasey.
Why don't you make your way there
Go there, stay there?
Once you get down Lambeth Way,
Ev'ry evening, ev'ry day,
You'll find yourself, doin' the Lambeth Walk.

Then, to latch on to the success of this, there came the dance-hall version of the Cockney song 'Knees up, Mother Brown', the words of which ran:

Knees up, Mother Brown,
Knees up, Mother Brown,
Under the table you must go,
Ee aye, ee aye, ee ahy oh.
If we catch you bending,
We'll turn you upside down,
Knees up, knees up, don't get the breeze up,
Knees up, Mother Brown.

The popularity of these cheerful, simple, miming dances was evident at all the hops, whether in barracks or schoolrooms, the Hammersmith Palais or the American Red Cross Club.

'It was great fun to look forward to an evening off duty,' wrote former WAAF balloon operator Barbara Boyce. 'We used to go to Covent Garden, dancing to Ivy Benson's band, and also to the Stage Door Canteen in Piccadilly, which was an American Forces Club, and this was the first time I had tasted Coca-Cola, which came out of a large machine, not bottled. I was only eighteen, and life in the WAAF was quite an eye-opener!'

Stella Pearson, a WAAF sergeant, took her boyfriend, Top Sergeant 'Buzz' Braddock, to a dance at the sergeants' mess at RAF Stradishall. On this occasion the band for the evening had come from the neighbouring unit – the Highland Light Infantry.

Never before or since then have I ever spent a night which demanded so much agility and endurance [she recalls]. It was far more energetic than any aerobic exercise session of today. I was pretty fit and nineteen, and it was great fun. Traditional dances like the waltz and quickstep were only put in, I'm sure, to give us time to catch our breath in between hectic Highland dances, 'The Dashing White Sergeant', 'Gay Gordons' and others I had never heard of before that evening. But everyone got up to have a go. And then towards the end of the evening there came the jive and jitterbug sessions. Buzz soon had his tie and jacket off, whilst the visiting HLI officers, resplendent in full attire, with kilts, white leggings, big buckled belt, sporran dangling in front, dirk in stockings, sweated rivulets.

It had not taken long for the Americans to take up the Scottish dances, keeping a watchful eye on a tiny major who always seemed to take the centre of the floor, performing amazing feats of spryness. At the end of the evening, though, many of my American friends were also taking the limelight, as they brought their own cries and capers into those dances. It was a wonderful night.

They were indeed great days for servicewomen. No longer were they suffering from the traditional shortage of men; now there were more than enough to go round. And this gave women a new feeling of confidence. They were in demand. Units organizing dances sent transport for them and to take them home afterwards.

Ruth Sims, an ATS ordnance technician, liked to go with her friends to St Lawrence's Church Hall or to the Co-op at Ipswich, where, from seven until eleven, they could dance to their hearts' content.

No one was ever a wallflower having to sit and wait for someone to ask them for a dance. There were men galore. And we were all jiving mad. Looking back now, I don't know how we did it or where we got the energy from. After a long, hard day on camp, with foot drill, route marches and PT on top of our normal work, we were transformed into animated youngsters, like primary school kids, faces alight with excitement the moment we entered the building and heard the trumpet and clarinet. The whole place seemed to be throbbing in time. One band in particular was a favourite; it played in the Artie Shaw style, and again and again I've seen that hall in my mind's eye during the last forty years whenever I hear 'Deep Purple' and 'Stardust' played. Since then I've become convinced that music has a power which we never use enough – a power to move us emotionally, to stimulate us physically, to relax us mentally. It can make us feel elated, give us a sense of buoyancy, infuse us with a fervour and dynamism not often seen today. I'm sure music could help us when we are sick and lift us when we are depressed. It certainly did a lot for us in wartime Britain.

One of the rare treats for servicewomen then was to dance to Glen Miller's band. Phyllis Carter recalls one occasion: 'We were all in our best uniforms but as the evening wore on they began to look a little crumpled and our faces were hot and shiny, but the band still looked cool and immaculate, a parade of trumpeters blowing in one direction, trombones in the other and saxophones weaving in unison through soothing smoochy arrangements of "Moonlight Serenade" and "String of Pearls". We swayed rather than danced under a haze of purple American cigarette smoke which hung like a thick cloud above us.'

Molly Urquhart has good reason to remember Glen Miller with sadness. She was at work in the Special Duties Station as a filter plotter in direct contact with radar stations when his plane disappeared from her screen. He was never to be seen again.

By early 1944 Americans found themselves in many parts of the British Isles – getting on for a million of them and, in British terms, fabulously wealthy. Even the lower-paid black GI would earn £15 a month, compared with the British private soldier's £3. To be pursued by a well-dressed American serviceman who looked more like an officer or film star than a soldier added a touch of glamour to a woman's life. For many it seemed that the promised land lay ahead, a land of oil wells and ranches and pretty white houses and Cadillacs. 'Even the ordinary US soldiers treated us like ladies, with tremendous courtesy and respect the like of which we had never known before,' said Ruth Sims. 'And sometimes, shyly, they would bring us presents, not just nylons, perfume and Camel cigarettes but things for the family as well. They loved to meet the families of girls they took out. They would come with tins of ham or fruit, sweets for the children and butter. My sister had her first banana from an American friend of mine.'

Near Liverpool, at Burtonwood, there was a big US Airforce base. Paula Cooper used to spend all her leave from the Wrens at her home in

Crosby and never failed to get the special bus from the Adelphi Hotel in central Liverpool to Burtonwood whenever she was home:

The dances there were sensational. You did not have to know how to jive or jitterbug. Once your partner gripped your hand and touched you deftly on the hip, you felt yourself performing in a way you had never thought possible. It was fabulous. There wasn't much drinking, never any trouble. Towards the end of the evening the tempo would slow down to a final smooch and then, sometimes suddenly without warning, the band would stop and the lights go up unkindly. Everyone would be blinking and looking annoyed as the duty officer would take the microphone and announce that the last buses were now leaving the camp for Liverpool, Widnes, Warrington and Manchester. There would be a universal groan, hurried last cuddles and kisses, an exchange of telephone numbers and perhaps an agreement to meet mid-week, as the braying brass of the band did its best to blow us all out into the cold.

And so Britain carried on dancing and took the American invasion in its stride, as it had Dunkirk and the Blitz, and it took the US GIs into their hearts too – 80,000 GI brides would later testify to that – whilst the rest of the country was suitably impressed by the ever-increasing numbers assembling and training in Britain for the day when they would be a formidable army landing on the beaches of Hitler's Fortress of Europe.

There was plenty of dancing in North Africa too. The victorious troops of the British Eighth and First Armies celebrated the end of their particular war by getting drunk, dancing and chasing the local girls to such an extent that the woman they loved to hate, a woman once described in the magazine *John Bull* as a 'hypocrite of the first water' the first woman to sit in Parliament, Lady Astor, stood up there one day and demanded of the War Minister that he send more servicewomen out to Africa to keep the soldiers away from the local women, thereby reducing the number of troops catching venereal diseases. She feared that these troops would one day be returning to Britain spreading the disease and that women would have to be told to 'Beware of the man with the V neck!' – referring of course to the tanned V on his chest exposed to the African sun by his open-necked khaki drill shirt.

In this lull between campaigns, the brief interlude before the next assault landing, the soldiers almost relapsed into being ordinary civilians again, resuming habits of normal living, letting themselves enjoy and revel in their innate desire for peace. But all the time there was a thought at the back of their minds which disturbed their own peace. Soon, all too soon, they would have to 'stiffen the sinews, summon up the blood' and carry on the war again.

However, as the men cavorted in the sun and rejoiced in the fact they were still alive, nurses in the base hospital were not always enjoying the same feelings of elation.

Sister Rubina Campbell,[17] for example, found it was not easy to answer questions like: 'What have I to look forward to, Sister?' from a man whose abdomen had been ripped open by a mine and who now had a permanent colostomy and no stomach. 'My job won't look at me like this.' In his plight he was not alone. Nurses in hospitals and sickbays along a thousand-odd miles of the desert road from Algiers to Alexandria were dealing with others like him, pitifully maimed British, Germans and Italians. For them the celebration bells jangled harshly.

Even those recovering from wounds were often gloomy when it came to thinking about the future. When Pamela Barker asked one of her patients how he felt about getting back very soon to his pals in his infantry battalion, he replied sourly: 'I feel bad. Bloody bad. I've had enough war for one lifetime.' At the back of his mind too was the thought, 'What next?'

Patients were not unaware of what was going on in their hospitals; they could see the nurses had other things on their minds than just caring for the sick and wounded. They were bustling about bringing everything up to one hundred per cent battle efficiency. The men saw too how the wards were being emptied in readiness. For what?

Inventories were being checked. Replacement stores arrived – sometimes erroneously. Brenda McBryde tells of one awful gaffe: 'When the nursing staff collided with the less well-known side of troop management, as on the occasion when rubber goods intended for a naval destroyer unaccountably turned up at a sick bay for WRNS, the Naval Sister in Charge handed several cartons to the ship's embarrassed medical officer with the words: "I wondered why they'd sent me so many finger stalls. We don't have that many cut fingers." '[18]

Soon the nurses were all ready and waiting and wondering: 'Where to now?'

The answer to that question had already been decided by US President Roosevelt, Prime Minister Churchill and US General Marshall. They had on their hands a battle-trained army. Could they let this army remain idle? Should they send it home to join the forces getting ready for the invasion of Europe? Or should they use this army to attack what Churchill liked to call the 'soft belly of Europe' – Sicily, 'a ripe fruit, fat for plucking'.

Whilst General Marshall wanted to keep the army for the invasion of France of 1944, Churchill and Roosevelt believed that there was an urgent need to divert the German armies away from the hard-pressed Russians. In this way they were supported by their own Army commanders, who wanted to invade Sicily, saying it would not take long to conquer the island, and then they would soon be able to overrun Italy.

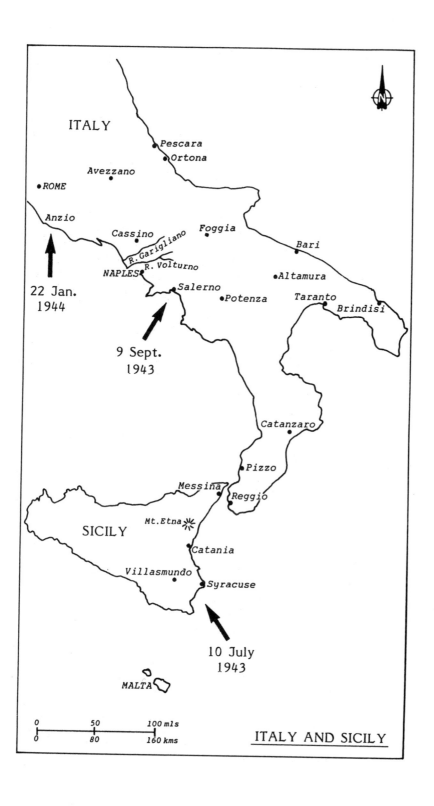

ITALY AND SICILY

The veterans of the gruelling desert campaign and the 'bloodly' Tunisian Djebels thought it was once again the 'old, old story' of a battle where there was going to be little opposition. And it was they, and not the generals, who were right.

Not many of those American, Canadian and British soldiers who set off for Sicily on Saturday 10 July would survive to see the Allies' triumphant entry into Rome. Many would be killed, or broken in spirit and body, on the way.

Now the brief interlude was over. The infantry soldiers got down to their last bit of letter-writing, but, for security reasons, the letters were not posted until the invasion was well launched. Eventually, after hours of hanging about in assembly areas and with battle-order webbing over their clean, sun-bleached khaki drill, the troops boarded the ships.

The nurses were ready too. Alongside the ships of the invasion fleet – the largest amphibious assault in history, bigger even than D-Day's – were the hospital ships and hospital carriers standing by for transporting the casualties back. The largest hospital ships could carry 500 wounded, and carriers, with their shallower draught enabling them to go inshore, between 200 and 400.

So it was that on 10 July 1943, as US General Patton's Seventh US Army and Montgomery's new Eighth Army sailed for Sicily, Pamela Barker was waiting aboard one of those carriers and hoping they would not be called upon to sail for at least a few hours. A terrible hot Khamsin wind was howling straight from the Sahara Desert and whipping the waves into white-crested mountains that buffeted the ships mercilessly as they left the shelter of the harbour. By midday the winds had increased to Force Seven! Some of the smaller ships were so swept by the breaking seas that they looked more like submarines than ordinary sea-faring craft. Fortunately for Pamela Barker – never a good sailor – and for the invasion fleet, the gale had blown itself out by dusk, and only a gentle breeze ruffled the waters.

On the following morning Sister Barker's ship sailed. It moved slowly, stopping for hours at times, but when she woke up the next morning, it was to a view she has never forgotten: 'Straight ahead was the awe-inspiring sight of the 10,000-foot volcano, Mount Etna, snow-capped and with a white trail of smoke from its flat crest. It made a fitting backcloth to the brilliant array of ships of all sizes anchored in the bay of a clear blue sky. Against the lighter blue of the sky, silvery barrage balloons glistened as they trailed from the ring of smaller ships circling the enormous convoy. And way above them were white vapour plumes left by aircraft.

That volcano, lighted in many different ways, was to loom above many nurses tending a constant stream of casualties coming in during the next few weeks.

Sister Marjorie Bennett had landed at Port Augusta, and after breakfasting with the Navy she and her colleagues drove northwards in trucks, through orange and lemon groves. 'I remember thinking what a beautiful place it was compared with the Western Desert. And then she drove through the battlefield of but a few days ago,' she shuddered.

'Bloated corpses lay stinking in the burnt-out wreckage of tanks, armoured cars. The place was littered with the debris of battle. Here and there were rows of crosses with a British or German steel helmet on top. Sometimes it would be just a rifle stuck into the ground to mark the spot of a hurried burial. We were very glad to reach that hospital, which we took over from the Italians.

Immediately we were working incessantly, snatching a bite to eat now and then, and a nap whenever there was a gap between the arrival of convoys carrying in battle casualties, dysentery and malaria cases.'

Gunner Lee Harvey was one of these casualties and recalls:

I fell ill with diarrhoea and then after that with malaria. I felt really bad and could hardly move from the plank of wood which was my bed, to answer the call of nature. I was transferred to an emergency tented hospital at Syracuse and here the severe attacks of chills and high fever culminated in an acute state of delirium, my speech became disorderly, and I suffered all too frequent attacks of hallucinations.

The first night there the enemy dive-bombed and machine-gunned the hospital continuously and it was a source of wonder to me that all were not killed, but the casualties were surprisingly low. A piece of shrapnel struck me on the top lip and left a red scar which is still there to this day.

There were in the Syracuse hospital German as well as British wounded, but they were all treated in the same way, as Marjorie Bennett said: 'They were no different to our boys. They were courageous, and I could see they were amazed to see women nursing so near to the front.'

Nurses were never far behind the forward troops. They were in Catania shortly after it fell, tending wounded in a civilian hospital set amongst olive trees, almond groves and the familiar cactus bushes or 'prickly pears'. Those cactus bushes were responsible for their fair share of casualties too. Pamela Barker was in that hospital and recalls:

It was a terrible sight to see those young men we had seen embark so smartly but a few weeks before. They came, bleached with dust, their khaki jackets filthy, shapeless and torn. Black patches of sweat showed on their backs, and their faces, glistening with the sweat of pain and the heat of the piercing Sicilian sun, were ugly with stubble and sores. We eased bleeding feet out of cracked boots.

One who came in with a shoulder wound wanted to give me a present before he lost it – soldiers still had the idea that RAMC stood for 'Rob All My Comrades'. He asked me to pass him his small pack and take out a parcel. I humoured him and passed him the tightly rolled parcel. He pulled the loop of string, and out fell a huge piece of parachute silk. 'A present from the Hermann Goering Parachute Division, I'll never get it home and I shan't be able to carry it. I'd rather you have it.' That silk was still being used years later, there was so much of it.

For the five weeks of the Sicilian campaign, British hospital ships ferried the wounded across the dangerous sixty-mile straits between Sicily and Tunisia. Though painted white and bedecked with large red crosses according to the Geneva Convention, they were not safe from the German bombers. Within a week of the landing, HMHS *Talamba* was attacked in the bay and sunk whilst embarking casualties. The wounded, who had been brought to her in anything that would float, then had to be taken back. When the bombs dropped, a surgeon had just finished amputating a soldier's leg. Hurriedly, as the ship sank, the surgeon strapped the stump, tied the man to a stretcher, said a little prayer and cast him into the sea. Amazingly the stretcher floated, the man was rescued and made a good recovery.

After the explosion Sister Makepeace found herself in the sea, the bones in one leg shattered, but she managed to keep herself afloat for ninety minutes until rescued. Her friend Sister Maud Johnson, though, was never found. Ship's Matron Violet Innes was not at all put out by the incident. As one astonished eye-witness put it: 'She shepherded all the wounded in her care into a lifeboat and got them safely away – without even soiling her veil.'[20]

At ten o'clock on 17 August, thirty-nine days after the landings, General Patton's 7th US Division stumbled over the piles of rubble that had once been Messina. In thirty-eight days of fierce fighting, Sicily had been captured. But not the German Army: most of it had escaped over the Straits of Messina to mainland Italy. That easy conquest the generals had promised had cost the Allies 30,000 dead, wounded and missing. That 'soft underbelly' of Europe was proving to be a 'tough old gut'!

For two or three weeks there was again a brief interlude for the troops whilst units regrouped ready for the long slog from the toe of Italy's boot up to the top. There was time for them to trail through the shattered towns looking for a long, cool beer. There was time too for the overworked nurses to take a look at the city sights.

Though the fighting in Sicily had stopped, the hospitals were still kept busy with cases of malaria and dysentery. Troops were issued with mepacrine tablets to prevent their catching malaria, but they did not all take them: some soldiers just didn't believe in taking tablets. (They were suspicious of what might be in them.) Some didn't care if they did catch malaria, for it would keep them out of the firing-line for a few weeks, and some soldiers even sold the tablets to gullible Italian girls as 'anti-baby pills'. So, despite all the military precautions – sleeves down and long trousers on once the sun went down, a mepacrine pill every day, there were always plenty of malaria cases to keep nurses occupied.

There was one case though which was something more than malaria, a case which Marjorie Bennett remembers as one of her 'tales of the unexpected':

I was nursing South African soldiers at the time, and in one of the beds was a giant of a black man who did not seem to be responding at all the usual treatment. Doses of quinine were given three times daily for ten days, blood slides taken for three days running, and if they proved to be negative, the soldier was sent back to his unit cured. In this ward of black South Africans, the huge man lay moaning and feverish still after his ten days. Furthermore, his right arm was paralysed. Other patients seemed to be avoiding him, and this too was strange, for usually they all helped each other. But the big man was different. No one would go near him. Though his blood slides showed negative, he was obviously far from well, and so, when the unit officer came to take his men back to their camp, the medical officers took him to one side to express his concern for the black giant.

'Ah,' said the unit officer, 'this looks very much like a case of voodoo. The witch doctor will have put a spell on him. But if you do as I suggest, you may cure him.'

I took the advice given by the unit commander and went along to the ward armed with a hypodermic syringe. I filled it with sterile water and then inserted a small white, sugar-coated pill in the barrel. I went to the patient saying, 'This injection will be cure your arm.' But all he did was to twist his lips into a half smile and murmur something in Afrikaans about voodoo.

I injected the sterile water and then showed him the pill in the syringe barrel. 'There is your voodoo, soldier,' I said. He jumped off the bed and saluted me with his paralysed arm. I'll never forget the sheer joy on his face. I felt I'd performed a miracle, but it was just a case of mind over matter.'

A similar, but sadly fatal, situation was encountered by ATS Company Sergeant Irene Smith in Jamaica: 'It was an odd thing which I had heard of but never witnessed. A Jamaican ATS girl was taken ill and went into hospital. The doctors could find nothing wrong with her but nevertheless she was kept in as a patient. I visited her two or three times, and on the last occasion she told me she would surely die as someone had "fingered" her. She did die, and I could never satisfactorily explain this to myself. Mind over matter?'

Such cases were unique.

Generally, though, it was more routine cases like malaria that kept the nurses busy at that time in Sicily, but they did get upset duty rosters.

We did have time to relax [said Marjorie Bennett]. We went to the
magnificent opera house in Catania and to concerts (Gracie Fields was one
of the first artists to come over and entertain the troops), and went to parties.

Eventually our mess gave a special dance to repay the hospitality we had
received from so many neighbouring units, and my life was never the same
again. There I met and fell in love with a handsome RAF officer stationed in
Malta but in Sicily then on a visit. From that moment on, everything revolved
around our relationship – our plans and our hopes. It was a great feeling.

Meeting one another was not going to be easy for the young lovers
though – one of them in Malta and the other in Sicily – for the war
suddenly moved on. A few days later 100,000 British and 69,000
American infantrymen set off for an assault landing behind the enemy
lines at Salerno, south of Naples.

These troops were in remarkably high spirits, though, for over the
ship's radio came the news that Italy had surrendered. What a relief the
news brought, not only to those infantrymen but also to all the nurses
now preparing to join them on the beaches. Number One British
General Hospital was embarking, and a hundred American nurses were
already aboard the hospital ship *Newfoundland*, bound for Salerno,
where they were going to set up their own American Evacuation
Hospital.

It was drinks all round for those who wanted to mark Italy's surrender
in that way, and prayer meetings of thanksgiving for those who favoured
an alternative way of dealing with the relief felt in knowing there would
now be no storming up beaches raked by machine-guns.

Days later, however, those same men and women found themselves in
the front line fighting desperately, not just to move inland but to prevent
themselves being driven back into the sea. The Germans had reacted
with speed as soon as the news of the surrender reached them; they had
rushed their own infantry and tank units onto the high ground
overlooking the bay and were gradually pushing back the American and
British infantry, which had no heavy armour to counter the massive,
frightening Tiger tanks.

As the hospital ship *Newfoundland* approached the bay, it was attacked
and sunk. The bomb which landed between the funnel and bridge killed
the British matron and five of her nurses. Rescue boats and hospital
carriers raced to the assistance of the foundering ship, now burning
fiercely too. Scores of badly burnt soldiers, with huge serum blisters
hanging from their charred bodies, were brought ashore.[21]

Twice after this attack, other hospital ships were bombed and
machine-gunned, despite being clearly marked with the Red Cross.

Meanwhile the battle on the beach-head raged furiously, with the
Allied forces desperately trying to cling on to a shallow strip of sandy

coast. As one soldier said, 'It was like another Dunkirk but this time there were no small boats.' Huge shells ploughed up the beach where nurses were tending the wounded and dying. In the midst of all this horror and carnage, where 700 British soldiers staged a sit-down strike, refusing to fight,* British and American nurses worked wonders, forgetting their own fears in their efforts to reassure and bolster the morale of their charges lying on blood-soaked stretchers without any cover save the occasional shallow trench.

Somehow the Allies held on to that strip of beach at Salerno, and the days of crisis passed. Then, painfully slowly, the US and British troops got moving again and fought their way inland to join up with Montgomery's Eighth Army coming from the south. Together they battled onwards towards Naples and Rome. It was tough going, through the slush and slime of the autumn rains and over a succession of rivers running directly across the paths of the American Fifth and British Eighth Armies, with every bridge blown up.

Then came another formidable enemy – winter. Snow fell on the mountains, and the valleys filled with icy streams. After six months of continuous fighting in Sicily and Italy, the armies were more than weary. Everything came to a halt.

Things were happening elsewhere, though. Orders came calling General Eisenhower back to Britain to take Supreme Command of the Allied Expeditionary Force, and General Montgomery went too, as Commander-in-Chief of the British Forces under Eisenhower. The meticulous preparations and elaborate deceptions for the Allied invasion of Europe were rapidly gaining momentum. Soon 1½ million Allied soldiers would be landing on the beaches of Normandy. Ahead of them already were women of the WAAF and SOE.

---

* See *Poor Bloody Infantry* by Charles Whiting (Century Hutchinson, page 192). Eventually most of the mutineers agreed to go to 46 Division, but 192 men, including three sergeants, refused and were placed under close arrest, tried by court martial and sentenced to seven years penal servitude – except the sergeants, who were to be shot. Thereupon immediately these sentences were suspended on condition the men would fight with new units. All agreed but many deserted at the first opportunity.

7 Dice on the Table

When we lasted long enough they gave us medals.
When we died they said, 'Our casualties were low.'

From Randall Jarrell's poem 'Losses'

Spring and Summer 1944
Listeners to the BBC nine o'clock news on the evening of 5 June 1944
were puzzled by an interruption which made no sense at all. The clearly
articulated words had no bearing whatsoever on world news. A dry voice
was saying: 'Eileen is married to Joe ... It is hot in Suez ... The compass
points north ... The dice are on the table.'

Germans monitoring the broadcast no doubt furrowed their
foreheads. Was it a local station perhaps breaking in with a faulty
transmission? It made no sense to them either.

But to a specially selected group of WAAF officers in France, to men
and women of the Special Operations Executive and to 500,000 French
men and women, the meaning of those messages was soon made very
clear by those few leaders who were 'in the know'. It was the secret,
long-awaited call to action. That night bridges on major roads all over
France erupted into dust and rubble; main railway lines leapt from their
tracks into a tangled, twisted mess; troop trains thundered down
dead-end country tracks as points were shifted; telephones went dead
and fuel dumps blazed.

By dawn the next day, D-Day, 6 June 1944, vital German troop
movements were slowed to a crawl; bottlenecks in sabotaged
communications delayed by forty-eight hours formations sent to repel
the Allied assault troops.

The powder keg of this uprising had been primed by SOE agents,
who had persuaded Resistance groups to abandon sporadic acts of
violence in favour of co-ordinated sabotage on receipt of a coded
message given over the radio.

Now it was time for those carefully selected WAAF officers to play
their part. French-speaking section officers, such as Sonia Butt,
Maureen O'Sullivan and Phyllis Latour,[1] dropped by parachute at night
into northern France in the months preceding D-Day. Their particular
role was to move among German troop formations and radio back

information which might make all the difference to the outcome of the savage battles that would rage around the beach-heads. A few morse signals from WAAF transmitters could bring RAF bomber squadrons to blast concentrations of troops and tanks in their woodland hide-outs.

It was going to be difficult, though, for these women to gain the co-operation of Norman farming families, who had a good working relationship with the German Army there. Their life had been going on for years with little interference from German troops. Indeed, 'Live like a king in Normandy' was the saying. Local people were impressed by the correctness of the German Army's behaviour, particularly when they heard of German soldiers being shot for incivility to women.[2] Naturally they would look with deep-seated suspicion on anyone likely to upset a way of life that was working well for everyone – no one went hungry. It was fortunate for the WAAF officers that Norman civilians could not imagine the horrific fate that would come to them soon, when heavy bombers began to pound their villages to rubble whilst trying to blast a way through German defences.

These WAAF volunteers came from all branches of the Service: some had worked in the ranks as clerks, others had been on balloon sites, and others were station wireless-operators. Section Officer Maureen O'Sullivan parachuted into France on 22 March 1944. Her special task was to act as wireless-operator for a British officer working with French Intelligence near Limoges. On her first liaison mission she hired a taxi to take her to a secret destination. Within her shabby suitcase was her radio transmitter. On the way, a German patrol stopped the driver. A sergeant stepped forward and wrenched open the door but then stepped back in surprise, finding himself facing a pretty, demure young girl sitting in the middle of the back seat, her legs drawn up on her case. Obviously embarrassed, the German sergeant asked, in his execrable French, where she was going.

He received a nervous, appealing smile from the girl, now perched nervously on the edge of her seat. 'I ... I am going to my aunt's ... she is ill ... I don't expect to stay long ... you see ... she ... I haven't much money ... and food ...'

The sergeant drew back, then remembered to ask for her papers. He flicked them over quickly. Stamps all in the right places. He thrust them back. 'On your way,' he said.

Such were the situations, and worse, with which these women had to deal. Sonia Butt, who parachuted in May, blended so well into the local community that she soon developed a nodding acquaintance with the local Gestapo chief. He was most surprised months later when he was visited in his prison cell by a young woman in the uniform of the Women's Air Force.

Phyllis Latour was a twenty-three-year-old WAAF flight mechanic before she parachuted into France. She was trained to work in the most dangerous areas of all – immediately behind the enormous concrete emplacements of Hitler's Atlantic fortifications. This was a '*Verboten*' area. While Gestapo and Secret Police combed the area for suspects, shot Norman peasants and set fire to their homes, Phyllis Latour collected a wealth of military detail vitally important to the Allied Command. In the early hours of the morning, she would sit with her headphones over her ears, sending signals to be picked up by the Wrens, ATS and WAAF at Bletchley Park. Despite all security checks – her area was once cordoned off and thoroughly searched, Phyllis Latour carried on gathering information, transmitting it and escaping arrest by the narrowest of margins. Several times her house was searched and she was questioned, but each time she seemed eager to tell her interrogators everything they wished to know, and they were convinced she had nothing of importance to tell them.

There was no glamour in the roles these WAAF officers had to play; they were not elegantly dressed Mata Hari figures but often scruffily clothed as they crawled through rain-lashed woods at night, skirting minefields and barbed-wire defences. Unknown to all but a handful of War Department planners, these women helped pave the way for the invasion of Europe. It was not until a year later that news of what they had been doing was leaked.

Late one evening in March 1945, the Secretary of State for Air, Sir Archibald Sinclair, rose to the House of Commons to introduce the Air Estimates, but before getting down to the subject of money he made the surprising disclosure about the WAAFs who had parachuted into France.

Not all women agents parachuted. Some, like Violette Szabo,[3] went by light aircraft to lonely landing grounds in France.

It was late one afternoon in April 1944 when Violette was driven up the Great North Road to that secret airfield of Tempsford tucked away amongst the beet fields of Bedfordshire. She was dressed in clothes specially made for her by a French seamstress – the small details of finishing and lining were different from the British way of dressmaking. Frenchwomen's jackets, for example, were then eight inches longer than those in Britain, and these details were important if the agents were to avoid the scrutiny of women Gestapo agents. Nothing was overlooked which might give her away. In her bag were toiletries from all over France. There was, however, one standard item of equipment which she refused to take with her, the 'L pill', the lethal suicide pill for those who preferred a quick, clean death to the extremes of physical torture practised on prisoners by the Gestapo.

Once at the airfield, the despatching officer searched Violette for the give-away, tell-tale bits and pieces which might blow her cover story: no screwed-up British bus ticket, no flakes of Virginia cigarette tobacco. She was given her papers, rations, clothing and identity cards – exact replicas of the French. At last the light aircraft of 138 Moon Squadron slid out of its hangar. It was a small monoplane with a black fuselage, sometimes called a 'flying hearse', which could take off and land in a restricted space. Stripped of all guns and armour, there was just room for passengers but not for a navigator. The pilot had to be really good to find a tiny field with perhaps three glimmering torches signalling him to land.

It was now time to go.

'*Merde*! – Shit!' said everyone, instead of 'Good Luck' – in the same way as actors will say 'Break a leg!', fearing that wishing 'good luck' might bring bad luck. Then, in the dusk before a rising moon, the 'Lizzie' took off. Soon below them a faint line of foam faded on a dark shore, and then the small aircraft began to soar gently downwards to within a few hundreds feet of the hedges of France, too low to be hit by anti-aircraft guns. The pilots had little difficulty in identifying the landmarks and was about to do a circle into a position to land when suddenly he turned into a steep climb. Violette caught a lopsided view of the landing-light markers, then she was flung from one side of her seat to the other as the small aircraft kept turning sharply and steeply. Just as suddenly it dropped, diving faster and faster. Muscles stiffened as terror flashed through Violette's body. All at once, the aircraft flew straight again, leaving its passenger collapsed and weak. An approaching fighter had made off.

The Lysander was soon back on course, and the pilot was pointing down below. As Violette looked, a cold wave of apprehension ran through her body, to be quietly replaced by a protective wave of insensitiveness which seemed to make her immune from fright, almost unconcerned, a total victory of mind over body, as it is with those who have accepted the possibility of death. It was a strange capability which women under stress seemed to develop. It was to serve Violette well.

Within a few moments the aircraft was bumping to a halt in a small field. The French Resistance group were waiting, looking businesslike and important, scarves tied round their necks, Sten-guns in hands and magazines sticking out of pockets. One of them carried a Bren-gun. Hurriedly they greeted Violette and thrust a bicycle into her hands. Before the German fighter could have had time to report his engagement, the Lysander and secret army guerrillas were well clear of the scene. They stopped a few miles away, at a resister's farm, and early next morning Violette, with her small, battered French suitcase, was put on the train for Paris, where she changed onto another train without having her papers examined and soon was in Rouen. There her mission was to give Resistance groups final instructions as to their tasks on receipt of certain coded amusements over the radio. When that all important D-Day came, a combined effort was imperative from civilians and military alike.

Passing such information to the right people was not easy. Each contact had to be checked carefully, for all too often plans had gone wrong through betrayal. The greatest hazard was with Frenchwomen whose husbands were already in German prisons, for these women could be tempted by concessions for their menfolk in return for information. And, of course, there were plenty of people eager to earn a few quick francs for passing on whatever of interest had been heard. Barmen and waiters were notorious for this, and many of them later paid for their treachery with their lives.*

Even those who were once keen members of the Resistance sometimes became disillusioned and frankly said to their British courier: 'All your talk about an Allied invasion is nothing but hot air. All talk. You'll wait until the Russians and Germans have worn each other out and half the French population have died in concentration camps and then you'll come in with flags waving and bands playing victory marches. It's all bluff and politics with you.' Many French farmers hated the Maquis and all those engaged in 'underground' Resistance work more than the Germans, and for very good reasons, as we shall see.

It was against such a background that Violette had now to make her contacts. Her first call was at a motor-repair garage, where a shock awaited her. She was appalled to discover that of the once flourishing Resistance group operating from the garage ninety-eight members had been taken away and shot by the Germans. She therefore moved north, to the villages closer to the highly sensitive area behind the Atlantic Wall, to investigate the position there. Around Le Havre security checks were intensive. Twice Violette was arrested and grilled for hours on end. But this did not deter her. She carried on with the linking process, encouraging the resisters, letting them know that they were part of a large organization with direct access to London. Soon fresh supplies of arms and ammunition would be dropped. At last her mission was completed, and she returned to Paris. There, as arranged, she met her British contact, Captain Charles Staunton, who arranged for Violette and himself to be picked up from a field near Blois.

The timing was perfect. As Violette and Staunton arrived at the appointed field, again on bicycles supplied by the local Resistance group, the Lysander came in. And once more Violette found herself bouncing over the rough field in the light aircraft. It seemed that the job

---

* There was a terrible national settling of grudges immediately after the liberation – 20,000 summary executions, says Robert Aras, in *De Gaulle Triumphant* (Putnam, 1964).

was not going to be as dramatic or difficult as others had made it out to be. It was, however, the last successful trip she was to make.

On that same stormy night chosen for the despatch of the Allied armies to Normandy, Violette took off from Tempsford again. This time she was in an American Liberator with arms and explosives, and she landed in countryside controlled by the Maquis. Everything seemed to run too smoothly to be true. Quickly Violette was whisked away to a safe farmhouse, and the arms were taken off to various other farms.

The following day, 7 June 1944, when the Germans were rushing troops from all parts of France and Germany towards the Allied bridgehead, the great D-Day plan came into operation. Roads and bridges were blown, railways and lock gates destroyed. Violette's job was to harness the resources of the Maquis in the most effective way, receiving instructions from Captain Staunton and from London. But by far the most important of her tasks was to prevent the crack German division SS Das Reich from moving from the south to the north of France. To do that, instructions had to be taken to the southern Maquis leaders.

So it was that on 8 June Violette Szabo set off armed with a Sten-gun and eight full magazines of ammunition – she was the best shot of all the women in the SOE – to go to Pompadour village. With her was a local Maquis leader called Anastasie, and it was his job to present Violette's credentials and vouch for her authority to the southern Maquis. It was a beautifully sunny June day and, as they bowled along the dusty, deserted country roads, winding up small hills and down narrow valleys, in an old Citroën, both Violette and her companion sang cheerfully the choruses of childhood songs. Then, as they approached the first houses of the village of Pompadour, Anastasie slowed down cautiously, suddenly jammed on the brakes fiercely and stopped alongside a high hedgerow. He peered ahead. 'There's something strange here,' he said hoarsely. 'Look behind that hedge.'

'Germans!' cried Violette, and they both leapt out of the car and flung themselves into the ditch. A platoon of Germans then rushed from behind the cover and began firing their Schmeissers, spraying the hedge bottom. Violette and Anastasie dashed off, zigzagging and bent double along the hedge, broke through another, crossed a field and took cover behind a farmhouse for a moment.

Quickly, Violette took stock of the situation. It was imperative that Anastasie should get back to his own group and take command. She saw two armoured cars bouncing up the track towards them. 'Come on,' she shouted, and dashed off towards a small copse behind an orchard. Bullets zipped and cracked around them. Violette felt a jolt in her left arm and fell. But it was not the bullet that had felled her: it was her ankle. Still weak after the parachuting injury, it gave way. Anastasie stopped to lift her, but Violette knew this was courting disaster. 'Go on. Run. Leave me. You have to get back,' she shouted, at the same time shaking herself free from his supporting arms. Leaning against an apple tree, clenching her teeth at the pain in her arm, she aimed low at the approaching black-uniformed SS soldiers. When the Sten magazine was empty, she clipped another on and with total disregard for her own safety kept firing short bursts into the sections advancing in a wide arc. The Germans were now firing their machine-pistols, first from one side, then from the other, covering each section's advance. Violette was firing the last of her magazines, drawing fire whilst Anastasie made the most of those few moments to make good his escape. Screams and cries of the wounded rose from the long grass of the orchard, yet Violette, now a perfect target, remained untouched. Suddenly all firing stopped. The black figures closed in and seized the struggling young woman. They brought her to their officer. He peered closely at her face and nodded patronizingly, as if admiring her performance. It was not yet finished: Violette screwed up her cheeks and spat full in his face.

Anastasie got away, but there was a price to pay. Two days later, on 10 June 1944, a battalion of Das Reich SS Panzer Division marched into the neighbouring village of Oradour-sur-Glâne, determined to teach those hit-and-run guerrillas and the villagers who supported them, a lesson. The entire population was summoned to the main square for an identity check. Complaining about being taken away from their tasks, but unsuspectingly, 640 civilians gathered. Children marched in orderly crocodiles from three schools; women were hustled from their homes, men from fields and workshops. In the square they were divided into groups. Over 400 women and children were packed into the church, 250 men pushed into barns and garages. There they waited under the guns of their guards, wondering what was to come next. They had not long to wait. A single shot rang out from the direction of the square. At this signal the SS soldiers pressed their triggers to pour rapid fire into the cowering groups of men, women and children. When the shooting stopped, other soldiers threw straw and brushwood onto the bodies, some still stirring and groaning. A firebrand was put to the heaped tinder, and the bodies and buildings went up in a crackle of flames. Five men survived, 642 people perished.

'Why did you do it?' the divisional commander was later asked at his trial.[4]

'It was necessary to provoke terror among the *maquisards* to deprive them of the support of the civilian population,' replied General Heinz Lammerding. He pointed out that the Geneva Convention formally forbids the action of '*franc tireurs*' (guerrillas) and warns that all such irregular fighters would be shot. (Indeed, the Canadians did shoot women snipers – wives of German soldiers – in Normandy after losing some good officers and men, and this was condoned by General Montgomery.)

Such brutal reprisals by the SS certainly had the required effect in France. Many French civilians grew to hate the Maquis and the SOE, who were supplying them with arms, ammunition and official approval. No doubt there were some in the Maquis who made the most of their opportunities to pay off old scores, for murder and for rape and looting. Thus it was plain to see that the women of SOE were not always assured of a warm welcome when they arrived on the doorstep of some country farmhouse. They had therefore to be on their guard against those of the French who wanted to be left alone to make the best of the German occupation, as well as the Germans.

In Oradour, the SS Das Reich division had demonstrated its determination to overcome all opposition in their way to the Normandy beachhead, but even so, they were a little too late in arriving to affect the outcome of that battle, thanks to men and women like Violette Szabo.

After her arrest, when she was taken to the headquarters of the Paris Gestapo at 84 Avenue Foch, she knew what to expect. She had heard tales of torture, of people screaming night after night in specially heated chambers, of their being brought with feet and bodies covered in blisters and burns, of teeth and toenails being pulled out with pliers between each question, and of people being tilted backwards into a bath full of ice-cold water until it dribbled down the nostrils, producing a terrifying feeling of drowning slowly. Violette received the interrogators' treatment: she was beaten, questioned and beaten again. She would tell nothing. Back and forth she travelled between the awesome prison of Fresnes, south of Paris, and the Avenue Foch to face a never-ending stream of questions: 'What were the Maquis's plans for hindering troop movement? Where were their stores of arms and ammunition? Where were the leaders? Who were they? What were the transmission codes?'

These men were pastmasters in the art of persuasion, in psychologically undermining the resistance of a captive, in inflicting plain brutal torture. But they failed with Violette. No matter what obscenities they inflicted, no matter what pain, Violette kept silent. She existed on a diet of cabbage soup and a hundred grammes of bread a day and an occasional fatty sausage. For eight weeks she lay in her cold, damp cell in the Fresnes prison, being questioned every few days until at last the Gestapo gave in. By this time the Allied armies had landed and successfully broken out of the beach-head and were making progress inland. There was only one thing left for the Gestapo to do with Violette Szabo. And the order came for it: '*Nacht und Nebel. Ruchkehr ungewunscht*' – she was to disappear into the 'night and fog' of the concentration camp, 'Return not required'.[5]

In Caen barracks that June of 1944 German firing squads were dealing with the first of eighty executions of French civilians summarily convicted of having helped the Allied invasion. The rest of the citizens held their breath in anxiety, fearing that even this invasion might fail, remembering the disaster of Dieppe and contemplating the harsher punitive reprisals which might be inflicted on them should Germany succeed in pushing the Allies back into the sea.

But the Allied success was already assured. All concerned had worked well to help the assault troops – French Resistance workers, Special Operations Executive agents and the WAAF officers had good reason to be pleased with their efforts.

Ironically, though, whilst WAAF officers in France had been doing so much for the success of the invasion, women in Britain generally were thinking less and less of joining the WAAF, as was evident in recruitment figures: women then preferred to join the ATS or Wrens. The low esteem in which the WAAF was held caused so much concern that Air Chief Marshal Leigh-Mallory, famed for his part in the Battle of Britain, wrote a strongly worded letter to the Chief of the Air Staff, a letter that is often quoted today in arguments on equal opportunities for women in the RAF. Writing in a 'formal official' style, he said:

It is a deplorable fact that the WAAF no longer holds as high a position in public estimation as formerly, and I submit that the reason for this is its failure to attract the best and most adventurous type of woman in the country. Its pedestrian Safety First policy can make no appeal comparable with that of the ATS whose members serve in large numbers in theatres of war abroad and who at home help to man Anti-Aircraft batteries in the danger zone. Even the WRENs man craft at sea and, although a much smaller Service, are more in evidence overseas than are the WAAF who, much to their chagrin, are only allowed in safe zones outside the UK and then in very small numbers.

Yet in the aeroplane the WAAF possess the finest medium of all three Women's Services on which to build morale, and it is astounding that the opportunity of forming its own flying branch should so long have been neglected.

It is even more deplorable, now that increasing numbers of women are required as ATA ferry pilots, that volunteers should be called for from the ranks of Service in order to learn to fly.

The WAAF is, I believe, officially recognised as an integral part of the Royal Air Force. It is therefore difficult to see why it should be prohibited from sharing in the latter's essential function, viz. flying.

The excellent work done by the women of the ATA is fully realised but there can be no reason why the two flying organisations – Service and Civilian – should continue. Amalgamation might prove advisable.

Finally I have always assumed that at least a skeleton WAAF would continue after the war; if so, a flying branch would enable a reserve of women pilots to be built up, so that in the future there would be no need to form an ATA (which must obviously end when hostilities cease) in the event of another war.

It is, therefore, most strongly urged that the women who volunteer, and are accepted for flying training (with ATA) should retain their WAAF identity and form the nucleus of a Flying Branch of the Service.[6]

No doubt it had not escaped Air Chief Marshal Leigh-Mallory's notice that women in the Soviet Air Force had fought magnificently.[7] The Soviet Union had three complete Women's Air Combat Regiments: the 586th Fighter, 587th Bomber and 588th Night Bomber Regiments. They had all seen action against German squadrons and bases, and they had contributed greatly to the destruction of von Paulus's Sixth Army at Stalingrad, taking a real part in inflicting upon Germany the greatest military disaster it had ever suffered.

Naturally, as one might have expected, even in the Soviet Union, these women were not at first accepted by their male counterparts, but soon their courage, dedication and skill overcame all objections. Their achievements were little short of miraculous. For example, the 588th Night Bomber Squadron flew an astonishing 24,000 sorties and dropped 3 million tons of bombs.

Despite all this weight of evidence of how women had coped with operational flying and despite the efforts of Air Chief Marshal Leigh-Mallory, the Air Ministry decided that women would not be trained as pilots. They held to the philosophy of the non-combat woman as firmly as had the Royal Navy with their own simple answer that: 'Ladies do not go to sea in grey-funnel fighting ships.'

Committees went through the motions of discussing possibilities of training women as RAF pilots, but the objections were many, the 'administrative inconveniences' legion. And so they have remained for the last forty-odd years.

Thus in 1944 women had to find flying-opportunities in other roles, often no less hazardous. For example, shortly after D-Day women in the Air Transport Auxiliary were extremely busy ferrying aircraft. At first they were restricted to Britain, though they wanted to be flying to the advanced operational stations in Belgium and France. Surprisingly, this was not allowed, because the very man who had so ardently advocated the training of WAAF volunteers as pilots, Air Chief Marshal Sir Trafford Leigh-Mallory, now commanding the Second Tactical Air Force and the Ninth United States Air Force for the invasion, positively refused to accept women volunteers as ferry pilots to the Continent.[8]

However, necessity eventually changed his mind. As the Allied armies advanced deeper into Europe, so the ferry trips to forward airfields grew ever longer. Winter was approaching, days were getting shorter and the weather was more uncertain; consequently RAF pilots on ferry duties tended to be away for days on end completing a single ferry duty, and this led to a shortage of pilots available. Thus, as it had so often before, the RAF turned to the ATA. From that time on, women played their full part in ferrying, flying Mitchells, Bostons, Mosquitoes, Dakotas, Wellingtons and Spitfires.

There were some particularly hazardous trips during the 'Battle of the Bulge' in the Ardennes. It was one of the coldest winters France had experienced for decades; Spitfires were frozen onto the ground when pilots came to collect them on the British bases, and navigating to the advanced French airfields was very difficult, for snow blotted out all landmarks except forests – rivers were invisible under ice and snow, railways indistinguishable from roads, and airfields often hidden under a misty haze.

Ferrying aircraft was not the only role played by the ATA. It also operated an ambulance service with specially converted Rapides and Ansons, bringing casualties from all parts of the United Kingdom to the Canadian hospital at Taplow.

The bulk of the Air Ambulance commitment from north-west Europe, however, was undertaken by the RAF. Here was an ideal opportunity for the WAAF to fly, and they jumped at the opportunities offered but, once again, recognition of their efforts was not always given wholeheartedly. One senior medical officer said:

> Some girls talk too much in the air; they worry the pilot and the patient, and nothing will stop them. I suppose they get excited. The others are very good. They have a test after training. They are taught how to put the stretcher in the opening specially made for it in the plane. They learn how to give oxygen and how to recognise the effects of lack of oxygen. The symptoms of this are different in various people. Difficulty in breathing is usual, but some appear as if they have had too much to drink; they become unco-operative and pugnacious. To those in normal health oxygen is given at fifteen thousand feet but people suffering from lung or heart conditions need it at a much lower altitude. No instructions on administering the oxygen are given to the Orderly, she has to recognise the signs of oxygen lack for herself.[9]

Nor did some aircrew like the idea of having a woman on their aircraft. WAAF Corporal Myra Roberts was given a bad time by her pilot:

> I joined RAF station Blakehill Farm, Wiltshire, for training in Air Evacuation of Casualties early in 1944. 'Farm' was the right word for the place, for we were knee-deep in mud. There were twenty of us WAAF attached to the crews of Dakota aircraft for air experience, and we flew whenever they did. In addition we had training in dinghy drill at Bath Swimming Pool, in case we ever came down in the sea. In the pool we learnt

how to get a huge rubber dinghy right-side-up in the water, how to climb in and how to pull wounded men in also. Part of the specialist nursing training was given at Wroughton RAF hospital. All this was fine; it was purposeful and enjoyable.

It was when we got airborne that my troubles began. I had never been bothered with air-sickness and enjoyed flying, but whenever my pilot, a Scottish warrant officer called Jock McCannell, got into the air, he flung the Dakota about the sky as if he were a circus stunt-flyer in a Tiger Moth. This happened on every occasion whatever the weather conditions, and I finally got the impression that he might have been trying to get rid of me. After a particularly gruelling flight one afternoon, I waited until we had landed and then I tottered towards him, feeling sick, weak and sweaty but still with enough anger inside me to keep me going as I asked him whatever did he think he was doing. Was he trying to get rid of me?

I was surprised by his answer. In his broad Scottish brogue he confessed that he came from a fishing family and in that village fishermen would never put to sea with a woman in the boat as it was bad luck. There was nothing personal about it. A few days later all the women were grounded. It was 6 June 1944. All our aircraft took part in the airborne parachute dropping. One of the few aircraft not to return was that of Jock McCannell. I couldn't help thinking of what he had told me of a woman in a boat bringing bad luck.

Six days later it was Myra's turn to be operational, and 13 June was not a day to be thinking of being unlucky. Her story of the first trip to be made by women air ambulance orderlies, like so many war-time experiences, had an ending more coincidental than a fiction-writer would dare to make it:

We, the Air Ambulance Pool, as we were termed, were summoned to headquarters for a pep talk by Director General of RAF Medical Services, Sir Harold Whittingham. He chose three of us: Edna Birkbeck, as she was then, Lydia Alford and myself. We were to collect our gear and be fitted with parachutes and spend the night in station sick-quarters to be ready for an early start. We were wakened before dawn, given our 'flying meal' – an aircrew breakfast of bacon and egg, sausage and beans, a luxury in those days of strict rationing, and then taken out to our aircraft with our medical panniers of equipment and the large flasks of hot tea which were to be so popular with the wounded. The aircraft was already loaded with supplies of various kinds, mostly ammunition and weaponry, so there was no Red Cross insignia on the plane. The Air Chief Marshal came to wish us 'bon voyage', and he gave me a newspaper to read on the outward journey. I recall thinking, 'How silly! Does he think I shall be reading a newspaper?' I was far too busy watching the accompanying fighter cover and wondering what the next few hours had in store for me …

Our three planes landed in Normandy on an airstrip which really was a cornfield with a metal strip laid down the middle as a runway. Having flown over the coast, which was an indescribable scene of boats and ships of every size and shape, barrage balloons and all the debris of the landings, our three planes were quickly unloaded of supplies, and we busied ourselves with the task of getting the wounded aboard. Lydia's plane took off for the UK almost immediately, but the weather closed in and Edna and I were told that we should have to wait for a couple of hours until the weather improved.

We were taken on a short tour of the area by a newspaper correspondent towards Caen, where the action was fierce. We could see the shelling and bombing ahead, and there were still snipers around, so it was not wise to hang about. We pulled into a farmyard where we were given some food. On the way back to the airfield we passed convoys of soldiers moving up to the 'front' and columns of soldiers marching along in single file keeping close to the hedgerows. When they saw us in the jeep, one yelled: 'Blimey, Women!' [How often now has that reaction been recorded?] I can still recall the scene so vividly. Whilst we were at the farm I was given a large bouquet of flowers by a very shy and pretty young girl called Giselle.

When we got back to our aircraft, they were ready to take off, with wounded stowed on stretchers packed tightly one against the other and with hardly room for me to move. Edna's plane took off and our pilot had just given his engines a final burst and was beginning to roll when an ambulance came tearing up alongside. We stopped. A young medical officer dashed up to our open door and said, 'I'm sorry to do this to you on your first trip but I have a very badly wounded soldier with no place to keep him. He probably won't make it but for God's sake don't let him die on the aircraft. Do your very best!'

My first thoughts were, 'Why me?' But I was soon busy fixing him up with oxygen should he need it and making sure that he knew he was going home. I held his hand tightly during take-off. He was repeating a few choice words in Welsh, which I understood and told him so. He was terribly smashed up. I gathered he was from Tywyn. I was glad to be able to hand him over, still alive, with the other casualties, and I wondered if he would make it but I didn't think he would.

As this was the first trip for women in the Air Ambulance Service, we were met with a battery of newspaper men and photographers as well as the BBC wireless team – as it was then called. Can you imagine my mother's shock when a neighbour ran into her house that evening shouting: 'Put your wireless on ... Myra's on ... She's in France!' This was the first inkling my mother had of what I was doing.

The strange coincidence happened six years later. I was living with my husband in Bryncrug, and he came home one day and said that an ex-soldier riding around in an invalid carriage had stopped him and asked, 'Who was that lady I saw you with last evening?' My husband said it was his wife. The man – 'I.G.' – told him that he had remembered my face as he had seen my picture in the paper the day after he had been brought home and that he knew I had helped him home. I met him the next day and we celebrated with a drink in his local. He was minus one arm and one leg but lived for another twenty years afterwards.

The long arm of coincidence stretches out frequently to touch us all, by somehow linking together actors in the drama of life. Myra, though, experienced an even stranger coincidence:

> It happened whilst I was working in the Central Middlesex Hospital in London after the war. A young Roman Catholic priest was doing his rounds. We got chatting and talking of war-time experiences. I told him that I had been flying over Europe, and he immediately asked if I had known a girl called Margaret Campbell. I said yes, but that she was the one girl in our group who was lost, presumed killed. He then told me that he had been a prisoner of war in enemy territory when he had been asked to bury the crew of an aircraft which had been shot down nearby. Margaret Campbell was amongst the crew he had buried. It all came back to me then. How Margaret had taken off that day with no casualties aboard and just before the door was closed she waved and called to me, 'I'll keep that date!' That was the last I saw of her. Now she had been in touch again. Almost from the dead.

The Air Ambulance Service, which had started as an experiment, worked so well that it was re-trained and expanded as a most efficient evacuation service right to the end of the war. There were some hiccoughs at first, when conditions for women were somewhat primitive:

> Finding a suitable hedge to get behind when your air ambulance is in the middle of a field could be a problem [said Myra]. 'I remember the day when several planes landed on the strip. We were waiting around for casualties to be brought in, and spending a penny became a problem. We were doing a little reconnoitring to find somewhere suitable when a young pilot officer came by and said: 'Can I help you, girls? Are you looking for something?'
> 'Yes,' said Rose. 'We're looking for a hedge that we can get behind.' Poor chap, he blushed so red that he did not know what to say and walked away muttering apologetically. He must have said something to someone though, for soon we had a little canvas thing rigged with a bucket and two RAF chaps on guard, bless him.

It was not always quiet on those airstrips. Being so close to the front, they would occasionally come under shellfire. 'One day we were walking around the aircraft to stretch our legs when an elderly Army officer with a lot of gold braid on his red-banded hat came up to us and said, "This is a very historic moment, ladies. Here you are, British women on French soil risking your lives for your country!" The next moment he was flat on his face on the ground. We thought he had fainted with the emotion, but not a bit of it! He was yelling at us to get down as they were shelling the airstrip. They were too! Shells were bursting nearer and nearer. We made a very quick get-away from that landing strip. And we never went back.'

Wounded troops were flown back to air evacuation centres in Britain. At one of the biggest of these worked Edna Treacy,[10] a nineteen-year-old airwoman, part of a team keeping the operating theatres working day and night. Apart from her daily duties, she was on call every second night, and it is one of those nights that she now remembers so vividly and sadly, for an unusual proposition was put to her.

'I was asleep in bed that night when the hooter sounded at 11.45 pm. Hurriedly I dressed, washed and raced across to the Reception Centre where the others were already scrubbing up and donning masks and gowns.'

Patients were wheeled in on stretchers laid on trolleys, and it was Edna's job to find out exactly what the injury was and then cut off the mud and blood-stained clothing so that the wound could be cleansed by either a nurse or herself. Porters would then push the patients into the operating theatre or one of the wards. It was the last of her patients that night whom Edna remembers so well.

He was a very young soldier who was thoroughly disgusted with himself for being brought home with a septic toe. But he was obviously suffering with it, although he insisted it was nothing. The doctor had a look at him and said he would operate as soon as he could that night, to stop the trouble spreading any further.

As I got him ready for the theatre he told me his name was Jim and that he hoped to be back with the lads in a week. He had some idea that he was shirking his duty in coming back with such an ailment.

I began to ask him the usual questions. When I got to 'Any false teeth?' he replied, 'No, or glass eyes, so will you marry me?'

I laughed and said, 'Certainly, when you are better.' I was quite sure he was joking.

Then I suddenly realised that he meant it.

Edna Treacy had met similar situations in the past where patients had told her they were in love with her – it is not an uncommon experience for nurses. But with this young soldier, Jim, she soon saw there was a difference. 'He did not see anything strange in the fact that we had never seen each other before.'

Any further progress with Jim's proposition was halted at that moment by the arrival of the theatre sister, who came in to say that he would be having a small operation in about an hour and that, if Edna would get him a magazine to read, she could then go off duty for the night. But on hearing this Jim sat up on his stretcher and begged the sister to let Edna stay with him, as she was his fiancée. The sister looked incredulously at Edna, who blushed with embarrassment, and took Jim's words for fact, saying, 'Wasn't it lucky you were on call tonight. But don't stay too long as you must be very tired.'

When the door had closed behind the sister, Edna turned to the young soldier and said he must be crazy – she had no intention of getting involved deeply with someone she did not really know. However, she felt sorry for him and stayed until he was called in the operating theatre. That was when Edna should normally have gone back to her room, but she did not.

Somehow I felt held back and went with him into the room. Before he had his injection he looked at me and said, 'Think over what I asked you and tell me your answer tomorrow.'

I thought to myself, this man is afraid. So I smiled and consented.

'Now,' said the anaesthetist, 'take a deep breath with me and you will soon fall asleep', and he clamped the mask over his face. This was all new to me for I had not worked in the theatre. But I had learnt all about it and soon realised that something was amiss. I saw an oxygen mask being put on the patient and realised that he was not breathing. I suddenly felt very tired watching the doctor. I knew Jim was dead.

Edna Treacy walked back to her room, wondering what it all meant. Why should this young man have come back from the war to die only an hour after they had met? And what of the ring he had said he had in his kitbag?

Later, looking back on that night, Edna was to write: 'Had some girl sent the ring back to him when he was away fighting? If so I was strangely happy that I had in some small way comforted him in his last hour on earth.'

In June 1944 a new hazard had suddenly appeared on those southern English airfields. In the early hours of 13 June, precisely one week after D-Day, the first flying-bomb hit Britain. Two hundred crashed down within the next forty-eight hours, and 3,000 more followed during the next five weeks.

Though they were aimed at the Greater London area, parts of Sussex and Kent – called 'Bomb Alley' because they lay on the route – paid a heavy toll. Bombs also fell far and wide over the countryside from Hampshire to Suffolk. One landed close to Churchill's home at Westerham, killing, by a cruel mischance, twenty-two homeless children and five adults gathered in a refuge made for them in the woods.[11] The bombs came over by day and by night, in all weathers, at irregular intervals, so that people never felt safe.

This new flying-bomb, the first of Hitler's so-called 'terror weapons', the V-1, known as the 'doodle-bug' or 'buzz bomb' by the British, was a small pilotless aeroplane carrying a ton of explosive. It flew at 400 mph on a pre-set course controlled by internal mechanism; when the course was completed, the engine cut out abruptly, and the bomb dived to earth, to explode viciously on impact and before penetrating the building or ground. It was this design feature which helped to save the life of Doris Whitehead (now Mrs Boon) who was serving at the Air Ministry that June, as she recalls:

We were billeted in a tall Victorian building, made into flats in the heart of South Kensington. I shared a room devoid of furniture, with three other girls. We slept on palliasses on the floor, uniforms folded neatly at our feet, steel helmets and gas masks at the ready.

One warm Sunday evening, I was taking leave of my parents after a forty-eight-hour pass. My father had been busy in the garden and, as I kissed him goodbye, he put into my hand a small pot containing a bright red geranium. 'This'll cheer the place up,' he said. But sitting on the bus with the pot carefully wedged at the side of my gas mask, I was wondering just where I could put it in the billet. When I did get in, there was loud laughter from my room-mates when they saw what I was carrying, and even louder when they saw what I did next. I lifted up the sash window and placed the pot on the ledge outside. I remember looking out at the night, calm and full of stars and very warm, so, as we had put out the light, I left the window open.

'We've got a spy amongst us. She's just signalled the enemy,' they giggled. After some more giggling and chattering, we snuggled down to sleep.

Soon after that the air-raid siren went, and with it, came the feared menacing 'zoom-zoom, zoom-zoom' of the flying-bomb.

All awake and alert now, we lay, straining our ears, listening for engine cut-out and the ominous silence which preceded the explosion. The first was frighteningly near, the second even louder and closer. The third one hovered overhead and stopped ... The explosion which followed seemed no louder than the previous ones, only this time the whole building shook and rocked, the dim lights on the landing went out and there were sounds of shattering glass.

Hurriedly and awkwardly I groped in the darkness for my jacket but couldn't find it. A disembodied voice issued commands in a quiet, even tone. Obeying these, we picked up our blankets to cover our shoulders, grappled with the steel helmets, put them on and made our way downstairs. The whole operation was entirely orderly; there was no panic, no screaming, and it seemed that none of us had been hurt, I thought. We reached the front door, now lying flat on the pavement and spattered with blood, in about three minutes. But it must have been longer for as we stepped outside there was the dreaded zoom-zoom of yet another flying-bomb. We did hurry then, across the road to the air-raid shelter. There were some Army lads there, with strong arms and reassuring chitchat, guiding us down the steps to safety. Huddled in groups, we saw an unusually silent crowd of girls, exchanging only whispers as we waited for the 'All Clear'. It sounded just as the sky was lightening, and shortly afterwards trucks manned by RAF lads came to take us to the deep shelters under the British Museum. There, beneath that solid structure, there were beds made up with sheets and blankets into which we tumbled thankfully.

After a short sleep we were awakened and provided with soap and towels and then, after a wash and brush up, but still in our pyjamas, for we had nothing else, we went up the wide staircase to the Egyptian Room for breakfast. The hissing tea urns and smell of reconstituted powdered egg had never been more welcome. High above us Pharaoh, with his bodyguard of spear-carrying fighting men and retinue of slaves, proceeded majestically along a cobalt-blue frieze, sublimely indifferent to the plight of the present warriors below.

Breakfast over, an emergency pay parade was organized. We had lost everything, including money, our immediate priority being to have something to clean our teeth with. But as toothbrushes were not on the list of RAF stores, someone doubled off to the nearest chemist, who was no doubt surprised at the sudden clearance of his stock of toothbrushes but left in blissful ignorance as to the reason. We had the warning branded on our breasts: 'CARELESS TALK COSTS LIVES.'

I hugged my toothbrush to me, refusing to be parted from it, even sleeping with it under my pillow. It was my only real possession. Not that any of us wasted time mourning over our losses, we were too thankful to have got out alive, though in passing I was sorry to have left my twenty-first birthday present, a Parker pen, in my jacket pocket. It seemed like a miracle to me when, the next day, my jacket was returned to me, complete with pen, wallet and usual contents all there, undamaged. The jacked had been picked up by a WAAF on the floor above mine as she stumbled over it on the way down. Such was the mysterious effect of blast, that the same blast which had saved my jacket by blowing it upstairs had killed six WAAF who were up there. Upon their bodies was not a sign of injury.

Because we had no clothes, it took three days before we were kitted out sufficiently to emerge, mole-like, from our burrow beneath the British Museum, to mingle in the bright sunshine with summer-frocked girls and men in shirtsleeves, who spared us not a passing glance. It seemed incredible how little the public knew of what was going on.

Secrecy was vital and strictly adhered to. For this reason the memorial service for our dead companions was deliberately low key, only local RAF personnel and relatives of the dead attending. By this time we were housed in a block of luxury flats, with bedsteads and lockers and a bathroom to every six girls. When finally we ventured to take a look at our old quarters, we were not prepared for the shock of seeing such a gaunt, empty shell which was all that remained. The bomb, we were told, had hit the tip of the roof and exploded upwards. Had it fallen to the ground before exploding, this account would probably never have been written.

It seems miraculous that anyone survived that particular bomb. Another WAAF, B.R. Marks, who was billeted at the British Museum then (as one of the women whom neighbouring soldiers called 'museum pieces'), remembers how she came out of the cellar that day and saw the poignant remains of the WAAF hostel, '... with personal effects, bits of clothing, handbags and hats dangling from the trees alongside the shattered remains of the building'.

These new bombing attacks imposed a far greater strain on the British than had the Blitz of 1940 and 1941. The suspense and stress were more prolonged, as Churchill was to write: 'A man going home in the evening never knew what he would find; his wife, alone all day or with the children, could not be sure of his safe return. The blind impersonal nature of the missile made the individual on the ground feel helpless. There was little that he could do, no human enemy that he could see shot down.'[12]

The women of the mixed anti-aircraft batteries could see plenty, though. Once again they were in the forefront of the action.

The Prime Minister's daughter Mary, serving in Violette Szabo's old battery, was quickly in action.[13] By this time the battery was stationed in Hyde Park, and on the morning of 18 June Mary had a visit from her mother, who had left the Prime Minister at Chequers. As she arrived, the battery went into action. One bomb had passed over it and flattened a house in Bayswater Road, and as mother and daughter were standing together on the grass of the park, they saw a tiny black object dive out of the clouds which looked as though it would fall on Downing Street. Churchill's car had just been sent there to collect mail, and as the driver turned into the street, he was astonished to find all the people in Parliament Square flat on their faces on the pavement. There was a dull explosion, and then they all went about their business. The bomb had fallen on the Guards' Chapel at Wellington Barracks, during a special service for which a large number of Guards Brigade members had gathered. There was a direct hit. The whole building was demolished in a second, and nearly 200 people, including many distinguished officers and their relations and friends, were killed.

It soon became clear that the anti-aircraft batteries could be far more effective if they were concentrated south of London, where their radar for fire-control would have more scope. Thus the Ack-Ack women were suddenly ordered to leave their cosy beds and huts, which they had made more homely with gay curtains and even carpets. They were hustled into trucks and driven to windswept areas further south, to live under canvas and fight the bombs in the Tunbridge Wells area.

So successful were they that within a few days the guns were moving right to the coast, where the gun crews had an uninterrupted view of the bombs as they approached Britain. 'The huts we lived in were holiday chalets with walls as thin as cardboard. I remember we always seemed to have wet feet and wet blankets,' said former gunner Lynne Griffiths.

Now these women were living and working with guns concentrated all around them, in the midst of the most terrific shellfire. The sky was dotted with explosions of thousands of shells, and around them were the awful explosions of the falling flying-bomb. The women's tin-hats never left them. They wore them on duty and at snatched meals and when they slept they balanced them over their faces. One news report was typical of the bravery of these girls then:

> She was a sentry on air duty, watching the sky when she saw a bomb coming directly at the gun site. In that split second when a decision had to be made, she did not run to shelter, but stood where she was and pressed the alarm. Her action meant that only three persons were killed instead of a certain twenty-four.
>
> The men on another gun site are fond of telling the story of how they shot down their first flying bomb – as the bomb fell all the men rushed to the shelter, but the ATS just stood and cheered, although the bomb crashed down only a few hundred yards from where they stood! Later the girls learnt to dash into their slit trenches for safety as quickly as any man.[14]

Another tribute to the Ack-Ack girls' courage and skill, in the same report, came from a visiting US colonel: 'I have seen some marvellous things in this country but nothing like the Ack-Ack girls. How calm they seem to be with the shells screaming all around them and knowing that any one of those missiles can bring a flying bomb on top of them!'

Ruth Negus, who had been roughing it on a Thames Estuary site, remembers well that hurried move to the southern gun positions and the pressure of non-stop action:

We lived in denims during the day and changed into battledress after work. The flying-bomb battle made life very intense. We slept completely dressed and in plimsolls. It was difficult for us to get a proper wash or any sleep as everyone was fully stretched. Even the cooks and orderlies were pressed into service. All leave was cancelled and mail censored. I was in personal agony then as I had a whitlow on my finger and the only primitive treatment was soaking it in hot water. When I went again to the medical officer, he just lanced it with a scalpel before it was ready and before even asking me to sit down. That was followed by an abscess in my ear for which the ear was syringed with cold water, and after that a series of sties. No antibiotics then!

Pearl Drake-Witts working with the Women's Land Army on farms in the area, had a strange story to tell of doodle-bug problems: 'Several of our cows were ill, and some died after swallowing bits of fallen doodle-bugs.'

Peggy Linington (then Corporal Hennessey) was in 627 (mixed) Heavy Ack-Ack Battery under canvas at Foulness Island. 'And foul it was!' she recalls. 'We pitched tents in the mud as it was reclaimed land.

A thick mist always hung there, and it was so cold that we were given rum rations at times. There were three of us to a tent with iron beds on duckboards with bits of sacks separating one from the other. The lavatory was so far away and we had to cross over a stream with a plank of wood for a bridge. Well, those tin helmets were useful; in lots of ways. And when we moved the tents later, there were little patches of yellow on the grass. There was nowhere we could bath on the camp, so we asked local people if they would let us use theirs. Whilst the doodle-bugs were coming, there was little chance of a pass for an evening out.'

By 6 July 2,750 buzz bombs had been launched against London, coming over a score at a time. Eileen Kisby was cooking Sunday dinner for her FANY unit at Oxted then: 'I went outside when they first started coming that morning, and the sky was full of them, going straight overhead towards London. They were like a plague of locusts almost but far more frightening. Nearby was a barrage balloon unit and we just hoped one of them would not hit their cables for we'd already been blown out of our billet twice. The first time the window of the front room sailed outwards, and the next time all our belongings were sucked straight out of the window, but none of us was hurt. Blast is a funny thing. I went under the stairs when things got really bad.'

Soon the Spitfires, anti-aircraft guns and balloon barrages got the measure of these doodle-bugs, so that Churchill was able to say at the end of August that not one bomb in seven got through the defensive screen.

He was to write: 'The record bag was on 28th August when ninety-four bombs approached our coast and all but four were destroyed. The balloons caught two, the fighters twenty-three and the guns sixty-five.'[15]

Lynne Griffiths remembers those days well: 'We were stationed at Folkestone, "Hell Fire Corner". In three days our battery shot down over a hundred. We were very proud.'

Clearly Hitler's terror weapon, the V-1, had been mastered, but by then 15,500 houses had been destroyed and 69,000 were in need of repair; 50,000 building workers from all over Britain were brought in to tackle the job of getting a roof over people's heads. Those who could leave London had already left, but the nerves of those who remained were frayed ragged, as US Captain Harry Butcher, on General Eisenhower's staff, noted in his diary: 'People are semi-dazed from loss of sleep and have the jitters which shows whenever a door bangs or a motor cycle engine starts'.[16]

'It was on a day when 122 buzz bombs landed in London that FANY driver Kay Summersby received a call from Eisenhower. She had to drive him in the bullet-proof Daimler, his 'Al Capone car', to Bushey Park to reconnoitre a suitable place for his new headquarters, away from the city and the bombs. Whilst driving there, he told her an alarming piece of news he had just heard. A captured German, aged eighteen, had told interrogators about a new chemical-filled rocket which on explosion would destroy, by burning, an area of twenty-five square kilometres (some fifteen square miles). These would be fired as Germany's last hope of preventing defeat.

To meet this new menace, reserve nurses all over Britain were mobilized to empty all London hospital beds; 36,000 were cleared ready for the onslaught. Dorothy Brody remembers how she travelled up and down the York to King's Cross railway line in a meat-wagon train converted to carry tiers of stretcher cases filled with the sick who could be moved to beds in the provinces. May Elliott was called up as a nursing auxiliary to St Mary's, Manchester; Freda Howard, who had not nursed for years, was sent to join a medical team in the Masonic Hall at Cheshunt. In a feverish rush to find beds quickly, buildings were being requisitioned as casualty reception wards.

The prospect loomed of London being devastated as never before. These new rockets, launched from the Netherlands, rose fifty miles into the air at nearly 4,000 mph. There was no warning of their arrival: the first one knew was the tremendously loud explosion, followed by the high-pitched whirring sound of their passage downwards through the air.

'There was nothing we could do against them,' said Ruth Negus. 'They could not be tracked on our radar, and it was for us a very worrying time, wondering what was happening to our relatives in London.'

It was also 'a very worrying time' for the Supreme Commander, General Eisenhower. His thoughts were mainly with the men fighting inland from the beaches of Normandy but, just as he was going over to France, Prime Minister Churchill shuffled into his office, and Kay Summersby recorded in her diary: that the Prime Minister was very concerned about the rockets. She asked Eisenhower to give the launching sites priority over everything except urgent needs of the battle.[17]

Kay Summersby now occupied a unique position with the Supreme Commander. She was at his elbow most of the time. No longer was she merely a driver: she was his intimate confidante and support, privy to problems that piled up on his desk on top of all the tactics and logistics of battle.

Every day brought new shocks, new distractions, that drained his energy. A trainload of German prisoners were found suffocated to death when the wagons were opened on arrival at the camp; both American and British troops were vandalizing and pillaging the French countryside; soldiers were refusing to take prisoners and killing them instead (partly condoned by their commanders); French civilians who had stayed behind in Normandy were being robbed, raped and murdered; French generals complained that Americans were a more drunken and disorderly lot than the Germans.

And so it went on, problem after problem. Kay Summersby, worried by all this, wrote in her diary: 'Many cases of rape and murder and pillage are causing complaints by the French and Dutch. Strong measures will have to be taken. E. suggests there should be a public hanging particularly in the case of rape'.[18]

The death sentences for murder that Eisenhower had to review multiplied. Executions were held at or near the scene of the crime, and the immediate family of the victim and civic officials of the town were present to see the execution, to prove to the civil population that everything possible was being done to bring about justice. In all 454 GIs were sentenced to death by courts martial.*

No wonder Eisenhower looked ill, drawn and tired, complaining of ringing in his ears, for he was fighting a war in two theatres: martial and matrimonial. His American wife, Mamie, was something special to him, but she was 3,000 miles away, whilst his British driver and aide, Kay, was with him constantly. He wrote passionate letters to Mamie, saying how much he missed her and how he looked forward to the war's ending so that he could spend his retirement with her, travelling. And, perhaps, as a fantastic after-thought, he added that he could also be writing his memoirs to make money for expenses and bring a secretary along to whom he could dictate for an hour or so a day. Mamie did not rise to that one and wrote one of her griping letters, spiced with darts like: 'Such tales I've heard!' Mamie's irritability upset the Supreme Commander, who then found solace in his Western magazines, endless cups of coffee, chain-smoking, bridge and holding Kay's hand.[19]

This strange relationship between the Commander with the driver had burgeoned in Algiers. Perhaps it had something to do with the quasi-Oriental atmosphere there, for many of the generals were afflicted in the same way with an urge for female company. The most notorious womanizer was the fifty-nine-year-old General George Patton, with his Buck Rogers image and pearl-handled six-shooters at the hip. He was a self-styled connoisseur of the European female form, savouring statuesque Frenchwomen, who reminded him, he said, of 'the British locomotive with two buffers in front and powerful driving wheels behind'. He boasted of ordering nine condoms for a four-day visit to London, and his constant companion was his young and beautiful

.

* Of the 454 GIs sentenced to death by courts martial only 70 were executed – all except 1 for non-military offences like rape and murder. Executions were held near scenes of the crime and immediate family of victims and civil officials were present to see executions.

niece from Boston (his daughter's age), of whom he boasted, in an oddly old-fashioned manner, 'She has been mine for twelve years.' He feared no man, only his wife, Beatrice.

Then there was Air Marshal Tedder's girlfriend in Algiers, a 'big bossy Belgian blonde', Mrs Marie de Seton Black, whom he later married. General Everett-Hughes had 'J.P.', and General Walter Bedell Smith got into 'some personal entanglement' with a Nurse Wilbur, whom Eisenhower wanted to fire but was persuaded not to.[20]

Ironically, the promiscuity of women at Allied Headquarters Algiers annoyed Eisenhower intensely, especially the activities of some of the Women's Army Corps, whom he accused of 'unsoldierly comportment', admonishing them to mend their ways or quit. Forty-one of them obliged and went home. Eisenhower did not mince his words when talking of that type of woman, and it is said that he was '... possibly the origin of the scurrilous definition of a WAC that found its way into Everett Hughes' diary: "A double-breasted GI with a built in fox-hole".'[21]

Eisenhower's paradoxical feelings about extra-marital love-affairs seemed, on the surface, to have had little effect on his own relationship with Kay Summersby. It became a juicy morsel of gossip not only for staff officers and their wives but also for soldiers. Eisenhower once complained to General Patton that one day, when he was out horse-riding with Kay, a soldier had 'Yahooed at us'. And, to Patton's disgust, Eisenhower had only 'glared at the man'.

Not surprisingly, Mamie Eisenhower was not left in the dark. Her friends could not help remarking how fortunate her husband was to have such a talented and attractive British woman to drive him round the capitals and battlefields of Europe, as well as acting as hostess at dinner parties.

Kay's unique position in the Eisenhower ménage caused many an eyebrow to be raised. When, for example, Prime Minister Winston Churchill, together with his Chief of General Staff, General Sir Alan Brooke, visited Eisenhower in his small 'forward headquarters', Kay Summersby presided at the head of the table. Brooke, accustomed to the rigid hierarchy of the British Army, was astonished.[22]

At that stage of the war in north-west Europe, Eisenhower was under tremendous strain. Allied tanks were proving to be much inferior to the German, with their four-inch armour plating. His generals were warring amongst themselves; Air Marshal Tedder wanted Montgomery to be sacked, and the French General de Gaulle was being particularly unco-operative, 'obstructing with even more virtuosity than in Algiers'.[23]

No wonder Supreme Commander Eisenhower looked worn, tired and older; his left eye was sore and 'angry', and he had had a ringing in his ears for over a month. He needed all the help he could get from his own personal staff, to whom he was later to pay tribute.[24] And who could say how right his deputy, General Everett-Hughes, was when he said to one of Kay's colleagues who was complaining about Kay's privileged position: 'Maybe Kay will help Ike win the war.'[25]

But that was not the only war to be won. On the other side of the world a different kind of war raged, and it was being fought by what Lord Mountbatten called a 'forgotten army' – the Fourteenth Army of the Far East Asia Command.

There, right up with the forward troops, were British and Commonwealth women.

8 Not for the Squeamish!

At first the women were kept carefully back at GHQ
and secure bases, but as their record for helpfulness
grew, so did the scope of their duties in positions
progressively nearer the front. Nurses had, of course,
long been accepted as a necessary contingent of a
fighting force. From the outset of this war our nurses
lived up to traditions tracing back to Florence
Nightingale. Consequently it was difficult to
understand the initial resistance to the employment
of women in other activities.

Dwight D. Eisenhower, *Crusade in Europe*

Spring 1944 – Spring 1945

The old Dakota aircraft lurched and fell like a lift out of control as it
approached a shallow depression in the bamboo-dotted, abandoned
paddyfields strewn with coils of rusty barbed wire, heaps of mangled
metal and burnt-out skeletons of planes that had landed there once too
often. Without circling or calling control, the Dakota came straight in
and bumped to a stop at the end of a roughly made runway. Its engines
cut, the fuselage door banged open to let in the glare of the mid-day sun
and a harsh voice shouting: 'Wakey, wakey! This is journey's end.' Sister
Winifred Beaumont had arrived at Imphal.

There, in the spring of 1944, the British Fourteenth Army –
'forgotten' by everyone except the Japanese – had fought a bitter
campaign to hold the key towns of Kohima and Imphal, blocking the
Japanese advance into India. For the whole of the month of April, each
of these towns had been surrounded by a Japanese army led by General
Sato, who cared not how many of his soldiers died as long as he took his
objectives. At Kohima and Imphal he failed. He lost 53,000 men; the
British, Indian and Nepalese forces lost 14,700.[1] Now the latter were
fighting back but suffering terribly in the process, clawing their way up
the hills, scrabbling ankle-deep in grey, clinging mud, their arms, legs
and faces so scratched, bitten and septic that they turned into
non-healing ulcers. Malaria, dysentery and malnutrition took their toll
too. All hospital beds were full. More nurses were needed.

As Sister Beaumont and her two colleagues clambered out of the

Dakota, screwing up their eyes in the strong sunlight, a huge, barrel-chested man with a bushy black beard shouted in astonishment: '*Women! This means screens round the latrines!*'[2]

Early the next morning the new nurses were busy at work in the tented thousand-bed hospital, moving quickly between tightly packed rows of iron bedsteads, each with a khaki mosquito-net fixed to the head-bars. Beds were never empty, for in that jungle war seven times as many men were out of action from sickness or disease as were killed or wounded by the enemy. In the Imphal hospital, Sister Beaumont recalled that every patient had a wound and a skin infection; most had jungle sores, dysentery and malaria as well. She was horrified to see a gritty film of dust lay over everything, including the patients. Equipment was battered or non-existent. In the dressing tent she found a small enamel bowl of dirty water which was the only means of scrubbing up between patients.

She found there was an appalling lack of hygiene, for traditional standards had disappeared altogether. 'I watched with horror,' she wrote, 'the first time I saw a meal served in the ward. An Indian orderly brought in a pail of stew, and using an enamel mug, went from bed to bed and filled a rusty mess tin for each man. To make sure every patient received a just quota of meat, he conscientiously scooped the bottom of the pail at each refill, plunging his arm up to the elbow in the brew each time.'

One of Sister Beaumont's first duties every day was the ritual of the mepacrine round, to check malaria. Each man had to say, 'Thank you, Sister', to make sure he had swallowed the tablet. Some men had been known to spit it out.

Threats to health came from all sides. Sulphonamide drugs were given to control dysentery; and the threat of dehydration, due to the intense heat of the day, was met by adding salt to all drinks. They never had a decent cup of tea. 'Tea was made from muddy, heavily chlorinated water and salt added to the milk and sugar.' To make the brew more palatable for troops and staff each bucket of tea was laced with a measure of rum.

Yet there were few complaints about food and drink, both of which were in short supply. Somehow the men and the women there managed to rise above their miseries. They were all part of a team doing a job that had to be done, fighting an enemy whose bestiality knew no bounds – an enemy who had, for example, marched twenty-four nurses down a beach into the sea waist-deep and mown them down from behind with machine-guns, as the only survivor, Nurse Vivian Bullwinkle, was later to testify.[3]

Pride in doing the job as well as they could gave everyone strength and fortified their morale. Letters from home helped too. But not always. Inevitably there were letters from self-righteous busybodies that did more damage to morale than all the hardships inflicted by the jungle or Japanese. Sister Beaumont has never forgotten the day when she was cheerfully handing out the letters which had arrived: she was, on this day, especially pleased to be able to give a letter to a little man who had just arrived back from the front. He was pleased too. A little later, when mosquito nets were down, she was serving the medicines by the light of a hurricane lamp. She heard a sound and knew what it meant. 'I swung round and swept up the little man's net. I was too late. He had cut his throat with a razor blade and managed to sever the jugular vein. It was another one of those letters telling him of "goings on that he should know".'4

The death shocked the ward. Sister Beaumont took the suggestion that a patient staggered out of bed to make. She unlocked the heavy box in which the rum was stored and went round the ward giving each patient a tot.

Before leaving their embarkation camp in Britain every nurse going overseas was issued with a Red Cross arm-band and told to wear it when in a forward area, but once she arrived in Imphal, Sister Beaumont soon had this notion knocked out of her head: The unit security officer explained to her that Japs always made a special target of the red-cross emblem. He went on to suggest that each Sister should be given a hand gun with at least one bullet in it, so that she could shoot herself rather than fall into Japanese hands.

The Japanese were fighting ferociously that May of 1944. They had been told that victory in Asia depended on defeating the British at Imphal. They resisted savagely the Fourteenth Army's advance, and casualties of every colour and creed came into that hospital. Some had the strangest of customs. The Gurkhas – among the finest fighters of the world – who would never sheath their lethally curved kukri knives until the task was finished, suffered very heavy losses. One night Sister Beaumont was tending a young Gurkha in the high delirium of cerebral malaria, sponging his face and body to comfort him, when her hand brushed against a smelly little bundle tied round the boy's waist. She was about to lift it when the doctor spoke sharply. 'Don't touch it, Sister,' he said. 'They are the ears of his enemies. He is a brave warrior.'

As the battle rolled further into Burma, so the casualties increased. Nurses had to face more gruesome cases than they had ever met or imagined before. Soldiers and civilians all came into their care, terribly mutilated. Refugees and displaced villagers returning to their primitive homes were massacred by booby-traps left for them by the Japanese. Sister Beaumont was on duty when a consignment of wounded women and children were brought into the 87th General Hospital: 'They were lying on stretchers all along the floor of the corridor. I paused beside one and saw two tiny babies lying on it. These two brown little mites were chopped as an ox-tail is chopped for the pot by an exploding bomb. We could not say one word to comfort them and their eyes were clear brown marbles of terror. Mercifully they died.'

Being a theatre sister, Winifred Beaumont was spared little of the shock horrors of war. And she also saw raw courage. An RAF pilot who was brought in one evening and was already on the table when she arrived for duty. His face was covered by a piece of gauze which she carefully lifted and looked into a pair of eyes and a hole. In the crash the joy stick had smashed his nose and mouth, and his lower jaw hung down upon his chest. 'As I looked, the edges of the wound twitched and wrinkled and for one wild moment I thought he was starting a fit. I was mistaken. He could see me and was trying to smile.'

All night long, surgeons, nurses and orderlies worked on the man, who, because of the nature of his injuries, could not be given gas or ether but had to have a series of injections. It was just as the first light of dawn filtered into the tent that the surgeon put down the last of his needles and said, 'He should have a decent face. It's as good as his passport photo now.'[5]

While the Fourteenth Army was pushing forward on a broad central front in Burma and the Allied Armies in Normandy were massing for a break-out from the bridgehead, nurses in Italy were recovering from terrible battle experiences.

In January 1944 British and American assault troops had set out in great secrecy from Naples for a daring landing at Anzio, a small bay between the German lines and Rome. At first, all had gone well, for the force took the Germans completely by surprise. They won a firm bridgehead and brought ashore armour, weaponry of all kinds, supplies and medical units. But then they paused to consolidate the position before making advances. The delay was disastrous. In a few days the whole bridgehead was being raked by machine-gun, mortar and artillery fire. In the thick of it all were the women of three British casualty clearing stations, an American evacuating hospital and American field ambulances.

Sister Sheila Greaves[5] later told how doctors, nurses and orderlies all took spades, shovels and picks and furiously dug deep trenches in which to put the tents for the wounded. Around the tent walls they piled further ramparts of sand and stones for additional protection against shrapnel and mortar bombs.

Off shore, the plight of the nurses was little better. In the hospital carriers *Leinster*, *St Andrew* and *St David* they were under almost continuous attack from artillery and bombers. One evening, after taking casualties off the shore by day, they pulled out to sea when darkness fell, to escape the nightly beach-shelling barrage. Brightly lit with Red Cross emblems fully illuminated, the carriers cruised in close formation waiting for daybreak. Such a target was too tempting for German dive-bombers to resist. They set fire to the *Leinster* and sank the *St David*. Nurses brought as many of the wounded as they could from below and over the rails in the six minutes before the ship sank, and some were still jumping off when the bows finally reared up out of the water as the ship sank, stern first, taking her captain, RAMC commanding officer, several orderlies and two nurses down with her.

For twelve long weeks nurses on that beach-head faced the same hazards and discomforts as the soldiers carrying out their duties, sleeping in wet slit trenches and all the time trying to keep a morale-boosting smart appearance. It was not easy. Beetles got stuck on the face as Sister Brenda McBryde described vividly: 'The cream some still applied at night and their hair was regularly smothered with sand and dust. Once darkness had fallen, no-one left her trench for any purpose whatsoever, and, in the morning, all the Sisters could be seen carrying their tins to the latrines in the most natural way.'[6]

Those latrines were primitive in the extreme. Placed centrally to each unit, they comprised crudely built wooden boxes placed over a roofless slit trench surrounded by waist-high strips of hessian. Like those ATS in the desert these nurses had to decide whether to sit it out brazenly with head and shoulders showing over the top of the hessian looking unperturbed or crouch down and pretend they never went near the place.

The nurses' days were long, working as they were constantly under the noise of gunfire, the explosion of shells and the whizzing of flying shrapnel. Lack of sleep affected everyone. January, February and March slipped by without any progress being made, and it looked as though nothing was going to break the stalemate either on the Anzio beach-head or on the Monte Cassino front to the south. When April sunshine began to warm those Anzio beaches, Rome seemed as far away as ever.

The depressing news from the battle fronts did little to lower the spirits of the chairbound warriors at Allied Force Headquarters in the marble-floored palace at Caserta. There, but a short drive from Naples, ATS Company Sergeant Major Betty Cullum was surprised to find an almost peace-time routine reigning. Personnel, Service and civilian alike, went about their work with little apparent concern for the fierce fighting going on but a few miles to the north. At Caserta the fighting was done with words.

Novelist Eric Ambler[7] remembers going to a concert in the Caserta opera house where, after the conclusion of the show, the staff officers stood and sang, to the tune of 'a well known patriotic folk song':

Stand up and sing the praise of General Clark,
Your hearts and voices raise for General Clark,
Red, white and blue unfurled upon the field,
Its message flaunts Clark's sons will never, never, yield.
We'll fight, fight, fight with heart and hand,
The Fifth's the best Army in the land,
FIGHT, FIGHT, FIGHT!

Betty Cullum, however, had other battles on her hands. She was responsible for, amongst many other things, the discipline and welfare of the ATS women in her unit. As she was to say forty odd years later:

There were 300 girls in the detachment. Most of them were very young and many were wild, men-mad and completely irresponsible. Most of them were conscripts, and some were very resentful at being in uniform at all. One girl refused to wash or change her clothes, and I had the unpleasant task of standing over her whilst the medical orderly scrubbed her from top to toe. Several women went absent without leave, and many of them stayed out all night. At one time there was a very disruptive attitude amongst a group of young girls who rebelled against any form of discipline. Homesickness was often the cause, and the long delays between mail deliveries gave cause for grievance. When letters did arrive, they often came in a bundle all at once with several covering a lengthy period so that they had to be sorted into a date order before you could read them.

Week-end leave was granted once a month as a morale-booster. Some girls went to the YWCA in Naples, Sorrento, Amalfi or Capri. One even stayed with Gracie Fields, who rang up one night to say that the girl had missed the last ferry but would be staying the night at her later famous villa on Capri and would be returning in the morning.

Naples was a den of vice, a most dangerous place for women. Murder, mugging, drug-peddling and prostitution were rife. Much of the city was 'out of bounds' to both male and female personnel. Even in those squalid slum areas not 'off limits', it was dangerous to walk alone. There people lived in the lower depths of degradation and dirt. Children ran about with naked bodies caked with filth; fat-bellied flies clustered over refuse, excrement and food alike; and out of doorways ran ragged children importuning any soldier within earshot: 'Hi Johnnie, jig a jig, *mia sorella, molto bella!*' Others begged for cigarettes, chocolate, petrol, meat, even mosquito-nets (from which they made underpants).

Betty Cullum remembers getting lost one night and finding herself in those narrow slum streets where gangs of Allied deserters, as well as Italian crooks, had their hide-outs with girlfriends. They could exist only by theft and dealing in stolen military goods, and they had no qualms about using their weapons if necessary. 'It was very frightening. There were so many beggars clutching at my clothes I just had to push them away and hurry on. One persistent man turned out later to be from a British Special Investigation squad trying to catch black-marketeers. One of our girls, a Palestinian, was caught in this way, trying to sell Army goods. Stealing was regarded as such a disgraceful and severe offence in Palestine that she went back to her billet and cut her throat.'

There was one even more frightful experience for Betty Cullum, on a night which everyone in Naples remembers to this day. It was the night when the volcano Vesuvius erupted.

Everyone who witnessed that awe-inspiring sight stood spellbound, as enormous fiery clumps shot out from the crater way above the city and fell one over the other as they rolled down the volcano's sides. Orange-red lava gushed from smaller craters lying under and at the sides of the principal cone. It took little imagination to be cast back to the year AD 79 when a similar eruption buried Pompeii and preserved the city in ashes until excavation revealed all its richness of Roman life in 1748. Betty Cullum felt privileged to have been in Naples that day in 1944 and to have witnessed such a memorable event.

As a leave centre, Naples was well supplied with officers', WOs' and NCOs' clubs, NAAFI canteens and leave centres. Wine flowed freely as men came down from the front with a spirit of 'eat, drink and be merry', and those who were not at the front made hay whilst they could. There was no shortage of female Italian company. Soon venereal disease became a problem of great concern. It was classed in Routine Orders as a 'self-inflicted wound' and punished accordingly. Doctors and nurses were kept busy enough with battle casualties and begrudged time spent on VD patients, whose buttocks were energetically pierced with needles and pumped full of the new wonder drug, penicillin.

Whilst the Allied Command was worried by the sexual activity of the soldiers (and officers), the German High Command was positively encouraging it! A truly remarkable letter* found on a German prisoner recently drafted from Germany revealed a new idea direct from the German War Ministry. The translation runs as follows:

State Office for Increase in Birth Rate,
Berlin.

Dear Sir,
As many men have died during the war, it is the responsibility of the living to care for the women and girls, in order to have a steady birth rate.

---

* The authenticity of this letter is vouched for by the Commanding Officer of the Gordon Highlanders, Lt.-Col. Martin Lindsay DSO, MP. The writer visited the location of one of the breeding units in the Harz Mountains in 1970. Details of the breeding programme are held by the Wiener Institute Library, London.

You are thought to be very fit and we ask you kindly to accept this honourable duty. Because of this your wife will not have the right to divorce you but must take it as a necessary consequence of war.

You are detailed to the 12th District of Berlin comprising nine women and seventeen girls. Should you feel unfit for this task, you have to send the name of a good substitute [*eines teuchtigen Ersatzmannes*], together with a certificate of incapacity signed by three doctors.

Should you be able to take over another district too, you become a Breeding Officer and also receive a breeding remuneration; you receive too the birth medal, first class, with red ribbon. You are also exempted from all taxes and have the right to a pension.

We will send you a list of the persons to be visited by you. You should start your fruitful work at once and report the results to this office after nine months.

With German greetings, Personnel Branch of the War Ministry, I.A.[8]

The Allied servicewomen had little contact with Italian men. There was no attraction with the abundance of American servicemen around. 'There were so many at Allied Force Headquarters that it became a problem,' said Betty Cullum. 'They had much more money than the British, who were left out in the cold. Americans always seemed to have silk stockings and make-up to give away, even in Italy. We were forbidden, however, to have anything to do with the black servicemen, and I, for one, felt sorry for them.'

Though the servicewomen had little to do with Italian men, they did frequently visit families, who entertained them as lavishly as their meagre rations permitted. On one occasion, a religious feast-day, Betty Cullum had the rare treat of a magnificent, tasty meal with a family living near Caserta. The family was quite poor, with three small children, and so she arrived with chocolate for them and cigarettes for the father. 'The meal was absolutely delicious. I thoroughly enjoyed it, and it was only when I was thanking them and saying good-bye that I found out what it was – cat! A delicacy for them.' It was a feature of Latin diet the German soldiers would taunt the Italians about, asking if they had eaten any 'roof hares' that day.

And so life at base went on until the hour of battle drew closer and the infantry shuffled into their start lines early in May 1944. For the next few weeks the whole line across Italy flared into fierce fighting. Ten thousand Allied soldiers died. Rome fell on Sunday 4 June, but the glory of taking the city, though sweet, was fleeting. For just one day it was headline news, then it was gone, replaced by greater news still: the Allied landings and advance into Normandy.

The reality of that advance was soon experienced by ATS Corporal

Margaret Doherty, who had landed at Arromanches, Normandy, by LST (Landing Strip Tanks) with twenty other ATS volunteers for duty with 21st Army Group Headquarters.

After Caen had been 'liberated' by the Allies, Margaret Doherty drove into the city, and she has never forgotten a strange sight that confronted her there: 'In the debris-littered square of Caen was a crowd of men and women forming a kind of circle as if they were watching a fight. We went closer and saw a man shaving the heads of women who had collaborated with the Germans.' The witch-hunt had begun. It would soon turn into 'the winter of long knives' as the Resistance, formed and nurtured by the Allies, turned into a monster beyond control, using the charge of 'collaboration' as a cover for avenging personal grudges and political grievances.

In Caen Margaret Doherty saw also the truth in Montgomery's words when he first saw the city: 'It's a queer sort of liberation.' The air raid on the afternoon of D-Day had killed 200 French people, including families taking children to their first communion. And so the advance went on, with the callous disregard for French civilians exemplified in Montgomery's handwritten memo to his Chief of Staff, Frédéric de Guingand: 'Montebourg and Valognes have been "liberated", i.e. they are both completely destroyed! I think Valognes probably wins; it is worse than Ypres in the last war'.[9]

No wonder not all the liberated French were rejoicing – much to the displeasure of General Sir Alan Brooke, who wrote to Churchill that: 'The French population did not seem in any way pleased to see us arrive as a victorious army to liberate France. They had been quite content as they were, and we were bringing war and desolation to their country.'[10]

The stench in those flattened towns and cities through which the Allied armour raced was sickening and all-pervading, clinging to the clothing of all who were near. Mary Walsh, correspondent of *Time*, reported that, 'The corpses are beginning to give off a smell of vinegar and sugar boiling together such as was given off when my mother was putting down 'homemade dill pickles' for the winter.'[11]

Nurses in the tented hospital of 80 and 88, following up the advance, had forsaken their traditional outfits (white caps and grey and scarlet uniforms) and were 'sensibly dressed in khaki silk shirts, drill trousers and with bandeaux round their heads', as the CO of the Gordon Highlanders wrote. 'They never had a moment to call their own.'

Mary Walsh, who went into these hospitals, was struck by the contrast between the bustle of the nurses rushing from bed to bed and the loneliness of those dying. She wrote: 'How terribly alone the wounded and the dying seemed in their anonymity, surrounded by bottles, tubes and medical apparatus. All that linked them to the world outside was the chart above their bed, listing their name, serial number, blood type and unit. That information represented all that was known of them. No one knew or cared which of the bodies had been High School captains or presidents of the local drama club, or hot men on the guitar. Truly, their identity had ceased to be of any account.'

Lieutenant Frances Slanger, a nurse with a forward US hospital, praised the fortitude of her patients in a letter to the *Stars and Stripes* newspaper. She stated: 'Yes, this time we are handing out the bouquets ... after taking care of some of your buddies, seeing them what they are brought in bloody, dirty with earth, mud and grime, and most of them so tired ... seeing them gradually brought back to life, to consciousness and their lips separate into a grin when they first welcome you. Usually they kid, hurt as they are. It doesn't amaze us to hear one of them say, "How are ya, babe?" or "Holy Mackerel, an American woman!" or most indiscreetly, "How about a kiss?" '[12]

This was Nurse Slanger's first and last letter to the *Stripes*. It was written by the light of a small electric torch in a tent in the middle of a thunderstorm, the hail drumming on the canvas, the whole tent swaying as if to take off at any moment. 'It all adds up to a feeling of uneasiness,' she wrote prophetically. Soon after she had posted that letter, a barrage came down from the German artillery, and Nurse Slanger was just another sad statistic: the first American woman to be killed in the European theatre of operations.

As the Allied armies fought through the hedgerows of the 'Bocage' – like a battle in a gigantic shrubbery, the losses were alarmingly high. But the effort was not to be sustained for long by either side. Then came the slaughter of the Falaise, one of the greatest 'killing-grounds' of any war area, where the dead lay so thickly strewn on the ground that Eisenhower, horror-stricken, was later to describe the scene in words that reflected his feelings of shock at the time: 'Forty-eight hours after the closing of the Falaise gap I was conducted through it on foot, to encounter scenes that could be described only by Dante. It was literally possible to walk for hundreds of yards at a time, stepping on nothing but dead and decaying flesh.'[13]

Still driving Eisenhower around the battlefield was Kay Summersby. Apparently she was not quite so emotionally moved as her boss, for she was later to write. 'The events of those days – the rapid advance from the Normandy beaches across France and across the Rhine – are all part of history now. What amazes me today is how very routine it seemed at the time. The extraordinary was quite commonplace.'[14]

For that routine-like race forward across the plains of France, a high price was paid by American, British and Commonwealth troops – 206,000 killed, wounded and taken prisoner of war. But in that crucial phase of the war the German losses were even heavier – 400,000 killed, wounded and prisoner.

Wren officers on Intelligence duties prepare for D-Day

A uniform hemline for the Wrens: '*But supposing we all wore our skirts above the . . . er . . .* 'Plimsoll Line,' *as it were.*'

Opposite: WAAF of a servie
team going over to a bombe
after an operatio

WAAF medical orderlies evacuating casualties from
north-west Europe in 1944. They arrived in France on
13 June, just a few days after the landings. The speed
of air evacuation saved many lives

Ready for take-off. WAAFs heave the chocks away

Trying on life jackets at the transit camp before leaving for France, 1944

ATS landing on the Normandy beaches in July 1944

The switchboard room in Brussels where news of the German breakthrough first came through in December 1944

Have gun, will travel. ATS on active service in north-west Europe

Wash and brush up in camp on active service

The Montgomery Club NAAFI in Brussels where service men and women could relax amidst facilities for hairdressing, sewing, ironing and bathing – as well as eating and dancing

Feet under the table. ATS privates Ducker, Mossman and Booth enjoy Dutch hospitality

Above: Nurse Frau Gabriel Furtwangler who told the author how women prisoners were treated in the concentration camps

SS woman guards of Belsen. British nurses had to work in the camp helping to clear the dying away and prevent the spread of disease

The author examines the ovens in the crematorium at Dachau. One of the SOE girls, it is alleged, was put into the oven whilst still alive and scratched the guard's face as she went in. Subsequently the guard was identified by this scratch and hanged by the War Crimes Commission

General Eisenhower with Kay Summersby at a concert in London shortly after VE Day. It was one of their last happy occasions together

Echoing the feelings of women and men who came back from the war, the film 'The Best Years of Our Lives' proved to be one of the best movies of the year starring Frederick March and Myrna Loy

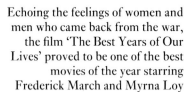

Wartime memories come flooding back on Remembrance Day. Marching smartly, servicewomen return from the War Memorial Service in York, 11 November 1987

And so, as the summer of '44 came to an end, the pundits were predicting that the war would be over in weeks. There was a feeling of euphoria at Allied Headquarters – that it was going to be roses, roses, all the way. Even Eisenhower was optimistic and had time to spare at his advanced headquarters to entertain celebrities who were now making their way in ever-increasing numbers to the theatre of operations, wanting most of all to have publicity pictures taken with the Supreme Commander. Eisenhower was not keen to have them around but, he felt they were entitled to hospitality and cordiality, so he, with Kay's help, managed to entertain all of them – from Fred Astaire and Bing Crosby to Madelaine Carroll and Katherine Cornell, from Anna Rosenberg and Bernard Baruch to Prince Bernhard of the Netherlands and a gaggle of Mexican generals.[15]

In all this, Kay Summersby helped take a load of responsibility from Eisenhower's shoulder, and for this loyalty and devotion to duty she was soon to get a longed-for reward: a commission in the United States Women's Army Corps. Kay was indeed most supportive to 'Ike', who was at that time in great pain with knee trouble. He often had to make his way about the house on crutches. But he never appeared that way in public. 'He would rather die than appear handicapped in any way in front of the men,' said Kay.

Thus, before the summer turned into the autumn of disillusionment for everyone, Kay's routine at Allied Headquarters was almost idyllic. The pressure was off, and it seemed that the war really would soon be over. Kay and Ike could even have time for themselves. Each morning she would go to the office, like a good Personal Assistant, take care of routine matters and then go to the house to have lunch with Ike and go over anything that might have come up. Afterwards, she wrote, we just sat and talked. We might hold hands or kiss.'

The feeling that the war would soon be over filtered through to the most remote and inaccessible parts of Germany. It was noted even by Violette Szabo and the other women within the confines of the concentration camp, that September.

Violette Szabo had been put on a train in Paris *en route* for Ravensbrück concentration camp as soon as the order condemning her to '*Nacht und Nebel*' – to disappear into the 'night and fog' – had been received. It was the beginning of a long and painful journey. In the full heat of that August sunshine she was packed aboard with hundreds of other men and women bound for the same destination. The train then baked for hours in sidings or crawled with difficulty and frequent stops through the rubble and ruins outside Paris. The rail network was a mess of twisted steel, engines lying upside down like dead animals, pylons and signals tottering at odd angles across the tracks.

On the afternoon of the second day, when everyone was desperate for a drink of water, the train suddenly stopped and there was a roar and a crashing of bombs. The RAF were attacking the train. The guards locked the carriages and leapt from the train to set up machine-guns. In the men's carriage there was panic – a mass of bodies squirmed on the floor, and then, in the midst of them all, there appeared the crawling body of Violette, holding a jug of water she had brought from the tap in the toilet. Crawling with her, still chained ankle to ankle, was another girl. 'Their presence calmed them all,' wrote Wing Commander Yeo Thomas after the war.[16]

The train never moved again. Trucks took the women prisoners off to the camp at Ravensbrück, built to house 7,000 but where there were at that time 40,000 women. There, jack-booted women ruled supreme, constantly on the look-out for breaches of discipline or refusal to work. But there were not just German women administering the beatings. There was at least one British woman wielding her thick leather belt there (p.223). In all, 120,000 women are known to have entered that camp, and of these fewer than 12,000 were alive when the Russian troops liberated it. They were appalled by the pitiful condition of those survivors.

Violette and her fellow-prisoners were well aware of the horrific scenes that were to witness there.

'It was like this,' said a reliable eye-witness. 'Women had to wait in queues five deep in the passage to the gas chamber. They could hear the motors of the gas generators, the screaming of women who had gone before and the imploring of those struggling to keep out. It was then that the death panic overtook those who waited; and in their death panic they let go, emptied themselves from front and rear and when their turn came to be pushed into the gas chambers they left behind rows of excrement.'[17]

Another eye-witness recalled: 'Outside beyond the huts there was frequently the crackle of gunshots and screams. Bodies were stacked like wood, they were buried like sardines, head to foot and when the gas chamber doors were open they fell out like potatoes. All this wasn't something belonging to this world, not to this humanity, but to Hell.'[18]

Yet another former inmate told of what Violette would have had to put up with whilst waiting and wondering what her own fate would be: 'It was my job to see them inside the gas chamber and to empty it afterwards. The women were given the order to undress. Only a few obeyed. Once, I could stand it no longer for I felt that life was meaningless and I went into the gas chamber with them but some women came over to me and said that I must live and tell the world of all that went on, and they pushed me out.'[19]

With Violette in Ravensbrück were two other British women with whom she shared the one blanket and one bunk: Lillian Rolfe and Denise Bloch. Towards the end of the war they were all three sent to Torgau to work in an aircraft factory – work similar to that which Violette had done in London before she joined SOE, and it was whilst they were there that news of the Allied advance filtered through. These were exciting rumours which filled them with hope that the end of the war was really drawing near. Freedom was surely in sight. But Violette was not one to wait passively. She attempted another escape and was caught. However, she was not yet sent back to the concentration camp at Ravensbrück but punished and afterwards sent back to the factory bench. Then, as Christmas approached, it seemed that it would be only a matter of time until the war would be over. But for those three British women time had already run out. The final executive command had been signed to process the '*Nacht und Nebel*' order. They were to be sent back to Ravensbrück.

Hopes of a quick ending to the war were dashed nine days before Christmas 1944. It was then, when Ike was getting his fifth general's star and Kay Summersby being recommended for the British Empire Medal, that things suddenly took a turn for the worse. German Panzers struck on the Ardennes front, taking the green, thinly spread new American troops by surprise. The situation was chaotic. American troops fell back in disarray. German commando units disguised in American uniforms, driving captured tanks and speaking good American, threw the defenders into confusion as the Panzer divisions punched through the line in two places and headed directly for Brussels and Antwerp.

In Antwerp, for the ATS of the mixed batteries, this time was the most hectic of their whole service. The greatest port of Europe was particularly valuable for the Allies – being so far forward, it made the supply lines much shorter – and naturally the Germans were keen to obliterate it. Compared with the attacks on London, those on Antwerp were much more horrific because of their concentration: 5,960 bombs out of a total of 8,696 fell within eight miles of the city centre; more than 4,000 people were killed, 3,470 civilian and 682 Service.[20]

Lynne Griffiths was on a gun-site by the River Scheldtenear and soon settled in with her feet under a Dutch table. 'The local people greeted us very warmly. We were entertained in their private homes and almost learned to enjoy raw fish!' she recalled.

Thus, despite all the flying-bombs, social life went on with little deviation from the normal; dances and theatre shows were held almost every night. One of the luckiest ATS girls there at that time was Sonia Corser, a twenty-year-old corporal who had just got engaged to be married to a Yorkshire sergeant. They had decided to celebrate by going to the theatre, but when they got to the box-office, they were turned away because all the seats were taken. Five minutes later they were sitting in a nearby wine bar when a flying-bomb went right through the theatre roof. Hundreds of Service and civilian personnel were killed; the bodies of many completely disintegrated and were never found.

The news of the German breakthrough in the Ardennes first came to Margaret Doherty in Brussels in the form of a 'buzz' from the telephone exchange, saying that all ATS were to be evacuated from Brussels immediately. But this rumour was quickly scotched. The ATS were to 'stay put'. In any case, how could they leave when there was to be a special Christmas 'Liberation' party arranged by the Belgians? They 'stayed put', and Margaret and her friends had a wonderful party. 'Our Christmas dinner was held in the Bon Marché department store, 1,100 of us sat down together,' she wrote later.

ATS Private A.S. Hall, then on that Brussels telephone exchange, was pleased to remain in the city that Christmas too. Shift-work meant that she and her friends always had time to spare for walking through the lovely parks and Treveuren Forest, for drinking coffee in the little cafés, for window-shopping and sight-seeing. Like most of the ATS there, she went to see the battlefield of Waterloo and then came back to her NAAFI, the Montgomery Club, where all 'mod cons' were available – from small rooms in which they could listen to records, to cubicles where they could wash their hair. And again, as with so many other servicewomen in Brussels then, it was where romance struck: there she met the man she would one day marry.

Brussels indeed was a fine place in which to be stationed. Selena Ringrose told how she lived in style in the Hôtel St-Continaire overlooking wooded parkland and the city beyond. It was but a short walk to the Hôtel Metropole Service Club, and she could travel free on the trams in the city. Over that bitterly cold Christmas-time, when the Allies and Germans were locked in fierce fighting in the snows of the Ardennes forests, if ever she and her friends felt cold, as she recalled: 'A few glasses of wine in the snug bar of the warrant officers and sergeants' club would soon revive our frozen bodies.'

The daily routine of Service life went on little influenced by the grim winter battles in the Ardennes. Monica Jackson and her colleagues in the mixed anti-aircraft battery were having a marvellous time. She remembers how, 'At that time the need for Ack-Ack was thankfully lessening, and the battery commander introduced Sunday afternoon teas! All ranks met in the canteen, and we had a musical request programme. We had a splendid radiogram, and I recall an excellent variety of music, from the classics to the pop of the day. Tea was served to everyone, crosswords were completed, conversations and discussions carried on, and a very happy and civilized afternoon was well spent.'

There were not only afternoon tea-parties but concerts too. 'One I remember very clearly was when the battery commander gave us permission to wear civilian clothes and we sent home for party dresses and shoes. Then we found to our horror that Army rations had put pounds on our hips and waistlines. But we altered and borrowed and eventually tottered around on our high heels feeling very feminine and glamorous. Some of the men turned up in dinner jackets and, even if they were straining at the seams, they looked great and we all longed for the day when we would always be in "civvies".'

Many were echoing those thoughts that Christmas, though some social engagements the ATS took on were of a very different nature. Corporal Vera Cole remembers that they disturbed her sorely. It began in this way, she recalled:

Our unit received a visit from a medical officer from the Queen Elizabeth Hospital. He asked if any of the ATS girls would be willing to go to the hospital for a social evening to help those servicemen, mostly RAF to get used to mixing again. You see, they all had been badly burnt and we were told that some of them were dreadfully disfigured and we might find it too much to cope with. My thoughts went out to my brother-in-law, Roger, who had been burnt and was in some prisoner-of-war camp in Germany, and also to my own brother who had been almost killed when a petrol dump blew up in the Middle East and had left him severely burnt. I could do nothing to help either of them but I could do a little for these men, so, along with several other girls, we went on the appointed evening and presented ourselves to the medical officer at the hospital. He took us to the men. They had most of their faces burnt away, eyes all tight-skinned, noses in varying degrees of being rebuilt, and yet they were friendly and once we got over the initial shock we spent the evening happily with them.

I chatted to one young man who told me that, after being burnt in his aircraft, he had been adrift in a rubber dinghy for weeks with very little food or water, and his face bore out the story. He made a remark that he would love to go to a pub for a pint. My heart went out to him, and on returning to headquarters I asked if we could have permission to take half a dozen of those disfigured men to a public house called 'The Mint', which was the nearest one to the hospital. Permission was granted and we got in touch with the publican, who gave his blessing to the idea. He said we could have full use of the public bar for the evening. The medical officer thought this was a splendid idea, and so we collected these brave young men and took them out for beer and darts. The evening was a great success and was repeated on many occasions. So, in some small way, we helped those men along the road to recovery.

For the Christmas and New Year of '44/45, leave was more generously given to women of all three Services, but it was not always without a backlash. Vera Cole remembers one such occasion:

A girl wandered into my room one evening and handed me a pen and a writing pad saying, ''Ere, Corp, write me love letter, will you? You can make it sound proper.' She sat down at the table opposite me and started telling me what to write. When I looked up at her once, my eye was suddenly caught by a movement in her hair. Her head was well and truly alive with nits and fleas. I put down the pen and told the girl to follow me. We headed for the bathroom where, having seen the medical orderly handle the same problem, I began to mix the lotion. 'Oh no!' said the girl, 'I'm not lousy again am I?' I told the girl to keep quiet and put her head over the sink. In no time at all the operation was complete and she emerged all clean and fresh-looking. It was not my job to clean heads but I felt sorry for the girl because she was a trier and whilst at work was always neat and clean. It was on leave that she got lousy. We got back to the table and finished writing her letter, and she went off saying, 'Corp, you're a real pal!'

The next evening there was a big jamjar full of flowers in my room, tulips and daffodils. It was her way of saying 'thank you' for what I had done. but the day after that I heard at headquarters that a complaint had been received from a lady in the village who had seen an ATS girl picking flowers from her garden. My junior commander had seen the flowers in my room and asked me where they came from. I was left with the nasty job of reprimanding the young girl. She said: 'I took them from the big house down the road. They had so many I didn't think they'd miss a few.'

With Christmas over, the weather in Britain and the Ardennes improved, the low cloud lifted and the Allied Air Forces were once more able to fly in support of the soldiers on the ground.

From then on, the Allies turned from defence to attack; the British forces from the north and the Americans from the south began to beat the Germans back from the River Meuse. Brussels and Antwerp were safe.

The German retreat was bitterly fought, both armies passing with little thought the purple-faced, frozen dead Germans and Allies – it made no difference. It made no sense to those infantrymen. Life elsewhere was going on oblivious to it all. No one seemed to be counting the cost any more. It was heavy: the Allies lost 77,000 men, the Germans 120,000. By 31 January the weary German Army, short of petrol, short of ammunition and short of food, was back where it had started from six weeks earlier. They had fought their last offensive. And they had lost.

Now the Germans had to face a new Allied offensive on the Western Front and at the same time meet a Russian push from the east. Then, on top of all the land operations, there was now to be a massive bombardment from the air – 'round-the-clock' bombing: the US Air Force by day and the RAF by night.

In the midst of these terrifying bombing operations were women of the WAAF in Bomber Command, living as never before or afterwards, with emotions fluctuating rapidly between the light-hearted fun of good companionship and the heavy grief of tragic bereavement.

Isabel Henderson[21] was later to write that, when she arrived at the Bomber Command station at Marham, she '... began the happiest and saddest time of her life'. Her work as station commander's secretary continually involved her with operations and aircrew. She was going out with a wireless operator of 218 Squadron and had just become engaged, so that, with each mission they shared a simple routine, for, like all aircrew, he liked to follow the pattern which had got him safely through the last mission – to disturb the routine could be unlucky.

After each mission aircrew were issued with chewing-gum, barley sugar and an orange (a very rare commodity in war-time Britain), and when they got back from the mission there would be a breakfast of bacon and egg waiting for them. Each time, on his return, after de-briefing, Isabel's W/Op would creep into her empty office and leave on her bare desk a little loving gift – an orange. It is not difficult to imagine the tautness of her nerves as she opened her office door each morning and looked to see if the orange was there.

Inevitably one day the desk was bare. No orange. He had not returned. Almost frantic with apprehension, she went to the operations room and waited for the familiar call-sign to come beeping through. As time dragged on, there came with it a creeping feeling of helplessness numbing all thought except the ever-growing certainty that the call-sign would now never come. Then, suddenly, when all hope had vanished, the ether was punctured by a voice from another station. Her fiancé had landed there. He was safe.

Edna Sheen, 'The Map Queen' of RAF Scampton, was part of a ritual too. 'After all briefings, each aircrew would touch me on the shoulder and say, "See you tonight". This was a ritual and they considered it bad luck if they went out without touching me on the shoulder.' On one occasion she had shown her annoyance with one of the navigators about the state in which he returned his maps; he was not going to take rebukes from a mere WAAF and a heated argument developed. Finally he stormed out of the briefing room. 'His aircraft failed to return that night and I felt so dreadful!'[22]

Several months after the war had ended, when Edna was demobilized at home, she was surprised to receive a letter. It was from the same navigator. He had been in a prisoner-of-war camp, and the argument had preyed on his mind all those months. After being repatriated, one of the first things he did was to trace Edna through the Air Ministry and write to say how sorry he had been for his behaviour. He also said that it was because he had not touched Edna's shoulder that he had been shot down.

Such was the stress of those men and women in the bomber offensive that engaged or married couples were rarely allowed to serve on the same station. Isabel's orange routine was not allowed to go on for much longer, for her fiancé was posted to the nearby station of Lakenheath. Isabel was no longer in quite the same position of knowing when he was on operations or not, and therefore she was not waiting up in the same way.

This nightly awfulness of waiting was recalled by Nellie Dumbrell, who was at that time a batwoman – one of the first batwomen in the RAF – at Linton-on-Ouse. She looked after four aircrew officers and naturally grew very fond of them. Her own steady boyfriend was a sergeant rear gunner, and she remembers well the night he was put on operations for Stuttgart: 'It had been a terrible day, sheeting down as it can in North Yorkshire, and we all thought operations would be cancelled. We had arranged to meet, and I was going to make something to eat in the batman's room so that we would not have to get wet going out. It was so difficult to dry clothing then. My boyfriend was due for leave, so I looked forward to an evening of quiet celebration. It was not to be. Ops were on. Stuttgart.'

The time waiting for the aircraft to return went by with its usual slowness. Some WAAFs went out onto the control tower balcony listening for the first sounds of the returning aircraft. The radio telephone was put on the loudspeaker, and eventually the silence was broken by the voice of the first pilot back asking for landing instructions. Then the air became full of voices asking for their turn to land or height to circle. There were problems. Bombers that had been to Berlin had been diverted to the station and were also trying to get down. Then it happened: a Halifax and a Lancaster collided in mid-air. They fell in a tangled mass of flaming metal. Thirteen were killed. One man was saved, a rear gunner.

Nellie Dumbrell recalled what happened the next morning: 'I was in the WAAF hairdresser's shop. An airwoman I did not know was about to leave, and then she began talking confidentially in a low voice to the hairdresser. I had the feeling she was talking about me. When the hairdresser came to my chair, she told me what had been said. The other airwoman worked in sick-quarters and had asked the hairdresser if she knew me. She had taken a photo out of a dead man's pocket and recognized me when I walked in.'

There were amusing moments too that Nellie recalled. One day, when she went to the airing cupboard and reached into the dark recess for a blanket, she touched a body. It was old Joe, a veteran of World War I, who had no family ties and on his half days always tried to hide away so that he would not be caught for odd jobs. Another favourite spot was under the ironing table: 'We couldn't see him and only knew he was there when he turned over and the table moved.'

Accidents took their toll of women as well as men. Joan Chamberlain, a Wren radio mechanic with the Fleet Air Arm, had to fly on air tests, sometimes in the cold open cockpit of Swordfish in winter, at other times in Albacores, Barracudas, and American Avengers. There were some very nasty and tragic moments, she recalled:

During the air test the pilot was required to stall the engine, a moment when one held one's breath and prayed for that reassuring roar as the aircraft came out of the dive. Air-testing of Avengers usually included firing the guns, which took place over Kirkaldy Bay. The armourer sat in a revolving turret immediately above the radio set, which meant that, whilst trying to maintain contact with the ground station, the poor radio mechanic was showered with spent ammunition cases as well as being choked with cordite fumes and deafened by the sound of guns.

The dangers involved in these air tests became tragically apparent when an Albacore crashed in the grounds of Fordell House, killing the pilot and the two Wrens in the crew. All three were our friends, and their deaths were particularly poignant. The funeral was conducted with full naval honours and, although it was some time since we had done any squad drill, the smart turn-out and the perfection of our slow marching was our way of paying tribute to our friends.

Winifred Blackham, who was at Bomber Command Headquarters in 1944, told of her unenviable job: 'I was in the section dealing with accidents in training, and there were many. It was pretty heart-breaking, especially when you came across someone you knew. This was especially true when a boy who had lived two doors away from me crashed in the quicksands at Morecambe Bay and was swallowed up, plane and all.'

The women in Flying Control could not help feeling emotionally involved in these crucial raids of 1944 that would bring the ending of the war so much nearer. Mollie Urquhart was often upset: 'We had many sad times when counting the aircraft back to base, and I was plotting on the day when we lost American band-leader Glen Miller from the radar.' And Peggy Dent, another R/T operator, recalled how after a long night she would go out onto the control-tower balcony and watch the sun coming up, with sadness in her heart:

It would look so beautiful and peaceful. There would be a slight misty look, the birds would be twittering, and there was a lovely soft silence that seems to come with the dawn. It was difficult to realise that just a short time earlier engines had been roaring overhead with tired crews glad to be home, and now everything so still. My heart would go out to the sleeping families of the missing airmen. I would think that some time today perhaps fourteen families would receive a telegram: 'We regret to inform you ...'. How wrong it all seemed on such a lovely morning.

But it wasn't all tears. In fact, after the first few weeks I realised that I couldn't break my heart over each and every crew that went missing, but it always hurt and one never got used to it.[23]

Jan Birch, a WAAF who had previously lost a fiancé, married another airman. He always telephoned her when he came back from a raid. One night he did not telephone. She waited and waited and then got the feeling that she must go to the station to find out what had happened, telling herself not to be silly and that everything would be all right. When she got outside the mess, an older WAAF officer came up to her and said, 'Oh, Jan, would you go and see the medical officer, he wants to see you.' Jan cycled over to sick-quarters, where the doctor was waiting. 'Jan,' he said, 'I've got to prepare you for something. Brian and his crew did not return.' To this day Jan can still feel the cold shudder that ran inside her.

> I think I said perhaps, 'Oh no! It couldn't happen twice,' [she recalled]. I couldn't cry. I couldn't say anything.
> I remember cycling down this lane, going into the woods and getting off my bike, and that feeling of being surrounded by beauty and solitude which wasn't sad in a way because amongst all the grass, were these wood anemones. They were just like a cloud of white delicate things blowing in the wind and I felt, well, it isn't all in vain. Whatever has gone wrong, life does go on. Brian would feel that, Colin would feel that, the other boys I knew would feel that. It wasn't as if that was a sudden solution to all my problems but it was a feeling that remained with me as a comfort.[24]

WAAF Controller Edge had her first taste of rye whisky when it was poured into her cup at three o'clock one morning as a thanksgiving for the narrow escape from being blown sky-high that she and the rest of the station had just had. Wittering had a three-mile-long runway and so became a 'distress station', and they took in any Lancasters, Halifaxes or B17s off raids when they were in trouble. 'Usually, this trouble was with the hydraulics, but one night we had a Canadian crew with a jammed bomb-rack holding 12,000 pounds of bombs. The tension was enormous. Fortunately it landed safely. We all felt in need of that whisky!'

Landing and take-offs caused most anxiety. One horrific moment was recalled by Vicky Barrett, then a leading aircraftswoman: 'I did a spell on the ambulance. That has a lot of sad memories. To see a plane take off with a full bomb load, not make height and crash, and to watch the medical orderlies and medical officer picking up the pieces of what remained of bodies and put them into weighted coffins was an upsetting experience.'[25]

A question which these women often asked themselves, and each other, was: 'How did the aircrew manage to keep going out night after night on those raids when they knew that, by the law of averages, they would be exceptionally lucky to survive more than ten?' Section Officer Grace Archer, herself 'Mentioned in Despatches' in 1944, was once asked by a much concerned RAF medical officer to look out for aircrew members who might be suffering from an advanced state of nervous tension, so that he could help them. As she pointed out, 'There were six other members in any crew and for one to have "the jitters" could be extremely upsetting for the others, and of course, highly dangerous, especially if it was the pilot of the aircraft. Extreme cases were invalided out – maybe grounded, but it was a stigma and that was sad.'[26]

Phyllis Bull, a nursing orderly at Marston Moor, had her own personal experience of such a situation. She was at the time emotionally involved with a wireless operator/air gunner stationed at neighbouring Bomber Command airfield at Rufforth, York. Shortly before Christmas she had bought him a little present, a lucky mascot in the form of a toy dog, which she gave to him one night in York. The next he was on ops, and she sadly recalls now how as she said goodbye to him at York railway station he suddenly said, 'Phyllis, I don't want to die!' There had been some previous discussion to prompt the remark and Phyllis had told him not to be silly and that of course he wasn't going to die.

On the following evening when the telephone rang in her sick quarters an aircraftsman at the neighbouring station, Rufforth, said there had been a crash but she was not to come with the others to help. Her boyfriend, Bernard had been trapped in the burning plane.

'Later I visited Bernard's widowed mother and did my best to reassure her about the nature of his death, though I knew in my heart what the true facts were likely to have been.'[27]

Rarely did relatives see the bodies of dead aircrew, and often the coffins contained little more than weights and a few bits and pieces.[28]

Such was the kind of life the women of Bomber Command stations were having to cope with. They coped well. Often they would balance the harrowing sides of their work with positive relaxation, practical jokes – like the medical orderlies who somehow managed to push the medical officer's 'baby' car into his surgery and place a card on its front listing the symptoms of its sickness. And the time the station commanding officer told an airman to strap a parachute onto his secretary before taking her up in his Tiger Moth aeroplane. She had never flown before, hated heights and certainly had little confidence in such an old-fashioned-looking machine dwarfed alongside the bombers: 'I was in my uniform skirt and I don't know who had the reddest face – the airman or me – when he fastened the straps between my legs!'

Bomber Command was certainly not for the squeamish!

Every day and early evening now, the great US and RAF air armadas rose, circled, assembled and set off to harass the German Army retreating to the Rhine and beyond. All roads, railways and bridges leading to Germany were littered with German dead, wrecked cars, trains and horsedrawn carts. Soon all resistance west of the Rhine collapsed. On 6 March 1945 US troops entered the devastated city of Cologne, and by the last week of March 320,000 German soldiers in the Ruhr were surrounded, their general, Model, killed by his own hand.

Victory on terms of 'unconditional surrender' was now so clearly in sight that the War Office was working flat out selecting and training troops to administer the disbandment of the German military forces. And this was where the women again were to play an important role – for a rather strange reason: *it was because they were more hard-hearted than men!*

This was the belief of the Director of the Women's Royal Naval Service who said, in a minute to the First Lord of the Admiralty when pressing for women to be trained for disbandment of the German *Marine Helferinnen*: 'Ministers and Parliament may have divided opinions about the Women's services executing the military clauses of the "Terms of Surrender" in respect of German women. As we see it, the value of the WRNS in this disbandment work is to have available the women's viewpoint, with perhaps a soupçon of hard-heartedness to stiffen a male disbandment organisation which might otherwise be too tender-hearted to the German Women's Naval Service.'[29]

She won her point. Soon the ATS and WAAF made similar proposals and had specially selected personnel ready to take posts with the British Control Commission immediately after the tide of battle rolled onwards through Germany. Private Peggy Roberts of the ATS was delighted to be selected for work with the secretariat for the Commission. Germany made an exciting change after two years on the Clyde, ' ...where the rain sometimes lasted for weeks and hair just would not curl'. She was to encounter some frightening and amazing scenes: 'Many of the villagers around Lübeck were most hostile. It was an unforgettable experience, the ruins, the smells and the people trudging off with their handcarts through all the rubble.'

But there were some revelations beneath all that rubble, as Mary Walsh found:

From what I saw jeeping slowly through bomb rubble in scores of villages and towns I am convinced we do not understand the thinking and feeling patterns of German people. If you want to see whether or not the German people have really suffered from our bombings, you check on the cellar of any German house you enter. The roof may be blown away, some walls may be down. But in the cellar there are rows of neatly put up glass jars holding chicken, vegetables, fruit, fruit cake. There is always the big earthenware jar holding eggs in waterglass. There are the makings of considerable comfort, rugs, the radio, couches, an air-intake system, the family pewter or china, the best clock. In the town of München Gladbach they were able to distribute milk onto the broken doorsteps two days after the 29th Division passed through there. One woman was complaining because the milkman overlooked her. In a dozen towns I saw what German looting of the continent meant – nylon or real silk stockings, shoes better than England or France have seen for years, thick warm coats. In Eschweiler a pretty young woman, sunning her baby in front of her house, was wearing a mink coat with a Paris label.[30]

Following closely behind these British and American armies were casualty clearing stations and British hospitals. Nurses were treating more than Allied soldiers: they were looking after released prisoners of war, civilian inmates from German labour camps and casualties from the German Army.

The Allies were now driving through all opposition at the rate of nearly forty miles a day. By 25 April the Americans and Russians had joined forces at Torgau, to the east of Leipzig.

Early in the morning of 29 April, Hitler married his mistress, Eva Braun, in a bizarre ceremony in his Berlin bunker, had his favourite Alsatian dog, Blondi, destroyed, gave his new wife poison and shot himself. The new Führer, Doenitz, broadcast that Hitler had died fighting at the head of his armies. On the following day Hitler's most faithful supporter, Dr Goebbels, killed his five children and then ordered the SS Guards in the bunker to shoot himself and his wife.

The war in Europe was over.

One week before the Americans met the Russians, the nurses of Number 32 Casualty Clearing Station had a meeting that most would have given almost anything to avoid. They met the dying and the dead of Belsen concentration camp.

As if they had not supped full enough of horrors, they moved in to Belsen to tackle a medical problem that would have strained the resources of several major cities. Amongst the 60,000 prisoners in that camp, 1,500 were suffering from typhus and a further 900 from typhoid. If these inmates had escaped into the surrounding countryside, a plague of disease could have spread across Germany. When the Divisional Director of Medical Services of the RAMC, a man who had seen horrifying scenes on the battlefields, first went into the camp, he had to turn aside to vomit, of such a nature was the shocking scene which met his eyes and those of the nurses there. They wondered what kind of men and women were they who could inflict such agony of mind and body upon others that they were brought to the condition of beasts – who could take joy in such devil's work?

Senior Sister, Miss Higginbotham[31] with a team of eight QAs set about the task of directing 200 German soldiers from a nearby barracks to remove all surviving inmates to suitable buildings in the vicinity.

To give some idea of the conditions in which these women were working one must look at the sober statement made by the Senior Medical Officer of the British Second Army. He said:

I am afraid you may think I am exaggerating, but I assure you I am not. It is the most frightful, horrible place I have ever seen. There were people dying in the compounds, dying in the mass before our eyes. There was one crematorium, but the Germans did not use it because they could not cope with the number of deaths.

We saw enormous covered death pits. One was uncovered. It contained a great pile of blackened and naked bodies. There was typhus in every compound, and in one compound the typhus cases were not even separated. People were lying dead in gutters outside huts to which they had gone to rest more comfortably, and died as they lay. In the women's compound, in full view of the children's compound, 50 yards away, we saw an enormous pile of naked dead women. It stretched about 60 yards by 30 yards.

The Brigadier hesitated before he mentioned his next point:

I cannot vouch for this, of course [he stated cautiously], but prison doctors told me there had been cannibalism. Prisoners were so far gone that they took out and ate the heart and kidneys of those who had died.

Starvation caused more deaths than typhus, and a large number of the prisoners must die before we can prevent it. Of the women, 18,600 were so weak that they ought to have been in hospital just to give them a chance of staying alive.[32]

One of Sister Mary Sands'[33] patients was typical of the type of political prisoner found in Belsen. He was not a Jew but had spoken out against the National Socialist régime in 1937 and had been in various concentration camps ever since. When Mary Sands gave him some clean straw for a bed, he was so delighted he just 'wept and wept for joy', she reported.

As soon as the patients began to build up enough strength to move about the camp, life became dangerous for the nurses. The commanding officer would not allow them to do night duty, because some patients, having lost all sense of social conscience, had taken to roaming the camp at night, breaking into stores and stealing food.

'The nearest comparison one could make with Belsen was the Black Death in the Middle Ages and the cries of "bring out your dead",' wrote Sister Mary Sands, for each morning when they went on duty they would find bodies lying 'all over the place in the most grotesque positions, half out of bed, on the stairs, and so on'.

In the camp the SS women were ordered to haul scores of naked corpses from lorries and fling them into a mass burial pit in which hundreds of sprawling bodies were already lying. But what most surprised the British nurses was that these SS women, the eldest of whom was only twenty-seven, were unmoved by the grisliness of their task. Brenda McBryde[34] was to write that these brutal women showed 'no outward sign of abhorrence or shame'. And Edwin Tetlow of the *Daily Mail* reported that, 'One even smiled as she helped to bundle the corpses into the pit.'[35]

Unfortunately, for some British servicewomen – like Violette Szabo and others from the WAAF, FANY and SOE who were incarcerated in concentration camps – the defeat of Germany came too late.

What happened to Violette Szabo after she was sent back to Ravensbrück from the factory at Torgau was not known until long after the war in Europe was over. It might never have been discovered but for the determination of one woman, a squadron officer of the Women's Auxiliary Air Force, who, as a war-time intelligence officer with SOE, had been largely responsible for preparing agents despatched on mission to Europe. Her name is Vera Atkins.

When hostilities ended, she was very much disturbed by the fact that so many of her women had disappeared without trace, and she set out to discover what had really happened to them. For the sake of relatives as well as for her own peace of mind, she resolved to get the facts.[36]

Vera Atkins was helped by the national press, which also took up the quest by publishing a photograph of Violette Szabo, asking if there was anyone with information as to her fate. A British woman, Mrs Julie Barry, came forward with a most unusual story. She claimed to be the last person to have seen Violette alive. In her story, published in the *News of the World* in 1946, she is reported as saying:

I was caught by the Germans for sabotage in Guernsey and imprisoned there at first and then in many other prisons in France and Germany before being sent to Ravensbrück. I spoke several European languages and the staff of the prisons made use of me as an interpreter. At Ravensbrück, I was made a prison policewoman and given the number 39785 and a red armband that indicated my status.

I was handed a heavy leather belt with instructions to beat the women prisoners. It was a hateful task, but in it I saw my only chance to help some of the condemned women.

It was into this camp that three British parachutists were brought. One was Violette Szabo. They were in rags, their faces black with dirt, and their hair matted. They were starving. They had been tortured in attempts to wrest from them secrets of the invasion but I am certain they gave nothing away.[37]

Mrs Barry went on to say that Violette had told her about her daughter, Tania and her dead soldier husband, Etienne. The three women knew why they had been brought to Ravensbrück, said Mrs Barry, but she added that even then nothing could break their spirits. She went on: 'One morning came the order for all three of them to go to the commandant's office. Mrs Szabo walked unaided. The other two were carried. Many of the inmates wanted to die but Mrs Szabo and her companions wanted to live to tell the world how they had been treated.'

In an effort to discover more, intelligence officers from the War Office interviewed Mrs Barry, but there were still many gaps in her story. Nor were the officers convinced of its accuracy. Corroboration was needed. Vera Atkins was shortly to provide this, for she had found by this time the second-in-command of Ravensbrück, Johann Schwarzhuber, in the north German prison of Minden. She went to interview him and caused him virtually to sign his own death warrant with a complete statement about what happened to Violette Szabo, Lillian Rolfe and Denise Bloch when they arrived back at Ravensbrück from the factory at Torgau.[38]

At about seven o'clock one evening, under instructions from the camp commandant, Fritz Suhren, three women were taken to the cemetery yard by the crematorium. With the camp commandant and his deputy were the camp doctor, Dr Trommer, Sergeant Zappe, SS Corporal Scheink and Lance-Corporal Schult.

The camp commandant gave the order. Each woman was led forward by Scheink, and then Schult shot each one through the back of the head with a small-calibre hand-gun. Death was certified by Dr Trommer, and the bodies were burned in the crematorium. In his statement, Schwarzhuber was moved to say: 'All three were very brave and I was deeply moved. Suhren was also impressed by the bearing of these three women and he was annoyed that the Gestapo did not themselves carry out the shootings.'

Annoyed and moved they might well have been but they were not to escape the consequences of the murders. Both Schwarzhuber and Suhren were tried and hanged in 1946. Later that year the courage and steadfastness of Violette Szabo were appropriately recognized. She was gazetted for the George Cross.*

According to the records of SOE, French Section, just over fifty women were sent to France as agents, thirty-nine of them from the FANY or WAAF. Of those thirty-nine, thirteen were murdered by the

---

* Great efforts were made to convert this to a Victoria Cross. Details of MP Irene Ward's fight to get this VC for Violette Szabo can be found in the ATS Museum at Guildford.

Nazis. Many of the remaining twenty-six were captured and tortured but survived. Brave women, all of them, fighting alone, pitting themselves individually against the evil powers of Nazi Germany in circumstances calculated the break the bravest of mortals. Yet these women managed not only to bear ordeals undaunted, and harrowing experiences which for most of us are unimaginable, but also to hand the torch on to others who took their place.

What was it that impelled women to undertake such tasks? It was surely something more than a zest for adventure, something more than sheer hatred of the Nazi system. It was a profound belief in a way of life that was threatened, a world in which tolerance, freedom and tranquillity were valued and safeguarded.

9   I'll Be Seeing You!

Trip no further pretty sweeting
Journeys end in lovers meeting.

William Shakespeare, *Twelfth Night*, Act III, Scene iii

The long, hard road of war had been travelled. Now the women who had reached the end of their journeys were beginning to hand in their kit.

Leaving the Service was not a pleasant experience for most servicewomen, despite the fact that all had been looking forward to the end of the war. Demobilization came as a disappointing anticlimax.

Vera Cole, for example, remembers well how it was. Like most of her colleagues then, she had been keeping a watchful eye on the unit notice board to see who was going to be the next for demobilization. Then one day it happened: 'I saw my name and suddenly realized that my days in the ATS were fast coming to an end … Before I left the unit, an officer, whom I had never seen before, called me over and gave me my Conduct Sheet, on which was written, "Exemplary", thanked me perfunctorily, wished me well and said good-bye.' Before she knew what had happened, Vera was on a train heading for the demob centre at Northampton.

When I arrived at the barracks, I followed the notices and arrows which led me to a reception bay where I was greeted by a corporal who asked for my name and number. Then, suddenly, she thrust a small jamjar into my hand and pointed to a door saying, 'Through there and aim straight!'

That was not only my urine test but my medical exam as well. I was declared fit, my papers stamped 'A1', and told to hand in my kit to the store. I couldn't believe it; all the strict medicals to get into the ATS and there, without even being seen by a doctor, I was out, services no longer required.

This was something everyone found to be true. Joining up was far more exciting than being demobbed. Said former LACW Brenda Robinson:

It was not the big thrill I'd been expecting. I was sent to a large room with a lot of other girls. 'Take off your tunic and greatcoat, said a sergeant, 'and leave them here because you won't see them again.' So there we all were, emptying our pockets of picture-house ticket stubs, cigarette ends, a lighter made out of aircraft perspex, the odd lucky coin, part of a NAAFI wad and a wash-basin plug. We took our last look at the familiar stains on the tunic, wondering which were coffee and which coke, and handed it in. And that was that. It was an empty feeling, as if we'd lost all identity. For years in the Service we'd had something to be proud of, a sense of belonging to something rather special which inspired intense loyalty. Now, as civilians, we had nothing.

Fortunately, some of the ATS women returning from north-west Europe had a more memorable home-coming. Lance-Corporal J. Melrose remembers to this day the details of it all:

I had never flown before and we were to fly back in a Dakota. I died a thousand deaths on the ground, but was all right in the air and saw everyone else looking calm, cool, and collected. I even ventured to look down on the ships below – they were like little toys.

When we got to London, we were 'processed' into Civvy Street. And there, as we finally moved out, was the daughter of the Great Man himself. She shook me by the hand and wished me well for the future – Mary Churchill. She was a very cheerful person, with rosy cheeks and bright blue eyes.

On demobilization both men and women did miss the order that Service life had brought into their lives. But if it was hard for the rank and file to readjust, how much harder was it for the Queen Bee of the unit, the Regimental Sergeant Major!

It was a traumatic experience, former RSM Hedges recalls: 'Running a house after having a batman all those years was hard enough to bear but having to do jobs myself which I'd been used to delegating to others was worse. No longer could I just walk around and look as though I was working! It all came as a nasty shock.'

There was another shock waiting for many servicewomen when they got home. Wren Moira Keaton found that, although by this time her uniform was tight, her civilian clothes were even tighter: 'I couldn't get into any of my clothes and feel comfortable. I'd grown bigger, stronger and chubbier because we had taken more physical exercise than ever before, and four square Navy meals a day had played havoc with my waistline.' For Moira, resettlement into civil life was not easy.

And Phyllis Linsdell, who had joined the ATS way back in 1938, agreed: 'The first time I put a dress on to walk out I felt awful. I had to put my uniform back on again. It was a terrible let-down being demobbed. You were never without somebody in the Service, and there was always something going on, no matter how humdrum it might have seemed at the time. Once in civil life, friends got married and you just had to re-establish yourself. It certainly was not easy!'

True enough. Pat Hall[1] came home from Egypt and Rome to find she was no longer the same woman to whom her husband had proposed in 1939, and they parted without undue acrimony, he to re-marry and she to use her experience in the Western Desert on expeditions for the Natural History Museum.

Many war-time marriages and relationships were casualties. Kay Summersby's experience with the Supreme Commander, Eisenhower was no exception.[2]

Everything seemed to be going smoothly right up to the Victory in Europe Day celebrations. Ike and Kay had a special day out from their Frankfurt headquarters and went with Ike's son, John, and his Wren girlfriend to see a London show, taking bottles of champagne with them. After their return to Frankfurt, the love-affair burgeoned. Ike assured Kay that the twenty years difference in their ages was not important, saying: 'Age is not going to change what we have.' And they even tried for a baby, but Ike was not up to this. 'He was tender, careful and loving, but it didn't work,' Kay wrote.

Two weeks later she went on a visit to Washington, and when she returned, she found Ike packing. On 10 November 1945 he left. The affaire was over.

The plan was for the General's personal staff to follow him later but soon a message came from Washington to the effect that Lieutenant Summersby's name was to be deleted from the list of those scheduled to go to Washington. For Kay the shock was devastating.

She did, however, go to Washington on her own and visited her war-time lover two or three times, but nothing further developed. Eisenhower was soon to be President of the United States. There could be no blemish on his character in the run-up to the election. As far as he was concerned, the love-affair had ended in November 1945.

Years later, when Kay lay under sentence of death from cancer, she looked back on it all and wrote, without any bitterness: 'We were two people caught up in a cataclysm. Two people who shared one of the most tremendous experiences of our time. Two people who gave each other comfort, laughter and love.'

That month, November 1945, was a sad month for Jean Gordon too.[3] The young niece and mistress of General George Patton returned to the United States but was never to see her colourful and beloved General again, for in that month he died in a car crash. Two weeks later Jean Gordon killed herself.

Many servicewomen felt as apprehensive as General Patton and faced the return to 'Civvy Street' with trepidation. For them, the post-war world of inadequate housing, job shortages and queuing for fags and food seemed altogether too drab to contemplate. So when the Government decided to form the WRAC, its call for experienced personnel to re-enlist met with an enthusiastic response.

Margaret Doherty was one who jumped at the opportunity. 'I had been home for six months buried in the wilds of Donegal. It was not my cup of tea at all. And then I saw the advertisement. It was like a godsend. It read: "There's so much that's new in the WRAC, so many friends to make and places to go. It's a grand life, full of variety and interest, offering you a choice of jobs – and training for them too. Good pay, good comfortable accommodation, and thirty days holiday a year. This is the way to move around and enjoy your work and meet people." ' Margaret Doherty remained in the WRAC for another twenty-four years.

Other servicewomen felt differently. All they wanted was a comfortable home life. Well, almost. Hilda Dopson felt there was still something missing from her marriage. It had been a war-time marriage, a very happy one, but she had been married in her WAAF uniform and she had always dreamed of a white wedding. She got it, eventually. Her children gave her one on her sixtieth birthday, forty years later. When she and her husband renewed their marriage vows in Wakefield parish church, this time they did the job properly: it was a white wedding.

Naturally, thousands of women met and fell in love with their husbands-to-be whilst in the Services. Some waited to get married after the war; others, like Sister Marjorie Bennett, married abroad. She had met a young RAF officer at a St Valentine's dance in the Syracuse hospital, Sicily. Meeting was difficult, for he was stationed in Malta. Nevertheless, after a whirlwind courtship of only weeks they were married by the hospital chaplain, with patients forming a guard of honour with crutches and bedpans!

There were some very difficult courtships and unusual marriages, and perhaps none more so than that between Joan Armstead and Karl Heinz. Indeed, their courtship was forbidden. But love, as they say, will always find a way.

Joan Armstead was a WAAF wireless-operator stationed at Pershore. There she met Karl Heinz, a twenty-year-old prisoner of war, and fell irretrievably in love. Although their courtship was forbidden in both their languages – the penalty for a prisoner being restricted detention – and though neither could speak the other's language, their love for each other grew rapidly.

Joan's eyes still sparkle as she tells how it happened all those years ago. 'It was just like a romantic novel and takes some believing,' she said. 'I was playing cricket with some other RAF people when I had a strange urge to turn round, a feeling that someone was looking at me. It was then I saw this tall, handsome figure, Karl. Our eyes met. A message flashed between us, and that was the beginning.'

The stuff of which memories are made.

Today there are many who look back nostalgically, with pleasure and pride, on those war-time years when they were part of the mightiest fighting force of all time, helping to turn defeat into victory. And that did something for them all. Dorothy Calvert spoke for the greater part of them when she said: 'I have a lot to thank the Service life for. It brought me out of my shell and helped to make me as I am today, more tolerant, I hope, and friendly, and so pleased to be alive.'[4]

These were ordinary women who became extraordinary, shop assistants, bank clerks, teachers, nurses, women who had worked in industry and women who had never worked in their lives. Women from every class who served with unsurpassed grandeur of spirit. They were the women who went to war, fighting for a world and a way of life they both prized and deserved.

Do they have it?

York, 1988   Eric Taylor

Appendix A: Notes on the Memorandum for Her Majesty the Queen on the Disposal of Pregnant WAAF Personnel

Her Majesty the Queen (now HM Queen Elizabeth The Queen Mother) was very much concerned with the welfare of servicewomen. She wrote to the Director of the WAAF asking what arrangements were made for those women 'who were going to have a baby'.

The reply, which covered thirteen pages, set out in detail the procedure taken. Summarized below are the main points of that reply. (It may be found in Public Record Office file AIR 2/4460.)

During 1943 there were 2,235 WAAF personnel discharged from the Service on the grounds of pregnancy. Of these 646 were unmarried. A third of unmarried pregnant airwomen managed to conceal their pregnancy until after the sixth month.

The policy of the WAAF was that airwomen who became pregnant were required to leave the Service at the end of the third month of pregnancy.

The Service would not accept responsibility for unmarried pregnant airwomen for the following reasons:
1. Adequate pre-natal, confinement and post-natal care was the responsibility of the Ministry of Health.
2. The provision of RAF hostels for pregnant airwomen would attract adverse criticism of the WAAF.
3. The particular problems of unmarried mothers needed help from experienced civilian welfare workers.
4. The Service could not provide nurseries for illegitimate children.

The regulations relating to discharge on grounds of pregnancy were:
1. Airwomen certified as pregnant were not allowed to carry their own kit when leaving the unit, and transport would be provided for this purpose.
2. Airwomen being discharged should receive an allowance of £12.10s. for civilian clothing.

231

3. An airwoman marked on discharge as 'suitable for re-enrolment' might apply to rejoin the Service six months after the birth of her child.

The problem of the married woman illegitimately pregnant presented a special problem. She was outside the scope of the Moral Welfare Society. Where her husband's allowance had been stopped and she was unwilling to return to her own relatives, she had no alternative but to seek Public Assistance.

The policy regarding unmarried pregnant airwomen under the age of twenty-one was that parents must be informed. No unmarried airwoman left her unit until the officer was assured that she was going to relatives or friends, or to the care of a welfare society.

Special problems arose with concealment of pregnancy. Airwomen were reluctant to leave the Service for they knew that, with increasing illegitimacy among the civilian population, there was a lack of hostel accommodation. In many cases commanding officers were reluctant to make a grant of money from their Benevolent Fund for this type of case but the Soldiers', Sailors' and Airmen's Help Society offered assistance and provided the airwoman with a layette for the baby.

The Ministry of Health had hostels for the accommodation of unmarried pregnant ex-service women. Airwomen who had been in those hostels and could not speak too highly of the kindness and attention shown to them. Matrons helped with arrangements for the adoption of the child.

Many women were forced to allow their babies to be adopted because of problems with work and accommodation with an illegitimate child. Concern was felt at the number of women who were leaving their babies with people not contemplating legal adoption; to all intents and purposes the baby was abandoned. It was difficult to keep an accurate check on such cases.

Efforts were made to inculcate a high standard of moral behaviour through regular lectures. Many younger airwomen entered the service ignorant of 'the facts of life'.

Appendix B: How Women Answered the Challenge of War

Never before had women undertaken so many varied tasks in the country's defence. Thousands joined the three highly organized military Services – the WRNS, ATS and WAAF. Others performed important work in industry in order to release men to active service.

There was no shortage of volunteers but in December 1941 a quite revolutionary move was made by the passing of the National Service Act (No 2), which gave the Government power to conscript women.

Women were badly needed for the Auxiliary Services and, although the recruiting drives had not been failures, it was realized that a slapdash voluntary system might be wasteful of womanpower, for it was just as important that some young women should be kept out of Auxiliary Services as that other should be drawn in. Women had, in fact, to be mobilized as carefully as men, and, of course, women had the same statutory protection and safeguards as men for conscientious objection, postponement of calling-up on grounds of exceptional hardship, and reinstatement on discharge from the Forces.

Royal Proclamations were issued making liable to service single women and widows without children between the ages of nineteen and thirty, at first, but these age classes were subsequently altered as the war situation, and the paramount needs of industry changed.

It is interesting to note a rather patronizing and presumptuous sentence in a Government pamphlet on Manpower Mobilization* which said: 'These Women's Auxiliary Services, whose trim khaki, light and dark blue uniforms are now seen everywhere, are being sensibly managed; the girls look healthy and happy, and clearly most of them will make better wives and mothers and citizens, if only because they have had some physical and mental training, and been given a glimpse of wider horizons after their years of national service.'

* *MAN POWER, The Story of Britain's Mobilisation for War* (HMSO, 1944)

Chart showing strength of the three Services and the Nursing Services (in '000s)

Women's Auxiliary Services

Date	Total	Women's Royal Naval Service	Auxiliary Territorial Service	Women's Auxiliary Air Force	Nursing Services
Sept. 1939	–	1.6	–	–	2.4
Dec. 1939	43.1	3.4	23.9	8.8	7.0
Mar. 1940	–	4.4	–	8.9	8.2
Jun. 1940	56.6	5.6	31.5	11.9	7.6
Sept. 1940	69.3	7.9	36.1	17.4	7.9
Dec. 1940	75.1	10.0	36.4	20.5	8.2
Mar. 1941	85.8	12.3	37.5	27.0	9.0
Jun. 1941	105.3	15.1	42.8	37.4	10.0
Sept. 1941	157.5	18.0	65.0	64.1	10.4
Dec. 1941	216.0	21.6	85.1	98.4	10.9
Mar. 1942	258.6	24.8	111.1	110.8	11.9
Jun. 1942	307.5	28.6	140.2	125.7	13.0
Sept. 1942	351.1	33.5	162.2	141.5	13.9
Dec. 1942	400.6	39.3	180.7	166.0	14.6
Mar. 1943	435.9	45.0	195.3	180.1	15.5
Jun. 1943	461.6	53.3	210.3	181.6	16.4
Sept. 1943	470.7	60.4	212.5	180.3	17.5
Dec. 1943	467.5	64.8	207.5	176.8	18.4
Mar. 1944	468.8	68.6	206.2	175.7	18.3
Jun. 1944	466.4	73.5	199.0	174.4	19.5
Sept. 1944	463.7	74.0	198.2	171.2	20.3
Dec. 1944	457.1	73.4	196.4	166.2	21.1
Mar. 1945	449.7	73.2	195.3	159.7	21.5
Jun. 1945	437.2	72.0	190.8	153.0	21.4

The Women's Royal Naval Service

The WRNS of the First World War was demobilized in 1919 but many of its original members enrolled again when the Service was re-formed in April 1939. It was set up to replace various categories of naval personnel in shore establishments and thus to release men for active service. Although serving mainly on shore, the Wrens conformed to naval usage and naval ways of speech. Though living in buildings, they 'went ashore', and slept 'below decks' in 'cabins'. They never used a kitchen but worked in 'galleys'.

Many of the first Wrens were recruited from the families of naval personnel living near the ports at which WRNS units were being formed. Many of these were classed as 'immobile' – that is, they continued to live in their own homes after they had joined the Service. Many of them later volunteered for 'mobile' service.

WRNS units were attached to nearly every naval shore establishment in the United Kingdom, and many served abroad in both the Middle and Far East theatres of operations. Many Wrens were employed in highly secret naval communications duties, and there was a specially trained class of cyphering personnel decoding German messages.

In all their duties Wrens displayed tremendous courage and spirit – as has been shown earlier in this text. There is one story which particularly typifies their sense of commitment. A Wren cyphering officer had just finished her watch and gone into a hotel during an air raid when the building was struck and she was buried up to her neck in debris. Fire broke out in the upper storeys of the wrecked hotel and crept steadily nearer to the trapped Wren as the rescue party worked frantically to get her out. They succeeded with a bare margin of time and were trying to put her in an ambulance for hospital when she struggled off the stretcher saying there was something she must do first. She had realized that the key to the secret cyphering office was still in her possession. Terribly bruised and shaken as she was, she insisted on going straight back to the duty officer to give up her key. Then she collapsed. Weeks later she was still in hospital recovering from her injuries.

Such was the spirit of the WRNS, proving the sister of the Senior Service not unworthy of its ancestry.

The Auxiliary Territorial Service

In the winter of 1937-8 the problem of increasing the manpower resources of Great Britain became a matter of urgency. Consequently, wheels were set in motion to consider the best and most economical scheme under which women could be made available for duty with the Armed Forces on mobilization. An advisory council was set up to plan the Auxiliary Territorial Service in 1938 and included representatives of the Territorial Army (to which the new corps was to be attached), the Territorial Associations and the three women's services recognized by the Army Council: the Women's Transport Service, the Motor Transport Section of the Women's Legion (dating from the First World War) and the Emergency Service (a recently created group of ex-servicewomen concerned with recruitment of previously trained officers in the event of war breaking out).

It was decided that in each county the TA Association should nominate a woman to be County Commandant; she, in turn, would put forward names of women to fill the appointments of junior officers. The status of these women, both officers and members, was that of 'camp-followers' as defined by the Army Act. In principle it was decided that women would receive two-thirds of the soldiers' pay. Such was the organization on 9 September 1938 when the ATS came into being by Royal Warrant. Some companies were raised for duties with the RAF but, on the formation of the WAAF in the summer of 1939, the War Department ceased to have any responsibility for them. The FANY was to help recruit and train a number of motor driver companies.

In September 1939 the ATS went into camp for the first time with the Territorial Army, cooking, clerking and storekeeping, while other members spent their holidays in the Army record or pay offices.

On 10 April 1941 the ATS became an integral part of the Armed Forces of the Crown. Its Director, Chief Controller Jean Knox, held the equivalent rank of Major-General.

Very soon the Army wanted more and more women. Three hundred were sent out to France, and on the evacuation of the British Expeditionary Force in 1940 ATS telephonists were the last to leave Paris, carrying on their duties at the exchange whilst lorries waited to rush them to the coast. Three times on the journey to Le Mans they were machine-gunned. The last unit of about twenty-five ATS embarked at St Malo and reached Britain on the day France capitulated.

A new army of women now grew rapidly. The age limits were set at seventeen to forty-three but veterans of the First World War were accepted up to the age of fifty. The range of jobs done by auxiliaries widened steadily and included confidential work of vital importance calling for the highest standard of integrity; some jobs involved duties needing characteristics formally regarded as masculine – manual dexterity and cleverness with gear and gadgets for the installation, maintenance and repair, the testing and so forth of technical apparatus. They also undertook secret work including the testing of ammunition and other gunnery experiments.

As they grew in strength, so also did they establish a distinguished war record for courage and devotion to duty.

The Women's Transport Service – FANY

The history of this corps is of unusual interest, for it has been in continuous existence since 1909 and its members were the first women, other than nurses, to serve with the British Army. It was originally called the First Aid Nursing Yeomanry and is still better known by the initials of this title. The first FANYs were recruited to do various forms of medical transport work and were also prepared to follow the Army on horseback to render first aid to the wounded.

In the First World War they were one of the first women's organizations to go overseas. When peace was signed, they trained drivers to serve the Army's need in emergencies – as, for example, with the General Strike in 1926.

In 1927 the Corps was officially recognized by the War Office, and when the ATS was created, the FANY provided the personnel of all ranks needed for the motor transport companies.

Almost all the original members of FANY joined the ATS and were called up for active service with Army transport services in 1939. In spite of this, the FANY continued as an independent organization.

The FANY of the First World War won many decorations for courage and resource. Those who served with them in the Second World War in all theatres of war, were no less distinguished. They lived up to their motto: 'I cope.'

The Women's Auxiliary Air Force

The WAAF was not formed until June 1939, although the Women's Royal Air Force had started at the same time as the Royal Air Force in the First World War. Before its formation in 1939 personnel of the WAAF had been on duty for nearly a year in the RAF companies of the ATS. This experience revealed the need for women who could undertake a different range of duties from those needed by the Army, and so a separate women's service was formed under the direct command of the RAF.

As in the other women's services, the main object of the WAAF was to release men for combatant posts. Recruits were accepted between the ages of 17½ and forty-four. They joined for 'the duration' and had to be prepared to serve anywhere, at home or abroad.

The work done by the WAAF covered nearly every activity of the Service barring flying. There were well over fifty different trades. They handled balloons – no light job – worked in 'operations rooms', where intelligence and quickness on the uptake were essential qualities, and at fighter stations acted as plotters, often under dangerous conditions. During the Battle of Britain they won high praise from the men of the RAF for their steadfastness under bombardment.

They were closely connected with the best-kept secret of the early days of the war, radio-location, specially selected for their perfect eyesight, clear voices and integrity of character, working side by side with men through long hours and often under conditions of great strain.

The Service appealed to girls and women with initiative and the spirit of adventure. In its ranks were women from all parts of the Empire, and many went overseas with Air Forces of the Dominions.

Appendix C: Report for the Director of the WAAF on a Visit to the Military Detention Centre at Fort Darland Barracks, Chatham

In connection with the proposal to introduce a form of detention for the WAAF, an exploratory visit was made to the Fort Darland Military Detention Barracks by Mr E.A. Shearing and Mr W.J. Cain of Air Ministry S.11, and Squadron Leader Baden-Fuller. Information was supplied by the Commandant, Major Newington, and after a conducted tour of the barracks the visitors were able to report to the Director of the WAAF.

Summarized below are the main points of that report:

1. The Commandant thought that stern measures as sanctions for use with undisciplined and violent airwomen were essential. The straitjacket and body belt, such as that used for men, were perhaps not suitable for women as a measure of restraint, but handcuffing and solitary confinement could be used.

2. Diet would be on a lower scale than ordinary rations. Unco-operative airwomen would be deprived of luxuries such as jam and cake. Smoking was prohibited at all times for everyone.

3. Staff would have to be very carefully selected and properly trained. The Commandant thought training at a civilian prison or corrective institute would be most suitable.

4. A welfare officer and chaplain should be on the staff to 'help change for the better the outlook of the prisoners'. A psychiatrist should visit once a week.

5. Each prisoner would be provided with a Bible and a library book for one hour in the evening.

6. The Commandant expressed an opinion that numerous pitfalls were likely to be encountered at first and that one camp should be started first as an experiment.

After receiving the report and considering other opinions, the Director of the WAAF decided firmly against the setting up of a WAAF detention centre.

References

For the published works cited below, see Bibliography for publisher and date.

At the head of references for each chapter appear the names of the women who supplied information to the author in letters or written or tape-recorded accounts and in conversation.

Prologue
1. Philip Gibbs, *Since Then*
2. Robert Graves and Alan Hodge, *The Long Week-end, A Social History of Britain, 1918-1939*
3. Public Record Office, File AIR/8 793
4. *The Women's Auxiliary Air Force*
5. *Roof Over Britain, The Official Story of the AA Defences*
6. Albert Speer to the writer in an interview at Heidelberg, 1972
7. Wing Commander Evans WRAF to the writer, 8 December 1987
8. *Sunday Times Magazine*, February 1977
9. Colonel Robinson WRAC, Ministry of Defence, to the writer, November 1987
10. Wing Commander Evans WRAF to the writer, October 1987
11. The report 'Inside the Family' from the Family Policy Studies Centre, in *The Times*, 16 November 1987
12. Pam Andrews in conversation with the writer, November 1987

1 'Give Us a Job. We Can Do That'
Marjorie Bennett, Doreen Atkinson, Phyllis Linsdell, Ruth Jewell, D.M. Hedges, Y.J.T. Kingdon, Irene Smith, Audrie Kearney, Jean Baker, Brenda Beeston, Hilda Dopson, Vera Cole, Selena Ringrose, Carol Thompson, Evelyn Light, Cora Myers, Dorothy Calvert, Anne Reeves, Chris Roberts, Kathleen Clarke, Alice Blanchflower, Barbara Thomas.
1. Pat Hall, *What a Way to Win a War*
2. C.A. Lejeune, *Thank You for Having Me*
3. *Daily Telegraph*, 9 July 1941
4. R.J. Minney, *Carve Her Name With Pride*

5. Grace 'Archie' Hall, *We Also Were There*
6. The Wren's name has been withheld but a full account of the correspondence can be found in the Public Record Office, File ADM 1/17100
7. The Wren's name has been changed for obvious reasons but details may be found in the PRO file dealing with the court of inquiry into the injuries she suffered: ADM 16887
8. *The Women's Auxiliary Air Force*
9. *The Auxiliary Territorial Service, 1939-45*
10. Dorothy Calvert's conversations with the author and also material from her book *Bull, Battledress, Lanyard and Lipstick*
11. At a meeting of the York ATS Association, Aldwark RAF Club, 1987
12. Peggy Makins, *The Evelyn Home Story* (Collins, 1975)
13. Peggy Scott, *They Made Invasion Possible*
14. Public Record Office, File ADM/1/15617 N1348842
15. Ibid., ADM/1/14692, N1464342
16. Ibid., ADM/1/14692, N1464342
17. Ibid., ADM/1 11385
18. *The War in the Air*, ed. Gavin Lyall
19. R.H. Ahrenfeld, *The Psychology of Military Command*
20. Captain Sir Basil Bartlett Bt, *My First War, An Army Officer's Journal for May 1940*
21. Brenda McBryde, *Quiet Heroines*
22. Eileen Bigland, *Britain's Other Army*
23. *Daily Telegraph*, 4 June 1940

2 All Together Now
Dora Clements, Edna Turnbull, Doreen Atkinson, Mildred Morton, Connie Brook, Ruth Negus, Ruth Jewell, Audrie Kearney, Ada Ryder, Betty Wilde, Y.J.T. Kingdon, Pam Andrews, Ellen Purdham, Agnes Ferris, Brenda Robinson.

1. John Masefield, *The Nine Days Wonder*
2. Ada Harrison, *Grey and Scarlet*
3. J. Masefield, op. cit.
4. *The Times*, 30 May 1940
5. *The Auxiliary Territorial Service, 1939-45*
6. Robert Graves and Alan Hodge, *The Long Weekend*
7. R.J. Minney, *Carve Her Name with Pride*
8. *The Auxiliary Territorial Service, 1939-45*
9. *Roof Over Britain …*
10. Ibid.
11. *Roof Over Britain …*
12. Lettice Curtis, *Forgotten Pilots*
13. Constance Babington Smith, *Amy Johnson*

14. L. Curtis, op. cit.
15. *Daily Telegraph*, 18 July 1940
16. Frank Illingworth, *Britain Under Shellfire*
17. Ibid.
18. Ibid.
19. Ibid.

3 The Back-Room Girls

Brenda Beeston, Brenda Robinson, Margaret Taylor, Moira Keaton, June Penny, Christine Courtney, Nancy Dawson, Mary Room, Kathleen Loomes, Diana Payne

1. Cajus Bekker, *The Luftwaffe War Diaries*
2. Ibid.
3. *The Battle of Britain* (Prepared for the Air Ministry by the Ministry of Information)
4. Edward Bishop, *Their Finest Hour*
5. Conversations with the writer
6. Grace 'Archie' Hall, *We Also Were There*
7. Graham Wallace, *RAF Biggin Hill*
8. G. Wallace, op. cit.
9. R.T. Bickers, *Ginger Lacey, Fighter Pilot*
10. G. Wallace, op. cit.
11. BBC TV documentary (TV South) shown on BBC 1, researched by Anne Faid
12. G. Wallace, op. cit.
13. Lettice Curtis, *Forgotten Pilots*
14. Norman Gelb, *Scramble – The Battle of Britain*
15. Ibid.
16. Ibid.
17. Ibid.
18. James Leathart, OC 54 Fighter Squadron, who retired as Air Commodore. See also RAF Manston magazine article by Rocky Stockman (1987) and Fraser and Stockman's *The History of RAF Manston* (RAF Manston, 1969)
19. N. Gelb, op. cit.
20. C. Bekker, op. cit.
21. Account given to the writer by Frau Maninen, former wife of Gestapo Chief Reinhardt Heydrich, Burg, 1972
22. E. Bishop, op. cit.
23. Nancy Spain, *Thank You, Nelson*
24. Winston Churchill, *The Second World War*
25. *After The Battle* magazine, ed. Winston Ramsey (1986)
26. Hugh Popham, *FANY*
27. Kay Summersby Morgan, *Past Forgetting*

28. E.H. Cookridge, *Set Europe Ablaze*
29. H. Popham, op. cit.

4 For Those in Peril ...
Kathleen Loomes, Sybille Phillips, Monica Jackson, Margaret Taylor, Gill Rowlands.
1. William Stevenson, *A Man Called Intrepid*
2. E.H. Cookridge, *Set Europe Ablaze*
3. 'Facing the Bismarck' in John Nixon, *Front Line of Freedom*
4. Ibid.
5. Ibid.
6. *The Merchant Navy at War*
7. *Daily Telegraph*, 9 July 1941
8. Mark Arnold Foster, *The World at War*
9. Brenda McBryde, *Quiet Heroines*
10. Ibid.
11. Charles McCormac, *You'll Die in Singapore*
12. Ada Harrison, *Grey and Scarlet*
13. Ibid.
14. Ibid.
15. Doris Hawkins, *Atlantic Torpedo*
16. Newspaper cutting sent to the writer by Margaret Taylor
17. *The Auxiliary Territorial Service, 1939-45*
18. Ibid.
19. *The Wren*, October 1984
20. Pat Hall, *What a Way to Win a War*
21. *The Wren*, October 1984
22. Ibid., June 1965

5. Blue Skies and Buzzing Flies, Where the Khamsin Blows
Marjorie Bennett, Dorothy Calvert, Vivienne Templeton.
1. Ada Harrison, *Grey and Scarlet*
2. Ibid.
3. Pat Hall, *What a Way to Win a War*
4. Ibid.
5. Captain Nichol's account given to the writer by the ATS Museum, Guildford
6. Noël Coward, *Middle East Diary*
7. R.J. Minney, *Carve Her Name With Pride*
8. Copy given to the writer by former Sister Lillie Muff (now Saxton), edition of 9 February 1943
9. Mary Kent Hughes, *Matilda Waltzes With the Tommies*
10. Ibid.
11. Kay Summersby Morgan, *Past Forgetting*

12. Brenda McBryde, *Quiet Heroines*
13. Ibid.
14. K.S. Morgan, op. cit.

6 *Where Do We Go From Here?*

Joanne Duprés, Brenda Weeks, Monica Jackson, Vera Cole, Ada Ryde, Joyce Taylor, M.J. Edge, Betty Davenport, Eileen Kisby, Barbara Boyce, Stella Pearson, Ruth Sims, Molly Urquhart, Paula Cooper, Pamela Barker, Marjorie Bennett, Irene Smith.

1. R.J. Minney, *Carve Her Name With Pride*
2. E.H. Cookridge, *Set Europe Ablaze*
3. M.R.D. Foot, *SOE*
4. R.V. Jones in the preface to M.R.D. Foot, *Six Faces of Courage*
5. M.R.D. Foot, *Six Faces of Courage*
6. Baroness Sue Ryder in BBC interview, Radio 4, December 1986
7. Peter Churchill, *Of Their Own Choice*
8. Hugh Popham, *FANY*
9. Field Marshal Viscount Montgomery of El Alamein, *Memoirs*
10. *The Auxiliary Territorial Service, 1939-45*
11. Public Record Office, File A 443036
12. Lt Z, Penguin New Writing, 31 March 1947
13. Court of inquiry file read by the writer at Colchester Detention Centre, October 1986
14. PRO, File A 443036
15. Ibid.
16. Ibid.
17. Brenda McBryde, *Quiet Heroines*
18. Ibid.
19. G. Lee Harvey, *D-Day Dodger*
20. B. McBryde, op. cit.
21. Ibid.

7 *Dice on the Table*

Myra Roberts, Doris Boon, B.R. Marks, D. Lynne Griffiths, Ruth Negus, Pearl Drake-Witts, Peggy Linington, Eileen Kisby, Dorothy Brody, Mary Elliott, Freda Howard.

1. Leonard Gribble, *On Secret Service*
2. David Irving, *The War Between the Generals*
3. R.J. Minney, *Carve Her Name With Pride*
4. M. Hastings, *Das Reich*
5. Anthony Kemp, *The Secret Hunters*
6. Public Record Office, File Air 8 793, 1005, 'Proposal to form a Flying Branch'
7. Bruce Miles, *Night Witches*

8. Lettice Curtis, *Forgotten Pilots*
9. Peggy Scott, *They Made Invasion Possible*
10. Edna Treacy, *True Stories of the Second World War*
11. Winston Churchill, *The Second World War*, Volume VI
12. Ibid.
13. Ibid.
14. Cutting sent by Connie Brook
15. W. Churchill, op. cit.
16. Harry C. Butcher, *My Three Years With Eisenhower*
17. Kay Summersby Morgan, *Past Forgetting*
18. Ibid. and D. Irving, op. cit.
19. K.S. Morgan, op. cit.
20. D. Irving, op. cit.
21. Ibid.
22. Arthur Bryant, *Triumph in the West*
23. D. Irving, op. cit.
24. Dwight. D. Eisenhower, *Crusade in Europe*
25. H.C. Butcher, op. cit.

8 Not For the Squeamish!
Betty Cullum, D. Lynne Griffiths, Sonia Corser, Margaret Doherty, A.S. Hall, Selina Ringrose, Monica Jackson, Vera Cole, Nellie Dumbrell, Joan Chamberlain, Winifred Blackham, Mollie Urquhart, M.S. Edge.

1. Field Marshal Sir William Slim, *Defeat Into Victory*
2. Winifred Beaumont, *A Detail on the Burma Front*
3. Catherine Kenny, *Captives*
4. W. Beaumont, op. cit.
5. Brenda McBryde, *Quiet Heroines*
6. Ibid.
7. Eric Ambler, *Here Lies Eric Ambler*
8. Martin Lindsay, *So Few Got Through*
9. David Irving, *The War Between the Generals*
10. Arthur Bryant, *Triumph in the West*
11. Mary Walsh Hemmingway, *How It Was*
12. Charles Whiting, *'44 – In Combat on the Western Front from Normandy to the Ardennes*
13. Dwight D. Eisenhower, *Crusade in Europe*
14. Kay Summersby Morgan, *Past Forgetting*
15. Ibid.
16. Bruce Marshall, *The White Rabbit*
17. Interviews with member of concentration-camp staff, Claud Landsman, Channel 4 film, December 1986
18. Ibid.

19. Ibid. and writer's interview with nurse at Dachau concentration camp
20. Public Record Office, File WO 205, Records 21st Army Group, V-weapons against Antwerp
21. Grace 'Archie' Hall, *We Also Were There*
22. Ibid.
23. Ibid.
24. In the BBC TV programme *Widows*, November 1987
25. G.A. Hall, op. cit.
26. Ibid.
27. Ibid.
28. Ibid.
29. PRO, File ADM 1 16195 MO12805
30. M.W. Hemingway, op. cit.
31. B. McBryde, op. cit.
32. Account by the Senior Medical Officer given to the *Daily Mail* and other Special Correspondents with the Allied Armies of Liberation
33. B. McBryde, op. cit.
34. Ibid.
35. Edwin Tetlow, *Daily Mail*, in *Lest We Forget* (compiled by the *Daily Mail*, Associated Newspapers Ltd, 1945)
36. Anthony Kemp, *The Secret Hunters*
37. *News of the World*, 31 March 1946
38. A. Kemp, op. cit.

9 *I'll Be Seeing You!*

Vera Cole, Brenda Robinson, J. Melrose, D.M. Hedges, Moira Keaton, Margaret Doherty, Hilda Dopson, Marjorie Bennett, Joan Armstead.
1. Pat Hall, *What a Way to Win a War*
2. Kay Summersby Morgan, *Past Forgetting*
3. David Irving, *The War Between the Generals*
4. Dorothy Calvert, *Bull, Battledress, Lanyard and Lipstick*

Bibliography

Ambler, Eric, *Here Lies Eric Ambler* (Weidenfeld & Nicolson, 1986)

Arbib, Robert, *Here We Are Together* (Longman's Green, 1946)

Bartlett, Captain Sir Basil, *My First World War, An Army's Officer's Journal for May 1940* (Chatto & Windus, 1941)

Beauman, Katharine Bentley, *Partners in blue: the story of the Women's service with the Royal Air Force* (Hutchinson, 1971)

Beaumont, Winifred, *A Detail on the Burma Front* (BBC, 1977)

Bekker, Cajus, *The Luftwaffe War Diaries* (Macdonald, 1964)

Bennett, D.C.T., *Pathfinder* (Muller, 1958)

Bickers, R.T., *Ginger Lacey, Fighter Pilot* (Robert Hale/Pan, 1962)

Bigland, Eileen, *Britain's Other Army* (Nicolson & Watson, 1946)
> *The story of the WRNS* (Nicholson & Watson, 1946)

Eden, Anthony, Earl of Avon, *The Eden Memoirs* (Cassell, 1965)

Bishop, Edward, *Their Finest Hour* (Pan/Ballantine, 1964)

Brittain, Vera, *England's Hour* (Macmillan, 1941)

Bryant, Sir Arthur, *Turn of the Tide* (Collins, 1959)
> *Triumph in the West* (Collins, 1961)

Buckley, Christopher, *Road to Rome* (Hodder & Stoughton, 1945)

Buckmaster, Maurice, *They Fought Alone* (Odhams, 1958)

Butcher, Harry, *My Three Years with Eisenhower* (Heinemann, 1946)

Butler, Ewan, *Keep the Memory Green* (Hutchinson, 1946)

Calder, Angus, *The People's War* (Cape, 1970)

Calvert, Dorothy, *Bull, Battledress, Lanyard and Lipstick* (New Horizon, 1978)

Churchill, Peter, *Of Their Own Choice* (Hodder & Stoughton, 1952)

Churchill, Sir Winston, *The Second World War* (Cassell, vols. 1-6, 1948-54)

Cookridge, E.H. *Inside SOE* (Barker 1966)
> *Set Europe Ablaze* (Barker, 1966)

Costello, J., *Love, Sex and War* (Collins, 1985)

Coward, Noël, *Middle East Diary* (Right Book Club, 1945)

Curtis, Lettice, *Forgotten Pilots* (Nelson Saunders, 1971)

Deighton, Len, *Fighter* (Cape, 1970)

Drummond, John D., *Blue for a girl: the story of the WRNS* (W.H. Allen, 1960)

Eisenhower, D.D., *Crusade in Europe* (Heinemann, 1948)

Farago, Ladislas, *Patton, Ordeal and Triumph* (Barker, 1966)
Fleming, Peter, *Invasion* (Hart Davis, 1957)
Foot, M.R.D., *Six Faces of Courage* (Eyre Methuen, 1978)
   SOE (BBC, 1984)
Foster, Mark Arnold, *The World at War* (Thames Methuen, 1973)
Gelb, Norman, *Scramble – The Battle of Britain* (Pan, 1986)
Gibbs, Philip, *Since Then* (Heinemann, 1930)
Graves, Robert, and, Hodge, Alan, *The Long Weekend* (Faber & Faber, 1941)
Gribble, L., *On Secret Service* (Burke, 1950)
Hall, Grace, 'Archie', *We Also Were There* (Merlin, 1985)
Hall, Pat, *What a Way to Win a War* (Midas, 1978)
Harris, Sir Arthur, *Bomber Offensive* (Collins, 1947)
Harrison, Ada, *Grey and Scarlet, Letters from War Areas by Army Sisters on Active Service* (Hodder & Stoughton, 1944)
Harrison, Tom, *Living Through the Blitz* (Collins, 1976)
Harvey, G. Lee, *D-Day Dodger* (Macdonald, 1985)
Hastings, Max, *Das Reich* (Michael Joseph, 1981)
Hawkins, Doris, *Atlantic Torpedo* (Gollancz, 1943)
Hemmingway, Mary Walsh, *How It Was* (Weidenfeld & Nicholson, 1977)
Horrocks, Sir Brian, *Corps Commander* (Sidgwick & Jackson, 1977)
   A Full Life (Collins, 1960)
Hughes, Mary Kent, *Matilda Waltzes with the Tommies* (OUP, 1943)
Illingworth, Frank, *Britain Under Shellfire* (Hutchinson, 1944)
Irving, David, *The War Between the Generals* (Penguin, 1981)
Jones, R.V., *Most Secret War* (Hamish Hamilton, 1978)
Kemp, Anthony, *The Secret Hunters* (Michael O'Mara, 1986)
Kenny, Catherine, *Captives* (University of Queensland Press, 1986)
Lejeune, C.A., *Thank You For Having Me* (Tom Stacey, 1964)
Lewis, Peter, *A People's War* (Channel Four Books, 1986)
Lindsay, Martin, *So Few Got Through* (Collins, 1946)
Longmate, Norman, *How We Lived Then* (Hutchinson, 1971)
Lyall, Gavin (ed.), *The War in the Air* (Arrow, 1968)
McBryde, Brenda, *Quiet Heroines* (Chatto & Windus, 1985)
McCormac, Charles, *You'll Die in Singapore* (Robert Hale, 1956)
Majdalany, Fred, *The Battle of El Alamein* (Collins, 1958)
   Patrol (Longman's Green, 1953)
Makins, Peggy, *The Evelyn Home Story* (Collins, 1975)
Marshall Bruce, *The White Rabbit* (Evans, 1952)
Masefield, John, *The Nine Days Wonder* (Heinemann, 1941)
Mason, Ursula Stuart, *The Wrens, 1917-77: a History of the Women's Royal Naval Service* (Educational Explorers, 1977)
Mathews, Vera Laughton, *Blue Tapestry* (Hollis & Carter, 1948)
Miles, Bruce, *Night Witches* (Mainstream, 1981)

Miller, Joan, *One Girl's War* (Brandon, 1986)

Minney, R.J. *Carve Her Name With Pride* (Newnes, 1956)

Minns, Raynes, *Bombers and Mash* (Virago, 1980)

Montgomery, Field Marshal Viscount, *Memoirs* (Collins, 1958)

Morgan, Kay Summersby, *Past Forgetting* (Collins, 1979)

Nixon, John, *Front Line of Freedom* (Hutchinson, 1946)

Patient, Alan, 'Mutiny at Salerno' (*Listener*, February 1982)

Philips, and, Lucas, C.E., Kohima – *Springboard to Victory* (Heinemann, 1968)

Pond, H. *Salerno* (Pan, 1960)

Popham, Hugh, *FANY* (Leo Cooper, 1984)

Reilly, Catherine, *Chaos of the Night* (Virago, 1984)

Scott, Peggy, *They Made Invasion Possible* (Hutchinson, 1946)

Seventy True Stories (Editor of *People*, Odhams Press, 1952)

Sherman, Margaret, *No Time for Tears* (Harrap, 1944)

Slim, Field Marshal Sir William, *Defeat Into Victory* (Cassell, 1957)

Smith, Constance Babington, *Amy Johnson* (Collins, 1967)

Spain, Nancy, *Thank You, Nelson* (Arrow, 1950)

Stevenson, William, *A Man Called Intrepid* (Macmillan, 1976)

Taylor, Eric, *Operation Millennium* (Robert Hale, 1987)

Tickell, Jerrard, *Odette* (Chapman Hall, 1949)

Treacy, Edna, *True Stories of the Second World War* (Odhams, 1952)

Wallace, Graham, *RAF Biggin Hill* (Putnam/Tandem, 1969)

Whiting, Charles, *The Long March on Rome* (Century, 1987)
          '44 – In Combat on the Western Front from Normandy to the Ardennes (Century, 1987)

Wilmot, Chester, *The Struggle for Europe* (Collins, 1952)

Winfield, Roland, *The Sky Belongs to Them* (Kimber, 1946)

Official histories

Book of the WAAF: A practical guide to the women's branch of the RAF (Amalgamated Press, 1942)

The Auxiliary Territorial Service, 1939-45 (compiled by Controller J.M. Cowper, ATS, The War Office, 1949)

The Merchant Navy at War (prepared by Ministry of Information, HMSO, 1945)

Roof over Britain: The Official History of the AA Defences (prepared by Ministry of Information for the War Office and the Air Ministry, 1943)

The Women's Auxiliary Air Force (Air Ministry, Historical Branch, 1953)

Index